SUBJECT TO

DEBATE

Katha Pollitt

SUBJECT TO
DEBATE

Sense and Dissents on
Women, Politics, and Culture

THE MODERN LIBRARY

NEW YORK

All of the essays in this work were originally published in *The Nation*.

MODERN LIBRARY and colophon are registered trademarks of
Random House, Inc.

LIBRARY OF CONGRESS CATALOGING-IN-PUBLICATION DATA
Pollitt, Katha.
Subject to debate: sense and dissents on women, politics, and culture /
Katha Pollitt.
p.   cm.
A collection of articles originally published in the author's column,
Subject to debate, in the Nation.
ISBN 0-679-78343-1
I. Title.
PS3566.O533 S83   2001
814'.54—dc21   00-056109

Modern Library website address: www.modernlibrary.com

Printed in the United States of America

2 4 6 8 9 7 5 3 1

For Sophie, and for the Last Marxist

ACKNOWLEDGMENTS

For offering me a page of my own with complete editorial freedom, I am deeply grateful to Victor Navasky and Katrina vanden Heuvel, publisher and editor of *The Nation*. For help with research, copy-editing, and clarification of thought, many thanks to the staff of *The Nation*, especially my editors Elsa Dixler, JoAnn Wypijewski, and Betsy Reed; copy editors Roane Carey and Judy Long; and interns Maura McDermott, Beverly Gage, Elizabeth Ratner, Sari Nelson, Stephanie Greenwood, Chisun Lee, Emily Gordon, Amanda Hickman, Jane Manners, Beth Johnson, Kytja Weir, Anaga Dalal, Amy Cash, Erin Smith, and Dan Honan. Ann Snitow, Barbara Ehrenreich, Frances Fox Piven, Doug Henwood, Ellen DuBois, Adolph Reed, Joan Bertin, Laura Flanders, Alan Wallach, Janine Jackson, and Donna Lieberman offered sources, ideas, facts, quotations, and controversies. Josh Freeman did not complain when I quoted him without asking first. As always, my deepest debt is to Paul Mattick, who challenged, discussed, encouraged, read, and reread till all hours of the night—even when, as sometimes happened, he thought my ideas were definitely subject to debate.

CONTENTS

INTRODUCTION

Feminism at the Millennium

It's the year 2000. Are we equal yet? Are we dead yet? Have the frontlash and the backlash met, grappled, and twisted themselves together like a pair of mating snakes? More than one hundred and fifty years after the Seneca Falls Convention, when American women first met to demand full legal, political, and social equality, including the right to vote, the position of women continues to provoke furious argument. For every gain hard fought for by women, someone manages to find a negative side. Speak of the recently won legal freedom of women to control the timing and number of their children through contraception and abortion—a right not yet thirty years old, and one that for many exists only on paper—and conservatives from Francis Fukuyama on down chorus that this has only licensed men to be sexually irresponsible, leaving women more vulnerable than before. Note the dramatic increase in women going to college and moving on to higher degrees and careers in the professions, and you'll get an earful from faux stay-at-home mom Danielle Crittenden about lonely lawyers who've missed their chance at marriage and family. (Interestingly, it isn't the lonely lawyers themselves who make this complaint, but the professional anti-feminist to whom, in a weak moment, they have supposedly confided.) Note the increased influence of women in politics, and *New York Times* columnist Maureen Dowd responds with a jeremiad against soccer moms and the trivialization of once grand political themes—honor! greatness! patriotism!—while male conservatives bemoan the "feminization" of America.

Some of the same ambivalence marks even the attempt to evaluate how powerful women are. On the one hand, we read constantly that women aren't interested in feminism, that it doesn't work, can't work, even our genes are against it: Men are programmed to dominate and spread seed widely among the young and fertile, women to nest and preen and cuddle up to wealth and power. On the other hand, some of the same "evolutionary psychologists" who argue that male dominance is in the genes see men on the defensive everywhere, with women poised to run the universe, in fact running large tracts of it already: Feminists have rewritten the age-old contract between the sexes—she gives sex in return for support—and in the process have revamped law, politics, religion, education, and the literary canon. Why women have been able to fly in the face of nature is never explained, much less why they would even have the desire to do so or, most mysterious of all, why men have cooperated with this mad plan. After all, men are still firmly in charge of all the institutions accused of excessive kowtowing to feminists—the courts, the legislatures, the corporations, the schools and universities and publishing houses and seminaries. Why have men allowed their privileges to be curtailed? We are constantly told that women themselves have little interest in feminism: Pretty young girls don't need it; working-class and minority women scorn it; young professionals think they've got it already. An article in *Talk* magazine about Lorna Wendt—the homemaker and corporate helpmeet who made headlines when she demanded an equal share of her CEO husband's assets when he divorced her after more than thirty years of marriage—refers to the audience at one public appearance of hers as "an old-fashioned feminist one, women in cork-soled shoes, their bosoms ample rather than augmented," staid members of the American Association of University Women and the League of Women Voters. But if feminism is so outmoded, and feminists so uncool and frumpish (imagine, no breast implants), it becomes even harder to understand where the continuing power of feminism to alter fundamental social arrangements comes from.

One answer to the conundrum is that feminism has much more of a following than is usually acknowledged. It's true that recent polls assert that only about a quarter of American women describe themselves as feminists, down from about a third in 1992. Yet the same polls show large majorities of American women sympathize with the women's movement and feel it has improved their lives. For all that feminist positions are often described as "radical" and out of sync with the mainstream, the large majority of women tell pollsters they want legal, economic, and social equality with men, and do not believe they have it yet. Many "radical" feminist causes, when fleshed out with particular cases and close arguments, have broad appeal to both sexes. Americans regularly tell pollsters they abhor "partial-birth abortion." But when they were made to vote on its legality in state referenda in Colorado, Maine, and Washington, and in the process had to think concretely about the wording of the law and what criminalization would really mean, they chose to keep it legal three times out of three. Or consider *Davis v. Monroe County Board of Education,* the much publicized Georgia case in which the Supreme Court was asked to decide whether public schools receiving federal funds were legally liable for student-to-student sexual harassment. Anti-feminist pundits spilled oceans of ink belittling the issue, denying the need for some sort of school response (in the *Davis* case, teachers had even refused so simple a gesture as changing the victim's seat in her fifth-grade class so she wouldn't have to sit next to the harasser) and criticizing the girl's mother for not having solved the problem on her own. You would never know from their accounts that the boy in question was convicted of sexual battery for the behavior they found so trivial (or that the victim was black and the harasser white). Still, the Court's 5 to 4 decision—which held public schools responsible for stopping harassment, but only when the harassment was "severe, pervasive, and objectively offensive," and only when school authorities could be shown to be "deliberately indifferent" to it—drew favorable responses in polls (and sighs of relief from school administrators, who had feared a judgment that would have held them responsible for *knowing* about harassment, reported or not). Almost a year later, the case hardly seems controversial—especially in the wake of the Columbine killings, which made many adults question whether schools were doing enough to counteract a general student culture of cruelty and hostility, and were too oblivious of antisocial behavior and troubled kids. Whether or not individual moms and dads think of themselves as "feminist," demanding fairness and equality and respect for their daughters is increasingly a part of what it means to be a good parent today.

That feminism is not a single, independent, all-powerful force, but is connected in complicated and even contradictory ways with other historical forces—egalitarianism *and* individualism, hedonism *and* puritanism, capitalism *and* the critique of capitalism—is not something its detractors often consider. They prefer to see it as a plot, or maybe a joke, in any case something foisted by the outlandish few on the resistant many. Thus we are repeatedly treated to feminism's obituary: *Time* declared it dead of terminal silliness in a notorious 1998 cover story; Maureen Dowd was only one of dozens of commentators who announced that the "hypocrisy" of the National Organization for Women and other liberal women's groups who opposed President Clinton's impeachment had killed the women's movement. And yet the women's movement—corksoled, sneakered, Blahniked, or barefoot—moves on. And surely some of its staying power derives from the way it speaks to so many different and opposing political tendencies, and to so many different kinds of women—not excluding the ones who insist that they are not feminists because a feminist is a humorless anti-child manhater who doesn't shave her legs. A woman may believe abortion is evil, do the lioness's share of the housework, enjoy having men pick up the dinner check, and refer to herself as a girl (not grrrl)—and still sue her employer for sex discrimination if she's passed over for promotion in favor of a less-qualified man.

The many guises under which feminist ideas travel mean that attempts to evaluate feminism's progress by looking at society too narrowly can give a picture that is either too positive or too negative. As Susan Faludi brilliantly demonstrated in *Backlash,* the 1980s saw a major onslaught of anti-feminist propaganda in popular culture and the media: Movies, magazines, pop psychology, and self-help books all pressed home the message that excessive liberation explained every female woe from dateless Saturday nights to infertility. Depressing as it surely was to be surrounded by these messages, and amplified though they were by twelve years of Reagan and Bush, they did not seem to sway women's important life choices. The march of women into higher education, the professions, and the workplace continued apace. For all the hype around the now notorious 1986 Harvard-Yale study likening women's chances of marrying past thirty to the odds of being kidnapped by a terrorist, women did not start marrying younger. On the contrary, in the thirteen years since the study—only one salvo in an ongoing barrage promoting early marriage—women's age at first marriage has risen without a break from 23.1 in 1986 to 25 in 1998, the last year for which the Census Bureau has data as of this writing, continuing a trend that began in the mid-sixties.

Why? For one thing, the media has less influence than it thinks. To be sure, it has the power to rouse anxiety and self-doubt, especially when, as with the singles study, it is putting a pseudoscientific gloss on messages women have received from the cradle. But who accepts a marriage proposal from a previously unacceptable suitor because she read an article in *People*? (Especially when, as is the way with *People*, it is immediately contradicted by another article—about deliriously happy single movie stars.) Lots of women bought *The Rules*—but how many followed them, and how many of those followed them for more than a week? No matter what *Newsweek*—or *The Nation*—says, the deep economic and historical forces transforming women's social position continue to operate, and they are moving fairly steadily in one direction: away from the two-parent, single-earner family; away from acceptance of the "natural" or divinely ordained subordination of one group of people to another; away from large families and from childbearing and child raising as women's all-consuming lifework; away from the modes of life that enforced a social code of conservative "family values." A cover story in *U.S. News & World Report* arguing that families can indeed get by on one income, so women really could stay home if they wanted to, is not going to persuade a family that is using the woman's salary to pay the mortgage or save for the children's college tuitions. Nor will bully-pulpit fulminations by politicians and conservative pundits reweave the complex web of social taboos that made white parents in the 1950s hide their pregnant teenage daughters in distant maternity homes and put their babies—the grandchildren!—up for adoption.

Unfortunately, however, the benefits of feminism have not been as evenly distributed as the forces that have brought it into being. A middle-class woman can find an abortion more easily than a poor one can find either an abortion or respectful prenatal care, not to mention decent child care and a job with good pay and benefits that will enable her to raise her child in security. Sisterhood has not been so very powerful after all, and part of the reason is the uneven success of feminism itself. The old ideal of sisterhood rested on the conviction that women shared a common predicament, regardless of class or race. Any woman might find herself needing an illegal abortion, or denied a job for which she was qualified, or treated like a child by her almost certainly male doctor. The basics of female existence—husbandcare, childcare, housecare, eldercare—were the same for all. In practice, of course, the Sisterhood of Woman, like the Brotherhood of Man, was always something of a theoretical construct—the tedium and isolation of tending a suburban colonial is not likely to get much sympathy from women who come home from work to toil up the stairwell in a run-down building where the elevator is broken *again*. Still, it was possible in 1970, in a way that is much harder today, to believe that "women" constituted a potentially unified interest group.

Feminism opened doors for those who were able to walk through them. It has done more, ironically enough, for anti-feminists like Christina Hoff Sommers, who, it's safe to say, would not have become a tenured professor of philosophy had she been of college age in the 1930s rather than the 1960s, than it has been able to do for women on welfare. As a civil rights movement, it has been a tremendous success. As a social justice movement, it has had no more success than other movements that have attempted to win for Americans the welfare-state provisions Europeans have enjoyed for decades—parental leaves and benefits, child care, universal health care—and whose diminishment Europeans are strongly resisting, even as Americans quietly endure, or even applaud, the shredding of our own safety net. A great deal has been written attributing this disparity in feminism's achievements to misguided political strategies, faulty leadership, class bias, and philosophical flaws in feminism. Is it too individualist? Too shaped by the Enlightenment ideals of rationality and progress? Too focused on "male" values? Too bound to inevitably exclusionary definitions of "woman"? And what is a "woman," anyway? Maybe the truth is simpler: Rights are free; social justice costs a fortune.

This is where, for me, feminism and the left come together. For many reasons—custom, history, the formal and informal segregation by sex of the labor force, women's biological and social role as mothers, the prevalence of violence against women that renders many freedoms theoretical—rights alone cannot transform women's social position, even to the extent of rendering men and women equally likely to occupy any position in an unequal social order. Gender equality requires general equality. A society in which one in six people has no health insurance, in which millions cannot afford dental care, eyeglasses, or medications, is not going to offer women free abortions on demand or pay doctors to spend time explaining to poor women the pros and cons of different methods of contraception. A country that tolerates tremendous race- and class-based disparities in public education—and that has never even funded enough places in Head Start to take care of all the poor children who could benefit—is not going to provide affordable quality public day care just because millions of mothers need and want it. A society in which the very idea of the public sphere has been denigrated, in which poor people are constantly portrayed as addicts, sluts, and criminals, is not going to treat struggling single mothers as playing a valuable social role that should be supported with public funds. But precisely because feminism's fortunes are in some ways tied to those of the left, it's too simple to lay the failures of feminism solely at the door of the women's movement.

Feminism has yet to create a society in which women are not socially subordinate to men—nor has it created a world in which women are equal to one another. And yet feminism has transformed women's consciousness, whether or not women want to admit it. It has made what used to look like fate, or God's will, or nature's plan, look like something else—a personal choice, a social convention, an injustice. There are feminists on both sides of the discussion over medicated childbirth, but there's no doubt that the pain of "natural childbirth" was a different experience when there was no other way to give birth than it is today, when it means consciously rejecting a range of painkilling drugs and procedures. Staying home with a child feels different when the other moms are going off to the office every morning, just as going to work feels different now that it is the norm and not proof that one married a failure, is hopelessly maladjusted, or both.

The danger is that women, once assumed to be equally subject to "woman's lot," are now assumed to be equally free to choose how to live. A few decades ago, the question asked of a battered woman was "what did she do to provoke him?" Now, it's "why does she stay?" The problem of male violence in the home is still located in female behavior, which is still judged harshly and by a single yardstick. The usual answers to the question of why a woman stays with a batterer—because she thought she deserved it; she had no money, no place to go, too many kids for the shelter; and besides, he said he'd find her and kill her if she left—sound to many ears like "excuses." But what would one expect in a society in which cancer is widely believed to be caused by personality flaws, and lack of "personal responsibility" is supposed to explain why millions live in poverty? To the extent that the women's movement is founded on principles of *mutual* responsibility, *collective* struggle, and empathetic support for women in trouble, it is fighting an uphill battle against the prevailing spirit of hyperindividualism and blame, in which the message to "losers" is "get over it."

———

Feminists are often accused of having abandoned their early ideals in favor of selfish personal advancement: "Perhaps the century's most important movement—feminism—has, in the United States, been largely transformed into careerism," wrote *Newsweek* columnist Jonathan Alter in an end-of-the century state-of-the-world roundup. One might ask why it is women's job to resist "careerism"—if by that is meant pursuing fame and fortune with gusto and determination, as Americans are constantly urged to do, and as Alter himself has done. One might also ask if opening up professions and careers and good skilled blue-collar jobs to the previously excluded half of humanity is such a small achievement. On the left, too, as on the right and in the middle, sneers at feminism have a long history, for complex reasons: Feminists challenged men's grip on leadership and theory; they disrupted the romantic picture of a working class conceptualized as male—burly steelworkers, not supermarket checkers—and of families conceptualized as having no internal conflicts of interest. Even today, "progressives" of various stripes seem less interested in appealing to the millions of women who share their views than in capturing the "angry white men" who have no use for them. Feminism in this view is just "identity politics," a psychological frill, or worse, divisive. The paradox is that feminism, along with environmentalism, is the most popular and most effective movement to emerge from the sixties left (the gay rights movement, another cause with strong appeal, came a bit later), but much of the left is unable to see this.

Yet the women's movement continues to have transforming power, and not just in the West. Twenty years ago, feminism in the developing world or the Soviet bloc was ridiculed as a Western import, a view still held by cultural nationalists, some American academics, Muslim fundamentalists, and the pope. Today, though, indigenous women's movements flourish around the globe. It is African women who are organizing against clitoridectomy, Iranian women who are fighting unfair divorce laws and subverting Islamic dress codes, Jordanian and Pakistani women who are protesting "honor killings" and the tacit permission given to these crimes by the legal system. Women all over the world are organizing shelters, hot lines, cooperative projects, literacy programs, and economic self-help groups, not to mention demonstrations and civil disobedience protests that prove how false is the persistent American idea of the contentedly subordinate and passive Third World woman. I find these struggles immensely inspiring; American women could learn a great deal from them. Even in the limited realm of electoral politics, countries as different as India and France seem able to entertain tactics, such as mandating that a certain percentage of political slots go to women, that in the United States are no sooner broached than squelched as patently absurd.

As in the United States, the global possibilities for women's rights are determined partly by other developments. The Chinese government embraces rapid capitalist development—and millions of little girls in the countryside lose a chance to go to school. The former Soviet Union comes unglued—and hundreds of thousands of jobless Russian women are driven to prostitution, while polygyny makes a comeback in Ingushetia and Turkmenistan. African dictators in collusion with the International Monetary Fund drain their countries of resources—and women in vast numbers die of AIDS. Poverty, war, religious manias, drastic global inequalities, nationalism that enshrines cultural and legal traditions that deny women the right to inherit, to choose their mates, to have legal custody of their children (and this at the very moment that urbanization and globalization are destroying traditional societies!)—one can say of women, in the United States and around the world, what Marx said of human beings: We make our own history, but we do not make it just as we please.

———

Reading over what I've just written, I wonder if I'm being too optimistic, if you can call optimistic a confidence in women's progress toward equality that acknowledges as obstacles AIDS, poverty, fundamentalism, and other disasters that aren't going to disappear any time soon. After all, feminism is not just a matter of rights, or even of money; for women to be freed from the limitations of gender takes more than the vote and a paycheck. In the United States, one could argue that millions of women have won what earlier feminists saw as the prerequisites of liberation: education, the ability to support themselves, a degree of sexual and personal self-determination unparalleled in history. And yet the ones who insist they are free are usually explaining why they are choosing to behave as if they were not—"this face-lift is for me," "I never liked my last name anyway"—and the ones who believe they are still confined by gender (the students in the women's studies course I teach, for instance) have immense difficulty articulating the sources of this feeling of constraint. Is it sexist advertising, one student wonders, that makes her feel so undermined, so judged? Or street harassment? Or pop culture? Or the fashion industry? Theoretically, and according to all the official sources, my students can make their own lives as they please. In actuality, they can't even enjoy an ice-cream cone on a hot summer day without paying for it in celery and sit-ups. My students are only vaguely aware of the legal and cultural restrictions Betty Friedan wrote about. It came as news to them that not so long ago married women had trouble getting their own credit cards, help-wanted ads were segregated by sex, and women were routinely expected to resign their jobs if they became pregnant. They had little sympathy for the cultural and social pressures that kept Friedan's educated middle-class wives home polishing their silverware. What was the matter with those women? But somehow my students felt themselves similarly hedged in, similarly unable to grasp and use a personal freedom that everyone told them they already possessed. One particularly beautiful and charming young woman wrote a whole paper seething with cleverly expressed rage at the "fact" that she had to spend a precious hour—or was it two hours?—every morning making herself up, doing her hair, choosing her outfit. It was a lively paper, bursting with feminist analysis, but the one thing that did not seem to occur to her was that she could actually change her behavior. In the same way, it emerged in conversation, she expected that she would end up doing most of the housework when she married, and expected she would marry, because that's the way life was: as her mother put it, "better a split-level than a studio apartment." Yet this same young woman argued in the most uncompromising way that what ambitious working mothers really needed was publicly funded twelve-hour day-care sessions for their kids, and dismissed objections to such arrangements on behalf of children as sexist balderdash.

For this young woman, and I think for many others as well, it is easier to fantasize America turning into a kind of workoholic version of Sweden than to imagine that she could transform her intimate life as part of a heterosexual couple through her own energies or choices. At least in her imagination, the government, or whoever she pictured starting those round-the-clock day-care centers, was more likely to enable her ambitions than the future father of her children, but it wasn't as if she was making a serious demand for the centers, either. Most women queried tell pollsters that their lives are better than those of their mothers, and that was certainly true for this student. She had gotten out of the working class; she had a job she liked; she was getting an advanced degree. But the openness to experience, the drive, the curiosity that served her so well at school and in the job market did not help her dismiss social and cultural expectations surrounding beauty, sex, love, and domestic life any more than getting A's in art history helped young women in the 1950s think of themselves as potential professors or critics. It wasn't that she didn't understand her predicament; she could dissect an episode of *Ally McBeal* or an issue of *Elle* as neatly as a Chinese chef boning a duck. It was that her understanding did not lead anywhere. Lacking a social movement, it remained an essentially ironic response, allowing her to distance herself intellectually from circumstances she did not think she could change.

We usually think of social movements as being about institutional change: calls and demands on business or government for new laws, new rights, new programs, new spotlights on old dark corners. It's an aged trope among politicos both left and liberal to mock as navel-gazing and trivial and hostile to collective action any movements that have a personal dimension. My *Nation* colleague Christopher Hitchens blamed the feminist credo "the personal is political" for the decline of the whole left! But the women's movement in its flowering shows how false this distinction can be. The women's movement wasn't just about fighting institutional discrimination and rectifying public injustices. A great deal of its energy came from women collectively transforming themselves as individuals: nudging each other, not always in a nice way, to shed ingrained habits of deference, prudery, conventionality, fear, and hostility toward other women. Together, women made it possible for one another to do all sorts of things each could never have done alone, much as she may have wanted to. Political action was one of those things, and so was looking at your cervix and refusing to do the dishes and throwing away your girdle. It's customary now to mock as trivial and nitpicking and "politically correct" the challenges to the sexism of daily life mounted by radical feminists of the Second Wave—insisting that women not be called "girls," splitting the check on dates, and so on. The resistance to those egalitarian gestures—the need to caricature as man-haters women who did not like being ogled on the street, for example—suggests that those changes are not trivial at all, but significant and rather difficult. Indeed, it took a whole social movement to bring them about even to the limited extent they exist today.

Where is that impulse now? I wonder. Political feminism is still with us: regulations are challenged and proposed, candidates funded and campaigned for, lawsuits fought and not infrequently won. In the 1990s we even had a new kind of feminism—academic feminism, "theory"—which absorbs vast amounts of female brain power and probably does less to liberate real women than Brandi Chastain's picture on a cereal box. And we have what one might call the feminism of necessity, for as I outlined earlier, the realities of modern life ensure that there will be no massive "going back" to premarital chastity and buttoned-up cardigans as envisioned by professional virgin Wendy Shalit; or to thinking of college as finishing school; or to making the boss's coffee; or to believing financial dependence on a man is the summum bonum of life on earth. What is missing is the feminism that would give young women like my students a way of challenging the new status quo in which they are expected to be babes and clotheshorses, aerobicizers and celery-nibblers, degree-getters and résumé updaters and career-hoppers—and also sensitive girlfriends who will gracefully accept their status as secondary earners, child-centered mothers, and stalwart wives picking up the living room after everyone else is asleep. The zines popular among hip young women aren't much help here. They have plenty of attitude, as their names—*Bitch, Bust, Moxie*—suggest, but not much hard thinking, new ideas, or useful information. Indeed, their relentless focus on pop culture, celebrities, fashion, boys, and sex makes them not so very different from the conventional women's magazines they mock. After a few issues, the ironies and in-jokes and unreflective personal narratives feel almost as processed as pop culture itself. Still, whatever their shortcomings, zines represent an attempt by young women to talk to one another about their situation as women, and to do it in a way that is not mediated and controlled by others— advertisers, for example, or circulation directors, or the male owners and publishers who stand behind most mainstream women's publications. That has to be a cheering development.

How do we restart the stalled revolution? Arlie Hochschild asks in *The Second Shift,* her insightful and depressing study of how two-job couples divide the housework. The feminism of necessity carries women only so far. For Hochschild, and for many who have written on this topic, what women—and men, too—need is paid parental leave, flextime, national health insurance, day care, after-school programs, a public structure of support that makes it easier for parents to combine homelife and work. I agree that these are all necessary and important benefits, although they do not address directly the basic issue of women as second-class citizens in every area of life. But what would it take to win them? Women have been saying they wanted these things for thirty years, with as little impact as minorities who've been calling for good schools and decent affordable housing and clean streets, and factory workers who want more, not less, government regulation of their workplaces. It's a left-wing rhetorical platitude to say that these struggles are all connected no matter how different they seem. But perhaps there's a level on which a connection really does exist. Perhaps for women—including women usually dismissed as "middle-class" and "privileged"—to get that shopping list of expensive, tradition-challenging services will require the same cultural and economic shake-up that would have to take place for blacks to be fully equal, or for the bottom 20 percent of Americans—whose income has stagnated or even lost ground for thirty years—to live decently. Perhaps it would not be so much the day care and paid family leave that would restart that stalled revolution, but the struggle to get them in the first place. And in such a struggle, who can tell how women—and men—might transform themselves? What steps might they find themselves suddenly eager to take that only months, or days, before had seemed unthinkable?

SUBJECT TO

DEBATE

CLARA ZETKIN AVENUE

Scurrying around Manhattan on a blustery morning a few weeks ago, I happened to glance up while waiting for the light to change in front of the public library. Beneath the green and white sign reading Fifth Avenue was another, also green and white, and printed in exactly the same lettering: Clara Zetkin Avenue. Gee, I thought for a split second, if Rudy Giuliani is naming a street for the grande dame of German socialism, he can't be as bad as I thought. But will New Yorkers really start telling taxi drivers to make a right on Zetkin? Then I saw the bent wires fastening the sign to the post, and realized what was going on: Some lefty prankster was reminding us that the next day, March 8, was International Women's Day.

Well, the great day came and went with barely a ripple of attention here in the United States—although I understand that, over at the United Nations, Secretary General Boutros Boutros-Ghali gave a speech about the need to do more for women, which in the case of the United Nations shouldn't be too difficult. Maybe the local indifference is why I find myself filled with gloomy thoughts about the worldwide situation of women. Here we are, at the end of the twentieth century, and not only have hundreds of millions of women around the globe yet to obtain even the barest minimum of human rights, but the notion that they are even entitled to such rights is bitterly contested.

Consider, for example, the horrors documented in the State Department's annual human rights report, which focused on women this year for the first time: genital mutilation in Africa and the Middle East, bride burning in India, sexual slavery in Thailand, forced abortion and sterilization in China. Imagine the firestorm of international protest if any of these practices were imposed by men on men through racism or colonialism or Communism! Well, you don't need to imagine: Just compare the decades of global outrage visited, justly, on South Africa's apartheid regime for denying political, civil and property rights to blacks, and the cultural-relativist defense advanced on behalf of Saudi Arabia and other ultra-Islamic regimes for their denial of same to women. Nobody's calling on American universities and city governments to disinvest in *those* economies. In Iraq and a number of other Middle Eastern countries that are not theocracies, a man can with impunity kill any female relative he feels is "dishonoring" him by unchaste behavior; in Pakistan, the jails are full of women and girls, some only nine years old, whose crime was to be the victims of rape. I suppose Benazir Bhutto will get around to them after she finishes persuading the world that her mother is trying to undermine her government because of a sexist wish to see a son, rather than a daughter, in power.

Well, enough about the Third World. Consider the formerly Communist countries of Eastern Europe and the Soviet Union, where women are losing their jobs in vast, and vastly disproportionate, numbers; day-care centers are closing; and abortion is, in country after country, being restricted. And lest you think I am focusing too much on the evils of Islamic theocracy, consider the Christian variety, as practiced in Poland, where, according to a National Public Radio report, the Catholic church seems hell-bent on living up to the worst fears of Protestant antipopery ranters: abortions illegal, with three-year jail terms for doctors who perform them; birth control hard to find and drastically high priced; religion permeating the public schools, where sex education is taught by priests using textbooks that eschew the word "penis" in favor of "the male source of life that is external to the body"; and at the village level, increasing reports of clerical tyranny, like that of the priest who insisted that two little girls whose parents had not had a church wedding wear cloth badges in the shape of black hearts.

And what about the First World, us? Abortion, preserved for the moment as a formal constitutional right, is ever more circumscribed. Just last week, the Virginia state legislature voted thumbs up on parental consent, and Ohio's package of restrictive abortion measures went into effect. "Welfare reform" gathers steam among both policymakers and pundits, and ever more clearly reveals its true motive, which is not to move the poor into viable employment—an economic impossibility given the current job market—but to make out-of-wedlock childbearing so burdensome and impoverishing for women that they will avoid pregnancy, presumably by just saying no. You will notice that the male-responsibility components of the single-motherhood discussion have largely disappeared. Coercive measures are all right for women—many state legislatures are currently considering programs to Norplant women on welfare—but no one is suggesting vasectomies for men who refuse to pay child support. It would violate their human rights, after all.

And if sexual harassment, domestic violence, rape, job discrimination and the demonization of day care weren't bad enough, I opened my *New York Times Magazine* on March 13 and found a debate over the First Amendment, now "under fire from the left." And who is the representative of this left? Catharine MacKinnon!

Say what you like about Clara Zetkin—and I must say the more I read about her the less I like the old Leninist hard-liner, reproductive-rights opponent and mystic of motherhood—at least she didn't think women's biggest problem was pornography. Nor, for that matter, would she have had two minutes for what passes for "feminist debate" in the media today, in which, by some bizarre alchemy, women who decry sexual violence and harassment are labeled puritans and whiners, and those who pooh-pooh it—or blame it on women—are covered with glory as radical free thinkers.

All in all, things look bleak for women. Still, I suppose we ought to count our blessings. At least no one is trying to rename Lexington Avenue after Camille Paglia.

April 4, 1994

NATIONAL TULIP CONVERSATION

According to a recent item in *The New York Times*, the philanthropist Mary Woodard Lasker "once contributed several thousand dollars to substitute pink tulips, which were her favorites, for less expensive reds and yellows" on the Park Avenue median. Now there, I said to myself, was a woman who knew what her values were. Alas, the same cannot be said for the rest of us, according to Sheldon Hackney, head of the National Endowment for the Humanities. Hackney has called for a "national conversation," to be funded by the N.E.H. and carried out in schools, libraries, museums and state humanities councils around the country, that will take up the issue of what it means to be an American, values-wise: you know, rights and responsibilities, unity and diversity, individualism and group identity. He's been going around the media chatting up his plan, and if his appearance on the *MacNeil/Lehrer NewsHour* last month was any indication, he's got some exciting evenings in store for us:

Charlayne Hunter-Gault: "Do you think there is something, some animal known as American, that we can define?"

Hackney: "I think so. I think so, though I don't know what it is. I don't have an answer for this question, but I think it's an important question. And it's worth pursuing. And I don't have any particular outcome for this. The important thing is that Americans talk to each other and learn from each other about the meaning of being an American."

Personally, I think the values issue is much overrated. After all, Hackney admits that he doesn't know what it means to be an American, and he gets to run the N.E.H. anyway, so how important a question can it be? Besides, if we're all so bewildered about our national values, what is it we will learn from one another by sharing our ignorance in library basements? Actually, I think we're better off in the dark—look what defining their national essences did to the values of the Serbs and Croats. Hackney seems like a very nice man, but drawn out by the ever-diplomatic Hunter-Gault even he succumbed to what is, I suspect, the inexorable logic of the national values discussion. You begin by talking about democracy and pluralism and the Constitution, but before you know it you're talking about immigration restrictions, the "deterioration of the family" and "the loss of the work ethic," and mourning the end of the cold war because "the enemy is one of the things that has made Americans willing to submerge their own individual self-interest from time to time in order to do something for the common good." I don't know exactly what altruistic activities Hackney is thinking of—turning in our neighbors to the F.B.I.? Depriving ourselves of good schools and health care in order to bankroll the military-industrial complex? Invading Third World countries? But if the death of Communism has indeed enfeebled our Americanness, I suppose we could always take the N.E.H. funding and buy a couple of Bradley fighting vehicles so that we can feel noble and miserable again.

The more I scrutinized Hackney's transcribed remarks, the more puzzled I became. I mean, if "the family structure has been eroding" because, as he suggests, both parents are employed, isn't the problem too much work ethic rather than too little? Or is Hackney conflating two different, unnamed villains: Middle-class working moms erode the family, and inner-city blacks neglect the work ethic. I begin to see how it happened that as president of the University of Pennsylvania, Hackney got so dreadfully tangled up in inconsistencies, permitting disciplinary proceedings against a white male student who called a group of noisy black female students "water buffaloes," while declining to move against black students who destroyed all 14,000 copies of the student newspaper because of a column they considered racist. It wasn't that he was, as *The Wall Street Journal* charged, a "political correctness czar." He was just in the throes of a midlife values crisis, and now he wants to enlist the whole country to help him think his way out of it.

Well, I'm certainly prepared to do my part to help Sheldon Hackney out of his quandary. Here are a few questions to get the national values conversation going:

1. "I didn't breed them, so I don't want to feed them"—Jeannie Stich of Nogales, Arizona, talking to *The New York Times* about the "tunnel rats," impoverished Mexican children, some as young as six, who cross the border through sewer tunnels in order to beg or steal.

Discuss with reference to class, race, ethnicity, "family values," NAFTA and the implications of the speaker's gender for the psychological theories of Carol Gilligan.

2. "Freedom is the recognition of necessity"—Hegel.

"Arbeit macht frei"—sign over the main gate at Auschwitz.

"Freedom is about authority. Freedom is about the willingness of every single human being to cede to lawful authority a great deal of discretion about what you do."—New York mayor Rudy Giuliani, speaking at a forum on urban crime.

Analyze these statements as they relate to the notion of historical progress.

3. President Clinton's assistants have drafted a plan for a "national mobilization" against teen motherhood, which they call "a bedrock issue of character and personal responsibility" and claim is the driving force behind poverty, crime, drugs and educational failure.

Discuss with reference to condoms in the schools, parental notification and consent on abortion, the double standard of sexual morality, the boom-bust cycle of capitalism and the deindustrialization of America. Role-play a White House discussion of personal responsibility in light of a recent study suggesting that 62 percent of pregnant and parenting teens had been raped or molested prior to becoming pregnant.

On second thought, we might all be better off discussing the merits of expensive pink tulips versus those of cheaper reds and yellows. Or just quietly planting, for the public enjoyment, whatever variety we happen to prefer.

April 18, 1994

THE LAST PRESIDENT

In March, when Richard Nixon met privately with Aleksandr Rutskoi two months after President Clinton met publicly with Boris Yeltsin, I found myself wondering, and not for the first time, if the reason American politics seems ever more deeply mired in triviality, our Presidents each more hapless than the one before and the electorate ever more bored and distractible, was that the whole thing was a fiction. It seemed unreal because it was unreal. Ford, Carter, Reagan, Bush, Clinton—none of these men were really President. Secretly, behind the scenes, Nixon was President.

Now Nixon is dead, and almost no one seems to want to say good riddance to the old unindicted co-conspirator and war criminal. Clinton, who evaded the draft for Nixon's war in Southeast Asia and whose wife served as a lawyer to the House Judiciary Committee considering impeachment in 1974, offered to hold a state funeral and declared a day of national mourning. His proclamation, which mentioned neither the V-word nor the W-word, blathered on about "statecraft" and noted admiringly that Nixon "suffered defeats that would have ended most political careers, yet he won stunning victories that many of the world's popular leaders have failed to attain." I don't know, that sounds a little values neutral to me, a little lacking in the politics of meaning. But then, as presidential adviser Lloyd Cutler told *The New York Times* in an unusual burst of candor, speaking of the close relations between current and former Presidents despite bitter campaigns, "It's what all of them do for each other—they give each other cover."

But what about the press? On National Public Radio, Daniel Schorr's basset-hound voice was tinged with autumnal wistfulness as he shook his head over the wasted promise of the man who put him on the Enemies List. In the *Times*, Tom Wicker attributed Nixon's dark side to "insecurities" that "may have been rooted in a lonely and emotionally deprived childhood"—an insufficiency of "warm motherly love" (an explanation with the true Nixonian ring of innuendo, sentimentalism and self-pity). Frank Rich wound up his column with the thought that "for an American who came of age with him in the second half of the 20th century, making peace with Richard Nixon proved in the end an essential part of growing up." *Tout comprendre, tout pardonner?*

Why this rush to forgive and forget? I think it's because Nixon really was the last President. He was the last Leader of the Free World who controlled events rather than being controlled by them, who acted—albeit deplorably, deceitfully, disastrously—in his own person rather than as the tool and mouthpiece of organized economic and political interests. He was the last President who actually had a personality about which it was meaningful to inquire.

I don't mean that Nixon was more sincere than those who came after; his duplicity was legendary ("Would you buy a used car from this man?"), and he pioneered some of the media manipulations that we now take for standard practice: the use of television to obfuscate scandal in a blither of family-values kitsch, as in the "Checkers" speech; the public announcement of a reformulated political self, as in the many "new Nixons." But in his day politics had yet to become a branch of entertainment (contrast Nixon's famously awkward cameo on *Laugh-In* with Bill Clinton's effortless charm on *Arsenio*). The machinery of public relations and popular-opinion manufacture was still crude enough that one could hear it whirring and thunking, and one could see too the man at the controls, eating his cottage cheese with ketchup. You had to be pretty gullible—and, of course, in four out of five of Nixon's bids for national office, the electorate was pretty gullible—not to have a good idea of what sort of man Nixon was. But who can say what Carter or Reagan or Bush or Clinton is really like; how much of what they've proposed flows from belief or from expediency? It isn't even an interesting question.

In Trollope's *Last Chronicle of Barset,* two aging clergymen muse regretfully on the changes wrought by High Victorianism on the ecclesiastical vocation. In the old days, says one, "there wasn't so much fuss, and there was more reality." That sense that things are getting less and less real has been gathering speed for more than a century, and now extends to just about every area of life. Clinton and his Big Mac belong together in the world of mass-produced illusions, where, according to the *New York Daily News,* Barbra Streisand is scheduled to speak at the Kennedy School of Government on "Women in Politics." I think the longing for authenticity of any sort, even evil, underlies some of the intellectual and artistic elite's fascination with Nixon: He may have been a phony, but at least he was a phony phony, as opposed to his nemesis J.F.K., who was a real phony. That's why Nixon has preoccupied a striking number of first-rank novelists—Coover, Roth, Mailer, Vidal—and even inspired an opera, while J.F.K. is mired in the world of as-told-to's and bad poetry.

Still, whatever his appeal as a fictional character, and however entertaining his many acts of terminal unhipness (wearing wingtip shoes for a stroll on the beach), it's a mistake to let bygones be bygones. Nixon was personally responsible for a staggering amount of damage. He fomented McCarthyism; prolonged the war in Vietnam and invaded Cambodia; devised the Southern strategy that capitalized on racist resentments to reshape the political landscape in the image of the Republican Party. The men whose careers he promoted—Kissinger, Moynihan, Rehnquist—are, amazingly, still around a quarter of a century later, making the world worse. The only good thing Nixon did, in fact, was to make the Watergate tapes, which revealed to millions of hitherto trusting Americans how power was actually exercised, and what sort of people held it. It's a lesson they've been trying to forget ever since.

May 16, 1994

Communitarianism, No

I did pretty well on the communitarian-virtue test drawn up by Jamie Stiehm in last week's issue of *The Nation*. I took the subway just the other day, *even though* I was carrying two suitcases. I know many of my neighbors by name, have served on a jury, eschew health club membership, use public libraries and other civic amenities and conduct quite a bit of business with the post office, in person. The only questions I failed outright were blood donation (can't) and religious attendance (don't believe in God, so it would be kind of pointless). Volunteer work? Well, once a week or so I walk through Riverside Park with a big garbage bag picking up disgusting items deposited there by my fellow citizens. And I bake cookies for the P.T.A., even though it's always the moms who do it. It's not exactly rescuing the homeless, but then, if Michael Walzer counts editing *Dissent* and Amitai Etzioni gets to claim that, as communitarians, "all we do is civic service," then surely I get credit just for writing these words—at *Nation* rates yet.

And so what? you are probably asking. Well, for one thing, it shows how toothless communitarianism is if I can meet its criteria for model citizenship while devoting my days to promoting the "radical individualism" it holds responsible for the breakdown of community. I'm even on the N.Y.C.L.U. board (does that count as volunteer work?). True, Stiehm's questions are not very demand-ing, and the communitarians themselves might not agree that they fairly represent their views. Still, I ran down the checklist of "ac-tion you can take to help your community" that was included with a wad of P.R. materials in my review copy of Etzioni's *Spirit of Com-munity,* and I did all right there too ("vote in all elections," "consider family counseling if divorce is discussed between you and your partner," "speak up when neighborhood children are rowdy or when trash is dumped on your street"). I fell behind on the numer-ous questions that measured one's willingness to be an insensitive busybody ("encourage people to volunteer for HIV testing as long as their privacy, job, housing and insurance are properly pro-tected") but I picked up bonus points on "drive slower"—I don't even have a license. Can't get much slower than that.

I have three overlapping theories about communitarianism. One is that it's essentially a marketing device, a way for a dozen or so po-litically minded academics to magnify their public presence by marching under a common banner. Poets do this all the time (the New Formalism, the New Narrative, etc.), so why not policy types? This would explain why, for all their claims to be tough-minded, bold and challenging, they take no group stand on divisive issues that people actually care about—abortion and gay rights, for exam-ple. It would explain too why the whole thing seems to be all chiefs and no Indians. Have you ever met a rank-and-file communitarian?

My second theory is that it's antifeminism redux. Note its nos-talgia for traditionally differentiated sex roles, its romanticized view of marriage and striking lack of interest in that institution's darker side (domestic violence, for instance), its absurd habit of blaming family breakdown on women's frivolous quest for self-development. Oh, don't get me started.

My third theory is that communitarianism offers a particular so-cial ministratum—middle-aged white academics with children and fading memories of once having been happier and more liberal—a way to see themselves as political actors without having to do much that is difficult, boring, scary or expensive. It's a little like those ar-ticles in women's magazines ("What's Your Love Quotient?" "Are You a Bad Mom?") that seem to identify all sorts of terrible quasi-universal problems but are cleverly rigged to exempt the reader. At the personal level, most communitarian prescriptions are either easy to follow, in which case you are probably already fulfilling them (Laid off and spending more time with your children? See, you're a communitarian and didn't even know!), or impossible to follow (Office insists you bring work home? Sorry, kids.), in which case you simply move along to the next item, drive slower and so on. There isn't a lot in the communitarian agenda that its intended audience will find much of a stretch: Knowing one's neighbor's name is nice, but it's not exactly loving him as oneself.

Just as communitarianism allows its followers individually to see themselves as virtuous, it encourages them collectively to see what's wrong with contemporary America as the fault of . . . other people. It isn't one's own divorce that causes social breakdown; it's everyone else's divorces. The communitarians like to speak of balancing rights with responsibilities, which sounds good, but somehow the objects of this trade-off tend to be others: the young (curfews, national service), the poor (checkpoints in drug-ridden communities, work requirements for welfare), women (family values—and what about that silence on abortion?).

What is communitarianism, finally, but Republicanism for Democrats—Reaganism with a human face? It's the perfect philosophy for our emerging one-party state: *Travail, Famille, Patrie,* plus campaign finance reform and paid parental leave. More volunteerism, less government activism; more "arbitration," less access to legal redress; more police, less Bill of Rights. (Indeed, its affection for the expansion of police powers—curfews, checkpoints, "drug-free zones" and such—is one of its salient features.) Although communitarians claim they represent a third way, neither left nor right, look what they blame for America's ills: not corporate capitalism, poverty, bigotry and inequality but "radical individualism." You'd think the A.C.L.U. ran the country.

Alas, no. Bill Clinton runs the country, and the communitarians like to boast that he is one of them.

July 25/August 1, 1994

Single-Sex Sexism

Being a feminist can take you to some pretty strange places. Consider the past few weeks: In my capacity as tooth fairy, I bought my six-year-old, Sophie, a baseball glove; I got a warm feeling (this is embarrassing) reading an article about a reunion of the first Episcopalian women priests; and I let out a *Yesss!* when the Supreme Court ruled in favor of Shannon Faulkner, the determined young woman who wants to attend the all-male-though-publicly-funded Citadel military college. Sports, religion and war, the three banes of human existence—if this coeducation thing keeps going, we won't be able to blame them on men anymore.

Isn't it strange, though, how the more similar the lives of men and women become, the more we hear about the supposed benefits of keeping the sexes apart? Recently the case for single-sex education has mostly been made by feminists, who, rightly, note the many ways girls can get pushed to the margins of the coed classroom and who, more questionably, attribute the achievements of single-sex female grads to the single-sex factor. But as we saw in the Citadel case, two can play this game. The Citadel's arguments included such anomalies as citations from Carol Gilligan and expert testimony from Harvard sociologist David Riesman, who argued that the absence of women allows the Citadel's students to express their "gentler side," and write "very contemplative poetry of high aesthetic sensibility." (Gilligan herself filed an affidavit on behalf of Shannon Faulkner; Elizabeth Fox-Genovese, usually to be found railing against the supposed separatism of women's studies programs, weighed in on the side of the Citadel.)

Leaving aside the question of whether we want to break out the champagne because women will now be able to get degrees in ritual humiliation and bombing Baghdad, when it comes to the merits of single-sex versus coeducation in general, I find I can argue both sides without quite persuading myself. I don't think my nine years of boyless private school did a thing for me in the math, science, leadership or self-esteem departments, but this was back in the bad old prefeminist days; surely *now* girls' schools aren't run by men like Dr. Shafer, who let me drop trigonometry because, and I quote, "I've always thought women only needed enough math to do their grocery lists." On the other hand, I note that at Sophie's coed public school, the kids are pretty much permitted to sex-type themselves—no girls in the chess club, a solitary boy in the glee club. The efforts of the most outspoken feminist mom (not me) to call attention to this and other instances of stereotyping were, to put it mildly, not appreciated by the female head of the school.

A look at the research doesn't clear things up much. True, a number of studies show that single-sex education benefits girls (there's much less evidence that it helps boys, and some that it hurts them). The trouble is, since coed and single-sex schools have so many differences, it's hard to know what, exactly, is being measured. Choosing single-sex is a pretty dramatic decision, with complicated class and social ramifications that go way beyond income levels and the other things researchers use as controls. Perhaps those positive research results reflect not the school itself but what kind of students—and parents—the school attracts. Maybe, for instance, parents who choose single-sex are more ambitious for their daughters, care less about producing a "popular" teenager, take a bigger hand in their children's education. Interestingly, researchers who compared coed and single-sex comprehensive (non-selective, neighborhood, public) schools in England, where single-sex education is commonplace, found no differences in outcome for girls.

What I suspect is mostly being measured is the degree of attention kids get. The public-school experiments now in vogue—all-girl math classes, inner-city "academies" for black boys—have energetic teachers who believe in what they're doing, new instructional materials and methods, a sense of mission, excitement and commitment to success. You don't need a Ph.D. in sociology to see why kids who languished in regular classes would perk up. But if single-sex programs were to become routine, they would more and more resemble the regular classroom—perhaps even down to the sexism. As we sometimes tend to forget, women have played quite a large role in enforcing on one another those damaging stereotypes all-female classrooms are supposed to correct.

Changing coeducation to meet the needs of both sexes will take work, but will it really be so difficult as all that? If, as students in one all-girl math class told *The New York Times,* they had been mocked, teased, belittled and interrupted by boys in coed classes, why can't the grown-ups read those boys the riot act? Why should girls be segregated because of what boys do? Similarly, it shouldn't take a barbaric regimen of military drill to get a teenage boy to write a poem—and in fact, it doesn't, as a glance at any campus lit mag shows.

At bottom, single-sex education is the counsel of despair. It says that the sexes can't be friends and colleagues and do serious work together—although the adult world (even the army!) increasingly requires this—and can only "be themselves" in the absence of the other. In her Citadel testimony, Fox-Genovese argued that single-sex education separates "the story of mating and dating" from "education." Leaving aside the question of what head-shaving, will-breaking, insults and the rest have to do with education—it sounds more like *The Story of O* than Matthew Arnold to me—Prof. F-G's argument is reminiscent of the one misogynists of an earlier day used to keep women out of the Ivy League and, I wouldn't be surprised, out of the University of Bologna in the thirteenth century.

No, for better or worse the future is coed. As Shannon Faulkner advised her detractors, "Wake up and smell the '90s." And that goes for both sexes.

August 22/29, 1994

OPINIONATED WOMEN

The other morning a Finnish radio journalist interviewed me about Richard Nixon. It was an odd experience in several ways, walking around West End Avenue with one of those little microphones clipped to my collar so that the Finns in their quiet forests could hear our exciting New York City traffic noises. And the oddest thing about it was that, for once, my ideas were being solicited on a subject other than women and feminism.

About a year ago in *The New Republic* Naomi Wolf asked why women's voices are so rarely heard in the national forums of debate—public affairs talk shows, Op-Ed pages, political magazines, newspaper columns. I thought her answer—one part "passive but institutionalized discrimination on the part of editors and producers," two parts women's "deeply conditioned, internal inhibitions" against self-assertion and conflict—would have rung truer if the proportions had been reversed. *The New Republic* may receive, as she says, from two to five times as many unsolicited manuscripts from men as from women (here at *The Nation* the ratio is about the same), but surely what counts is not the slush pile, very little of which is usable, but assignments—the writers that editors recruit, cultivate and encourage in the perpetration of "think pieces" that will get them on *Crossfire*. Most of those editors are men. They just don't think of women, except when they absolutely have to.

And sometimes not even then. You can turn on your TV any night of the week and see a panel of male "experts" chatting away on a topic one would think a knowledgeable woman would bring a useful perspective to—single motherhood, for example, which was the subject of an all-male talk spectacular with Ben Wattenberg in April. But have you ever seen a panel of female "experts"—forget the female moderator—analyzing, say, deadbeat dads, much less gun control or the November elections? Even those silly televised catfights—Date Rape: Good or Bad? Find Out Tonight!—usually have a male guest or two to help the ladies out of their perplexities and remind us that these aren't women's issues, they're *human* issues.

Still, the cultural space that does exist for female opinion is mostly about those "women's issues," just as openings for blacks, Latinos, Asians and even uncloseted gays tend to be around their issues. The resulting situation illustrates both the usefulness and the limitations of identity politics as a way into the mainstream for either groups or individuals. One wins access because, besides being fabulously talented and all that, one can claim to bring a new perspective into the debates of the day; indeed, since so many of those debates are precisely about identity issues, these perspectives must be included, however grudgingly, if the forum is to have credibility. Even *National Review,* which firmly opposes the entire project of modern womanhood, beginning with bobbed hair, makes room on occasion for women who attack the women's movement: Christina Hoff Sommers, Cathy Young, Elizabeth Fox-Genovese, all of whom would be shocked and insulted, I'm sure, to be told that their presence in William F. Buckley's pages had anything to do with... their *gender*.

Of course it does. How many women, after all, does *National Review, The New Republic* or *The Atlantic Monthly*—or for that matter *The Nation*—publish on topics unrelated to gender? How often do women appear on *Nightline* or *Crossfire* when the subject isn't "Hillary Clinton: Does Whitewater Stigmatize All Women?" or "Is the Wonderbra Sexist?" How often, even, does a woman review a book that isn't either by a woman or about a women's issue? Identity politics has helped women get a crack at "their" topics, and it has helped enlarge the space allotted to those topics. But it has also boxed women into those topics. As Saint Augustine put it, men need women only for the things they can't get from a man. For procreation (the one thing Saint A. could come up with), substitute 1,000 words on breast implants or day care, and that view still holds a lot of sway.

All this encourages women to specialize in women: That's where the openings are. (This, too, is true across the political board: It's Phyllis Schlafly's antifeminism, not her anticommunism, that made her name a household word.) Within this world the Gilliganian taboos on space-claiming and confrontation are relaxed. In fact, I have to say that what I've seen firsthand of feminists and antifeminists in the media doesn't support Wolf's shrinking-violet theory at all. Strong opinions, interrupting, waxing on? No problem! Like actresses, opera singers and rock stars, women whose subject is women are allowed to be flamboyant, egocentric and attention-demanding, even rude, because they are safely ensconced in a gender-bound category, in which they compete with one another and not with men. Camille Paglia can get away with a lot more than Eleanor Clift.

The unfortunate thing isn't that lots of women specialize in opinions about women—feminism is, after all, one of the central movements of the century. It's the way the culture labels those women, and the way it shunts feminism itself away from what are perceived as general topics. Barbara Ehrenreich wrote a fine, prescient book about the economic anxieties of the middle class, but she's in the Rolodex under Women, so you don't see her on those mumblefests on the economy. The feminist critique of welfare policy gets a nod when the subject is feminism, but dead silence when the subject is welfare reform.

Am I being too cynical in arguing that female opinion-meisters specialize in women's issues partly as a cultural adaptation? I'm not suggesting that the interest isn't genuine, the work compelling or the commitment real. But that's how cultural adaptation works: You *want* to do the thing that is laid out for you to do. I'm a perfect example, having begun this column thrilled at being queried about Nixon, and having ended by writing . . . about women, after all.

October 17, 1994

"Sex in America"

The big sex story this month falls in the No News Is Good News department: "Faithfulness in Marriage Thrives After All," "Survey Finds Most Adults Sexually Staid," "Turns Out We Are 'Sexually Conventional.' " The occasion for these ecstatically ho-hum headlines was the publication of *Sex in America: A Definitive Survey* by a trio of social scientists (Robert T. Michael, John H. Gagnon and Edward O. Laumann) with Gina Kolata of *The New York Times*, which set off the sort of press-embargo-breached-by-furiously-competing-news-outlets frenzy usually reserved for the racier passages of presidential memoirs or sensational revelations by K.G.B. turncoats. So now it's official: Other people are not having more fun than you are. You (married, monogamous, straight, once-or-twice-a-week-but-nothing-too-kinky-please) are normal; 75 percent of husbands and a whopping 86 percent of wives do not stray. And it isn't 10 percent of Americans who are gay, it's 10 percent of *New Yorkers*.

Whew. This, after all, is the study whose original, federally funded version was deep-sixed by Jesse Helms, who said it would be used to legitimize "homosexuality, pedophilia, anal and oral sex, sex education, teenage pregnancy, and all down the line." At least according to Michael et al., he needn't have worried: The vast majority of Americans (83 percent) have one or no sexual partner, eschew exotic practices and—while they enjoy sex, especially if they are male and even if they are "conservative Protestants"—they're not about to go out and do something wild, like marry someone from a sharply different background or fool around with sex toys. While the media have played up the cozy, comforting side of the study's findings, *Sex in America* actually makes a rather dark point about American life: People exist in particular, distinct and rather isolated social milieus that mold, channel and limit their sexual choices and behavior in myriad subtle and not-so-subtle ways. We may believe in *Romeo and Juliet* (or *Debbie Does Dallas*), but we live on *Main Street.*

Well, far be it from me to suggest that the study, widely hailed as the most scientific in world history, may not be the last word on the subject of sex. Certainly it is better designed than its steamier predecessors—Kinsey, Hite, *Redbook, Playboy*—in that the subjects were randomly selected rather than solicited volunteers, who tend to be the more sexually oriented and active, not to say exhibitionistic and verbal, portion of the citizenry. I will merely observe that it is extremely difficult to speak truthfully and without reserve about intimate matters, and that it would be surprising if the pressures toward conformity and social acceptability that the authors identify as key shapers of American sex lives did not also shape the answers to a sexual questionnaire. As the psychiatrist Karl Menninger said, pooh-poohing the Kinsey report, Women *pay* me to listen to their sexual confessions, and even then they can't tell me the truth. You can apply Menninger's insight as you like to the study's finding that only six in a thousand men visit prostitutes in a given year, that virtually none find the idea of forced sex "very appealing" and that the lifetime median number of sex partners for women is two.

There's another news angle to *Sex in America,* though, which has tended to be overlooked in the general rejoicing at the robust health of monogamy, and that is the considerable amount of forced sex the study uncovered. Seventeen percent of women and 12 percent of men report having had a sexual experience as children with an adolescent or adult. Twenty-two percent of women report having been "forced to do something sexually" by a man, almost always one who was not a stranger (4 percent of the incidents) but an acquaintance, boyfriend or husband. Among women eighteen to twenty-four, the figure is 25 percent—the much derided one-in-four figure that Dr. Mary Koss came up with in her endlessly attacked 1985 study of campus date rape. True, it is unclear whether the experiences women are referring to are rape—in the legal or colloquial sense or in their own mind. Certainly they would not be so defined by most men, only 3 percent of whom said they had ever forced a woman to do anything sexual. But to my mind, once we are outside a courtroom, whether we call "forced sex" rape is not the most important question. What matters is that many women say they have been made to comply with a man's sexual wishes when they did not want to, and it seems pretty clear that they have not been brainwashed by Catharine MacKinnon.

You can turn that finding a number of different ways, of course. There's a big difference between a fraternity gang-bang, a boyfriend who says he'll drop you if you don't go down on him and a husband who pins you down and sticks it in when you've made it clear you're not interested. But there really isn't a way to interpret the forced-sex data that supports the views of the voguish critics of the antirape movement, Katie Roiphe, Cathy Young, Christina Hoff Sommers: for example, that reports of sexual coercion are really morning-after regrets that have been put through a Dworkinite blender; that the sexes are equally aggressive toward each other (significantly, almost no men said they had been sexually coerced by a woman); that the bedroom is an even playing field where women have as much power—and as much pleasure—as men.

Will Roiphe, Young, or Sommers attack the authors as "victim feminists," "gender feminists," "new Victorians"? *Sex in America* ought to help us cut right through the absurd contention that to say there's lots of sexual coercion is to render women weak and helpless, and that to imagine sex without aggression is "utopian." Here, after all, are three plain-spoken, middle-aged, social science sobersides, not a deconstructionist among them, and they rather like the way that consent is being redefined from "She didn't say no" (or "She was a slut, so I didn't have to listen") to "She said yes." They even have kind words for the much-ridiculed Antioch Rules, which require explicit consent for *everything*.

"Sexperts Say: Ask First Is Best." Now, *that's* a news story.

October 31, 1994

SCHOOL PRAYER?
BY ALL MEANS

For reasons I have never understood, my left-wing, cosmopolitan parents—he the agnostic Episcopalian, she the atheistic Jew—sent me to a private nondenominational Protestant school for girls. Prayer in the schools? For nine years I had chapel *every day*: three hymns, the doxology, the Lord's Prayer, a Bible reading (or was it two Bible readings?) and, on Fridays, a sacred-music solo from Mr. Crandall, the organist. Never mind that one-third of the student body was Jewish and another third Roman or Eastern-rite Catholic. You don't have to say the prayers, our teachers used to tell us, but you should bow your head as a mark of respect. Not praying was easy, not bowing somewhat less so. It was not singing that was the real challenge. I loved choral singing, which is surely one of life's great pleasures, but since I didn't believe in God, to take part was to participate in falsehood. Truth or beauty? Principled isolation or join the fun? Reign in Hell or serve in Heaven? These questions obsessed me for years and, indeed, still do.

What was the effect on me of all this compulsory religion? Well, I don't remember a single word of the doxology, but I do have by heart the words to dozens of hymns that no one sings anymore because the lyrics are too imbued with cultural arrogance or sectarian crankiness. Once I was trapped alone in an elevator and, believe me, I was glad I knew all the verses of "From Greenland's Icy Mountains" and "The Church's One Foundation." Then too, without all that force-fed Christianity I probably wouldn't have even the modest sense of Jewish identity I possess today. There's nothing like being excluded to make one embrace one's otherness.

Mostly, though, chapel made me loathe religion. I know nonbelievers who find in the occasional church service or high holy day something pleasant and nostalgic. I know believers too who don't trouble themselves over the outmoded or bloodthirsty bits of their faith; they just take what they want and leave the rest. Not me. For me, religion is serious business—a farrago of authoritarian nonsense, misogyny and humble pie, the eternal enemy of human happiness and freedom. My family may have made me a nonbeliever, but it took chapel to make me an atheist.

That's why I'm in favor of prayer in the schools. Now that Newt Gingrich has called for swift passage of a school-prayer amendment, just about every liberal columnist in America has pointed out that the separation of church and state is a great boon for religion and has helped make ours easily the most observant country in the West. Quite right. The state-backed religions of Western Europe are pallid affairs compared with our robust industry of Virgin-spotters, tongues-speakers and Mitzvah-mobilers. Where is the English Jimmy Swaggart, the French billboard in whose depicted bowl of spaghetti thousands claim to discern the face of Christ? You could say that state support waters down the Living Word, or you could say that when the state underwrites religion the buried links between these two forms of social control stand too clearly revealed for modern, let alone postmodern, people to accept. Or you could say that wherever the state gives it permission, religion invariably overplays its hand and starts acting like it's the seventeenth century. Look at Poland, where it took the Catholic Church only a few years of temporal power to squander the moral capital it had garnered during the Communist era as the self-proclaimed defender of human rights and personal liberty. Look at Israel, where civil marriage does not even exist. Look at Iran.

In our country the constitutional separation of church and state has obscured the nonetheless real connection between the two as fellow enforcers of conformity, mystification and hierarchy. Prayer in the schools will make it plain to see. It's never too early for the young to take the measure of the forces arrayed against those who would think for themselves. Right now religion has the romantic aura of the forbidden—Christ is cool. We need to bring it into the schools, which kids already hate, and associate it firmly with boredom, regulation, condescension, makework and de facto segregation, with business math and *Cliffs Notes* and metal detectors.

Prayer in the schools will rid us of the bland no-offense ecumenism that is so infuriating to us anticlericals: Oh, so *now* you say Jews didn't kill Christ—a little on the late side, isn't it? I see a big boom in theological casuistry, denominational infighting, schisms and scandals of all kinds. Anti-Semitism will thrive, as it tends to when Christian soldiers start marching as to war, and that will be a good lesson for Midge Decter and the other neocon Jews who have been cozying up to the religious right.

Many editorial hands have been wrung on behalf of minority-religion children who will be singled out and humiliated by school prayer, which cannot possibly be formulated so vaguely as not to violate someone's conscience. This too can be a valuable lesson in alienation. And there's a way out: I heard a Christian Action Network fellow, Tom Kilgannon, suggest on the radio that local standards should apply, so that if a neighborhood had, say, a lot of "Islams," the Islams should get to write the prayer. Who knows? We may yet see graduations blessed by anything from the sacrifice of a chicken to a Latin mass.

After a few years it will become clear that prayer in schools does nothing to lower crime or teen pregnancy, much less raise S.A.T. scores. The religious kids will still be devout, but the others—the ones from nonobservant homes, who supposedly need to be forced into piety—will have been moved from apathy to open disgust. And they will be entirely justified. Nothing reveals the bankruptcy of the new conservatism more than its promotion of school prayer. The message to youth is clear: We have nothing for you here, start thinking about the hereafter.

December 26, 1994

Beggar's Opera

"Ah, New York City," the Last Marxist said expansively the other day as we emerged from the subway at Fourteenth Street and Union Square, "where the nineteenth century meets the twenty-first, with nothing in between." Riding the subway does turn the mind to grand reflections on the sweep of history. For example, can we really have gone in less than a single lifetime from the senti-mental solidarity-in-misery of "Brother, Can You Spare a Dime?" to the Transit Authority's ad campaign against giving spare change to panhandlers? In addition to being entertained by the latest car-toon installment of the adventures of Julio and Marisol, the AIDS-education sweethearts, and ads for the tattoo-removal services of "*your* dermatologist," the appropriately named Dr. Zizmor, the rider is now being indoctrinated at taxpayer expense in downward class resentment through a ubiquitous poster campaign.

"I'm *SOOOO* glad I got this seat," reads a thought balloon clev-erly positioned to seem to be rising from an actual passenger's head. "Good, *NOW* I can relax." But no: "Hey, buddy. Over here—over my head. See that? It says it's illegal. Come onnnnn! Can't I just *SIT HERE* without getting hassled?!!" and so on. I give the T.A. credit for capturing the pugnacious whine of our local vernacular, but it's got a nerve assuming the hapless rider seated beneath the poster shares its views. Never one to shirk a challenge from the state, the L.M. immediately handed out quarters to both beggars on board our train, and scribbled "HATE SPEECH" over the offending ad in big Magic Marker letters.

I will spare you the plangent appeals for mercy, tolerance, fellow feeling and kindness, the references to Dickens and Christ. I've discussed the subway-panhandling question with many members of the cognitive elite, and I know that the bleeding-heart approach cuts no ice these days.

"I *hate* them," said one lefty academic friend of mine, who proceeded to mount a spirited defense of civility, public space, social order, peace and quiet, newspaper reading and meditative calm. This is the subway we're talking about, I protested—you know, perverts, thieves, crazy people? The place where I witnessed an actual murder in 1976, when things were still supposedly O.K. in the city? Where in one week in December a handmade incendiary device set three teenagers on fire, and in the next week an even more terrifying bomb explosion injured forty-five people, some critically? But I know what he means. I too feel a shrinking sensation when some poor wretch stands up in the middle of the car, takes a deep breath and announces his determination not to rob or steal to get the $14 he needs for a hot meal and a room, as passengers stare unseeingly at their newspapers or look stonily off into space. I too would like to be left alone to read about O.J.'s closetful of bloody garments.

There's a free speech issue here, of course—you can say just about anything else in the subway, after all, and over the years I've been riding, many people have. But what gets to me is this: Who would have thought that the times would require each of us to develop a personal philosophy of almsgiving? A while back Brian Lehrer did a segment on his call-in show on WNYC radio about street giving, and it was truly amazing how much mental energy people had devoted to ensuring that their little quarter did not find its way into an undeserving pocket. I know people who give to women but not men, to blacks but not whites, to the ones who look crazy or crippled but not the ones who look addicted or ablebodied, to the ones who open bank doors (because at least they're trying to be useful) or especially not to those (because it feels like a shakedown), to the ones they know by sight from around the neighborhood or never to those, because giving would be to deny Mr. or Ms. Homeless Person the dignity of a relationship untainted by financial motives. If people devoted as much close analysis to their tax dollars, the arms budget would have been slashed to zero years ago.

I say, give what you can without thinking too much about it. Better a panhandler than the Hare Krishna costumed like Bozo the clown, who is louder than any panhandler and much more obnoxious, or that beautiful black nun, doomed to spend her rapidly fading youth silently holding her bowl near the Times Square token booth. At least with panhandlers, you know your money isn't going to build ashrams or convert the heathen. Panhandlers need the money, even if their spiels aren't always the gospel truth, but more than that, the rest of us need to see them. It's crazy to expect that in New York City, where about a third of the children are poor, where whole families camp out in welfare offices and 1,500 people live squirreled away in the transit system's tunnels and passages, middle-class people can live untouched by squalor.

Sure, there was a time when the subways did not resemble an open call for *Threepenny Opera* extras. But it isn't the breakdown of civility that changed that, it's the explosive growth of poverty. To shoo away the beggars is not to solve their problems. They clearly need more than tough love and a cold shoulder, and it's not as though Mayor Giuliani—or President Clinton, who is contemplating things like abolishing funds for public housing as he stalks the elusive white male vote—is offering drug treatment, services for the HIV-positive, jobs, rooms, help on anything like the scale required.

The Transit Authority's antibegging policy is intended simply to allow the rest of us to pretend that the immiseration of the poor, with all its attendant madness, hysteria, violence, addiction, disease and bad smells, is not taking place, is not, indeed, the flip side of the mayor's plan to make lower Manhattan and midtown the world capital of the symbolic analysts beloved by Robert Reich. It's not for nothing the *New York Times* front page two weeks ago set "Giuliani Plans Inducements to Revive Wall Street Area" next to "Mayor Is Planning to Trim Programs That Assist Poor."

Let the panhandlers ride the trains, making the rest of us uncomfortable. Step lively, please, and watch out for teens in flames.

January 9/16, 1995

DEADBEAT DADS:
A MODEST PROPOSAL

"You start out with the philosophy that you can have as many babies as you want . . . if you don't ask the government to take care of them. But when you start asking the government to take care of them, the government ought to have some control over you. I would say, for people like that, if they want the government to take care of their children I would be for something like Norplant, mandatory Norplant."

What well-known politician made the above remarks? Newt Gingrich? Jesse Helms? Dan Quayle? No, it was Marion Barry, newly installed Democratic mayor of our nation's capital, speaking last November to Sally Quinn of *The Washington Post.* The same Marion Barry whose swearing-in on January 2 featured a poetry reading by Maya Angelou, who, according to *The New York Times,* "drew thunderous applause when she pointed at Mr. Barry and crooned: 'Me and my baby, we gonna shine, shine!' " Clarence Thomas, Bill Clinton, Marion Barry: Ms. Angelou sure knows how to pick them.

One of my neighbors told me in the laundry room that it wasn't very nice of me to have mentioned Arianna Huffington's millions when we "debated" spirituality and school prayer on *Crossfire* the other day. So I won't belabor Mayor Barry's personal history here.

After all, the great thing about Christianity, of which Mayor Barry told Ms. Quinn he is now a fervent devotee, is that you can always declare yourself reformed, reborn and redeemed. So maybe Mayor ("Bitch set me up") Barry really is the man to "bring integrity back into government," as he is promising to do.

But isn't it interesting that the male politicians who go all out for family values—the deadbeat dads, multiple divorcers, convicted felons, gropers and philanderers who rule the land—always focus on women's behavior and always in a punitive way? You could, after all, see the plethora of women and children in poverty as the fruits of male fecklessness, callousness, selfishness and sexual vanity. We hear an awful lot about pregnant teens, but what about the fact that men over the age of twenty account for two-thirds of births to girls fourteen and under? What about the fact that the condom is the only cheap, easy-to-use, effective, side-effectless nonprescription method of contraception—and it is the male partner who must choose to use it? What about the 50 percent of welfare mothers who are on the rolls because of divorce—that is, the failure of judges to order, or husbands to pay, adequate child support?

Marion Barry's views on welfare are shared by millions: Women have babies by parthenogenesis or cloning, and then perversely demand that the government "take care of them." Last time I looked, taking care of children meant feeding, bathing and singing the Barney song, and mothers, not government bureaucrats, were performing those tasks. It is not the mother's care that welfare replaces but the father's cash. Newt Gingrich's Personal Responsibility Act is directed against unmarried moms, but these women are actually *assuming* a responsibility that their babies' fathers have shirked. It's all very well to talk about orphanages, but what would happen to children if mothers abandoned them at the rate fathers do? A woman who leaves her newborn in the hospital and never returns for it still makes headlines. You'd need a list as thick as the New York City phone book to name the men who have no idea where or how or who their children are.

My point is not to demonize men, but fair's fair. If we've come so far down the road that we're talking about mandatory Norplant;

about starving women into giving up their kids to orphanages (Republican version) or forcing young mothers to live in group homes (Democratic version); if Charles Murray elicits barely a peep when he suggests releasing men from financial obligations to out-of-wedlock children and divorced moms have to hire private detectives to get their exes to pay court-awarded child support, it's time to ensure that the Personal Responsibility Act applies equally to both sexes. For example:

1. A man who fathers a child out of wedlock must pay $10,000 a year or 20 percent of his income, whichever is greater, in child support until the child reaches twenty-one. If he is unable to pay, the government will, in which case the father will be given a workfare job and a dorm residence comparable to those provided homeless women and children—that is, curfews, no visitors and compulsory group therapy sessions in which, along with other unwed fathers, he can learn to identify the patterns of irresponsibility that led him to impregnate a woman so thoughtlessly.

2. A man who fathers a second child out of wedlock must pay child support equal to that for the first; if he can't, or is already on workfare, he must have a vasectomy. A sample of his sperm will be preserved so he can father more children if he becomes able to support the ones he already has.

3. Married men who father children out of wedlock or in sequential marriages have the same obligations to all their children, whose living standards must be as close to equal as is humanly possible. This means that some older men will be financially unable to provide their much-younger second wives with the babies those women often crave. Too bad!

4. Given the important role played by fathers in everything from upping their children's test scores to teaching them the meaning of terms like "wide receiver" and "throw weight," divorced or unwed fathers will be legally compelled to spend time with their children or face criminal charges of child neglect. Absentee dads, *not* overburdened single moms, will be legally liable for the crimes and misdemeanors of their minor children, and *their* paychecks will be docked if the kids are truant.

5. In view of the fact that men can father children unknowingly, all men will pay a special annual tax to provide support for children whose paternity is unknown. Men wishing to avoid the tax can undergo a vasectomy at state expense, with sperm to be frozen at personal expense (Republican version) or by government subsidy (Democratic version).

As I was saying, fair's fair.

January 30, 1995

AFFIRMATIVE ACTION
BEGINS AT HOME

When people argue that we don't need affirmative action anymore, I remember an interchange I had a few years ago with the friendly mom who was showing me around her child's preschool. The place was adorable, I agreed, the teachers imaginative and kind, and no question my daughter would be happy there. But where were the children of color? It's a problem, the mother agreed with a rueful smile. We just don't seem to be able to find them! Then she brightened: Next year would be different—one family would be sending its adopted Chinese toddler, another its adopted Paraguayan. The school was so excited!

You may laugh at this peculiar definition of multiculturalism. Did she think the little Paraguayan would show up wearing a serape and tootling a wooden flute? But this was not Mississippi or Cicero, or even, God forbid, Long Island. This was the Upper West Side of Manhattan, the most liberal congressional district in America and, at least on paper, one of the most racially integrated neighborhoods in New York City, where people still read *The Village Voice* for its politics and the churches can't decide whether to be early-music concert halls or soup kitchens. If the Good Woman of West End Avenue "can't find" black and Hispanic and Asian children to share her child's classroom, and persuades herself that cultural diversity can be handily supplied by foreign adoption, how likely is it that the country as a whole has reached *either* the color-blind society conservatives claim to want, or the delight-in-difference that multiculturalists promote?

Across the media spectrum, opinion journalists have been falling over themselves to depict the 1994 elections as the White Man's Revenge, and affirmative action seems to be emerging as the chief culprit, worse even than the Antioch dating rules or deconstructionism. On talk radio, where Angry White Males conduct their drumming sessions, Al on his car phone and Joe in Chicago speak openly of blacks and Hispanics as unqualified, lazy and stupid. In the mainstream media, the objection is put differently. The civil rights movement has been such a success that affirmative action is unnecessary, say Linda Chavez, George Will and the other usual suspects; to rightward-moving liberals like Jim Sleeper, it's a bureaucratic hindrance that fuels white resentment and condescends to deserving nonwhites.

I'm not sure whether those who make these arguments are naïve or devious. But in my little corner of the work world—liberal opinion magazines—nothing could be further from the truth.

In the thirteen years I've been associated with *The Nation,* we've had exactly one nonwhite person (briefly) on our editorial staff of thirteen, despite considerable turnover. And we're not alone: *The Atlantic* has zero nonwhites out of an editorial staff of twenty-one; *Harper's,* zero out of fourteen; *The New York Review of Books,* zero out of nine; *The Utne Reader,* zero out of twelve. A few do a little better, although nothing to cheer about: *The Progressive,* one out of six; *Mother Jones,* one out of seven; *In These Times,* one out of nine; *The New Republic,* two out of twenty-two; *The New Yorker,* either three or six, depending on how you define "editorial," out of one hundred plus. Interestingly, in view of the bromide about feminism as a white women's movement to which nonwhite women are justifiably indifferent or hostile, *Ms.* comes off rather well, with three out of eleven, including the editor in chief, Marcia Ann Gillespie, who is African-American. (These figures do not include columnists, correspondents or contributing editors, who are also overwhelmingly white, and at *The Nation* exclusively so.)

My point is not to bite the hand that feeds me, or to attack particular people. Clearly, if so many liberal magazines share this particular limitation thirty-one years after the passage of the Civil Rights Act (and five years before the opening of the twenty-first century), something more is at issue than personalities. Nor do I wish to dwell on the hypocrisy factor, the liberal genius for avoiding the medicine one prescribes for others, for claiming extenuating circumstances one would *never* accept from one's political opponents, and for confusing, like that preschool mom, a heart in the right place with a major talent for cognitive dissonance. On second thought, let me dwell—because surely the widely noted and much-ridiculed ineffectuality of liberal politics is connected to the inability of that vision to command even its own adherents. If we don't live our politics, why should anyone else? Maybe the personnel is the political.

The real lesson I draw from these demographics, though, is that far from living in the color-blind America of conservative fantasies, or the multicultural America of left-wing ones, we still live in a society that is segregated in many ways. People are carefully slotted—and slot themselves—into remarkably precise positions in a complex class, racial and social order that then determines what they see and what they know. For that preschool mom, reality was families exactly like her own. For the denizens of the tiny cocktail party that is liberal journalism, it's the other denizens, plus their friends, classmates and former students and interns, plus all those people's grown children and *their* friends, all twined together in an eternal golden braid of networking and schmooze. The workplace is white because the social world is white, and vice versa. Merit doesn't really come into it.

It was to break open such closed worlds that affirmative action was originally designed. And, it's important to note, the benefits are not one-sided. Affirmative action would not only diversify our offices, it would invigorate our pages, which sure could use new voices, new perspectives, new questions. It might even—who knows?—refresh our politics.

Racial integration. It's such a crazy idea, it just might work.

March 13, 1995

WE ARE ALL MARCIA CLARK

Poor Marcia Clark. The tabloids criticize her hair and clothes, Judge Ito pounces on her every extra word, and now her estranged husband says she's spending too much time at work and he should have custody of the kids. Even by the admittedly high standards of male chauvinism set by the O.J. Simpson trial—which, besides the crime itself, offers the spectacle of not one but two of the defense lawyers having been accused of wife abuse in earlier marriages—Ms. Clark's custody problems set a new record for imposing on women a double standard and a double bind. You want to know why women are angry? This is why.

I used to quip, back when welfare reform was just a gleam in Candidate Clinton's eye, that you could tell the liberals from the conservatives because the liberals wanted poor mothers to stay home and prosperous ones to work, and the conservatives wanted exactly the reverse. That was before what the mainstream media like to call "the emerging consensus on welfare" had fully consensed. Now, it seems, everyone agrees that poor mothers should be compelled to work, and the only dispute is over whether they should receive actual wages. We don't hear too much about whether stressed-out moms, and day care, and coming home to an empty, cookieless apartment, and constantly shifting baby-sitting arrangements are bad for poor kids. On the contrary, as long as a mother is toiling in the low-wage female-ghetto part of the economy, her long hours on the job and frazzled mothering are supposed to be sources of pride for the whole family.

Look what happens, though, as you go up the income-and-education scale. Exactly the same behavior the government is on the verge of demanding of millions of welfare moms—and threatening them with loss of their children to foster or group care should they "refuse"—is being used by fathers to challenge the custody rights of mothers who are in the professions, or preparing for one, like Jennifer Ireland, who lost custody of her daughter last summer to the hitherto uninvolved and child-support-resistant dad after she enrolled the tot in day care so she could attend the University of Michigan. Are middle-class children so much needier of parental attention than poor ones? Or is it that when mothers take powerful, demanding jobs in formerly all-male fields, or go after higher education, not "job training" or basic literacy, the outdated, idealized image of the stay-at-home mother is mobilized to punish them for stepping out of line? I'm reminded here of the old "protective" labor laws which chivalrously protected women right out of fields in which they competed with men but left untouched their dismal working conditions in the jobs men didn't want.

When is the United States finally going to accept the modern reality that mothers have complex lives—and *should* have complex lives? They have ambitions, just like men. They get degrees. They go to work. Sometimes their work cannot be squeezed into the home-by-the-school-bell pattern that, according to *Newsweek*, half the probate judges surveyed in Massachusetts felt was appropriate for mothers. It isn't just high-profile women like Marcia Clark whose jobs sometimes require late nights and bouts of flat-out effort. The same bad-mother argument can be mobilized against *any* woman by a man alert to his opportunity: the office crunch, the big deadline, the evening classes, the job-required travel. She can be a working-class mom who needs overtime or moonlighting to survive. She can be a student, like Jennifer Ireland, who was denied custody by a barnacle-encrusted judge not because the child's father was some sort of household saint—he had a busy schedule too—but because his *mother* had offered to baby-sit, and thereby save the little one from the horrors of the University of Michigan's day-care center. The fact that Ireland had been her child's only parent for the child's whole life counted for nothing.

In pseudo-enlightened America, we like to think we are moving domestic law toward a single standard of gender neutrality. Officially, today's working mothers are to be evaluated against their working husbands, and the "better" parent—that is, the slower-track one—will win. That was the way the media first played the case of Sharon Prost, the lawyer on Orrin Hatch's staff who lost custody of her two sons to the father, whose job was supposedly more relaxed. But if you look at the court papers, it seems evident that Judge Harriett Taylor—yes, a woman—applied, perhaps unconsciously, a double standard. She gave the father extra credit for every minute he spent with the kids, and docked the mother for every minute she spent away from them. He was in charge of the kids in the evening—*bravo!* She gets up at dawn to be with them before work—*so?* Prost and her husband weren't judged against each other (actually, they invested about the same amount of energy in parenting); rather, each was judged against old gender stereotypes of the distant-breadwinner father and the stay-at-home mother. When that's the standard, modern women are set up to lose.

Put Marcia Clark and Jennifer Ireland and Sharon Prost, punished for working, together with welfare moms, punished for not working, and what's a girl to do? Single mothers are the demons of the moment, blamed for everything from crime to the deficit, and although divorced moms don't come in for quite the level of abuse visited upon never-married ones, they raise the same specter of women out of men's control. Of course, men are, and always have been, out of women's control—just ask the women who are owed those billions of dollars in unpaid child support, and the ones who, far from preventing visitation, would give anything to have their kids' dad come round on a regular basis.

Call me paranoid, but when I look at custody issues across class lines today, what I see is a society in which women get the kids if the men don't want them.

March 27, 1995

VICTORIA'S SECRET

Have you noticed that the retro cycle is getting shorter and shorter? The Bloomsbury revival went on for decades: the novels, the diaries, the biographies and memoirs, the notecards and datebooks, the fashions in everything from gardens (Vita's famous white one at Sissinghurst) to sex. Subsequent historical moments haven't fared nearly so well, with good reason—remember the Reagan-inspired attempt to glamorize the Great Depression?—and in the last few years the whole phenomenon reached the absolute nadir with the resuscitation of . . . the seventies: bell bottoms, platform shoes, disco, *The Brady Bunch.*

Faced with the prospect of donning daisy-printed polyester and watching nightly reruns of *The Louds,* is it any wonder people are fleeing in droves to the Victorian Age? I don't blame them a bit. The only other direction is forward through the eighties (too painful—all that lovely money, vanished!) and then, uh-oh, here we are in the nineties again, standing next to ourselves on the unemployment line. Much pleasanter to dream away the afternoon with the glossy photo spreads of *Victoria* magazine, or its highbrow counterpart, Gertrude Himmelfarb's *The De-moralization of Society: From Victorian Virtues to Modern Values,* the latest effort in the ongoing bipartisan attempt to rescue our eminent ancestors from charges of repression, hypocrisy, cruelty and cant. Newt Gingrich likes the way the Victorians humiliated unwed mothers, alcoholics and the unemployed. In *The Moral Animal,* Robert Wright argues that upper-class Victorian sexual mores, especially premarital virginity for women only, are the ones our genes want us to have. Indeed, the only person who's missed the bandwagon is Rene Denfeld, whose Roiphesque tract, *The New Victorians: A Young Woman's Challenge to the Old Feminist Order,* uses a cartoon version of the nineteenth-century social purity movements as a stick to beat a cartoon version of contemporary feminism. Let's see: If there are no significant differences between the National Organization for Women and the Woman's Christian Temperance Union, does that make Gertrude Himmelfarb my sister under the skin?

Well, I like the Victorians too. Gilbert and Sullivan, Mrs. Gaskell and George Gissing, Hardy's poems, the *O.E.D.,* Morris wallpaper, Queen Anne houses, workingmen's choral societies. I like their energy and their seriousness, their love of language and their homemade amusements. True, they had child labor, workhouses, orphanages, capital and corporal punishment galore, not to mention plenty of the stuff Himmelfarb sees as evidence of modern breakdown, like pornography and prostitution and the sexual exploitation of children. True, women had no rights outside the home and not many in it, racism and anti-Semitism flourished, and there were those vast inequalities of wealth and privilege denounced by Dickens, Carlyle, Ruskin, George Eliot, the Brownings et al. But nobody watched the O.J. trial. You have to give them that.

Why this fascination with the Victorians? Chalk it up to the Shirley MacLaine syndrome, which causes people to imagine themselves back in time incarnated as one of the privileged few. *(Yes, Professor Himmelfarb. . . . I see you in . . . ancient Egypt,* murmurs the channeler, *and that gorgeous man at your feet . . . my God! It's Ramses the Second!)* The fact is, had Gertrude Himmelfarb, an ambitious female intellectual and a Jew besides, been a Victorian herself, she would have been as miserable as the "New Women"—Eleanor Marx, Olive Schreiner, Amy Levy—whose flailing attempts at personal liberation she sneers at, just as I would have been helping my great-great-grandmother run her tiny shop in Wigan, an English town so destitute and cheerless that my grandmother used to say her single childhood visit there made her a socialist for life.

The promoters of Victorian virtue see themselves as making a bold protest against the tide of modernity: all those out-of-wedlock mothers and disrespectful dark people that so upset the *Commentary* crowd. But while they claim they are arguing for the primacy of values over economic conditions in determining social behavior, they themselves are proof that they're wrong. *Of course* Victorian values are making a comeback; Victorian social conditions are coming back too. We already have sweatshops, child labor, soup kitchens, beggars, tuberculosis, filthy streets, families doubling up in dangerous slums. And what is a homeless shelter but a workhouse minus the work?

As the standard of living is reduced for the working class—good-bye decent schools and health care, livable pensions, unions—it becomes ever more necessary to find an ideology that allows those who are precariously "middle class" to distinguish themselves from those who have slid down the social scale, or even off it. As Mickey Kaus acknowledged in an amazingly unguarded moment in *The New Republic,* given "the growing economic gap between skilled and unskilled workers" and the difficulty of delivering tangible improvements like health care, "another way to appeal to struggling, underpaid workers is to honor their work—by dishonoring the non-work of those who stay on the dole." And if welfare is to be reduced, or even abolished, marriage must be remoralized and "illegitimacy" stigmatized so that the poverty of single women and their children can look like the inevitable consequence of licentiousness, mental feebleness or (as in *The Bell Curve*) both.

From prayer in the schools and the death penalty to the absurd idea that charity and volunteerism can substitute for government programs, the nineteenth century is already once more with us, if indeed it ever went away. The only thing that won't come back is what made the Victorian Age, for all its grimness, glorious: the conviction, shared by persons as different as Karl Marx and the Queen herself, that humanity's story was one of progress and hope.

April 10, 1995

Opportunity Knocked

Equality of opportunity, not equality of result. Like "class, not race," this anti–affirmative action sound bite sounds so reasonable and pleasant I almost agree with it myself. What's not to like about opportunity? It's such an optimistic, Statue of Liberty, free-enterprise, log-cabin sort of a word. It is, after all, what America is supposed to be the land of. "Result," on the other hand, sounds harsh, mathematical, ruthless. Think tax auditors armed with rawhide whips. *The Bridge on the River Kwai*. Trains running on time. Stalin.

I wonder, though, if the pundits now bumper-stickering this phrase across the media know what they are asking for. Perhaps they think they have merely come up with one of those brilliant obfuscatory phrases, like "victim feminism" and "welfare dependency," the purpose of which is to plant the debate so firmly on false ground (i.e., that it's insulting to assert that women are the targets of sexual violence and discrimination; that poverty is a psychological problem to be cured homeopathically with the "tough love" of even more poverty) that by the time the unwary opponent has straightened out the terms of the discussion the credits are rolling and the theme music is up. It certainly seems unlikely that those who find affirmative action too burdensome, expensive, intrusive and unfair would prefer the sweeping measures required even to begin to equalize opportunity for all Americans regardless of race, gender, ethnicity. Assume for a moment, though, that the call is sincere. What would it involve?

Well, *The New York Times* recently reported the results of yet another study demonstrating the crucial role of socioeconomic status in early childhood development. Researchers from Emory University and the federal Centers for Disease Control have found that children born to poor black women and to uneducated mothers of all races are more likely than others to suffer mild retardation. The researchers, taking issue with Charles Murray, argue that their study provides yet more evidence that intelligence is not race-related; they also believe that the mental deficits they've found can be reversed with enriched day care and maternal education programs. Even that would be a major undertaking in today's political climate—here in New York City, the Giuliani administration is cutting day-care slots—so it's not surprising that the federal government has responded to the study with promises of a pilot (i.e., very small) program to start . . . next year.

How much more it would take to prevent the problem in the first place! We'd need to ensure children of whatever race safe housing (no lead poisoning, no gunfire, no crack dens), healthy diets, doctors, fresh air. We'd need to mount a serious campaign against domestic violence, emotional neglect, child abuse (including the kind that involves the impregnation of underage girls by older boys and adult men). We'd need to keep girls from dropping out of high school. We'd need to do something about the desperation, depression and isolation that blight poor women's lives, and give men a stake in responsible parenthood. We'd need well-stocked libraries open all week. I could go on and on, and so, I'm sure, could you.

It wouldn't be impossible to give poor children, if not an *equal* opportunity, at least *some* opportunity: The Ford Foundation's Quantum Opportunities Program achieved considerable success in keeping a randomly selected group of adolescents from Philadelphia welfare families in school and on the path to higher education. It just costs money, time, effort, the imagination to see as valuable those we now treat as disposable. We *could* have good schools for all—but not if we fund schools with property taxes; rely on parents to pay for "frills" like art, music, library books, guidance counselors and computers; and let senior teachers work at the whitest schools. We could have integrated housing too. But when the federal housing voucher program, Moving to Opportunity (that word again!), actually moved a handful of black inner-city Baltimore families to large white middle-class suburbs, look what happened. Working-class whites—manipulated by racist local politicians who warned of a black deluge—rebelled, even though, in an irony Karl Marx would have savored, their own communities were too poor to serve as relocation sites. Showing the true bipartisan spirit of the age, it was Maryland's Democratic senator Barbara ("Year of the Woman") Mikulski who scuttled the program as "too controversial."

If there is so little enthusiasm for even the minimal efforts I've mentioned, how likely is it that Americans are about to embrace the sort of broad measures necessary to place everyone on a truly "level playing field"? The fact is, to eradicate the opportunity-diminishing effects of poverty, we would have to eradicate poverty itself. Affirmative action is thus a good example of the right hand not caring what the left hand is doing: American society generates inequality in every conceivable way, which affirmative action then palliates for a handful of lucky people.

The proposal that class should replace race and gender as a criterion for getting a leg up has been criticized, properly, as ignoring the fact that racism and sexism do, after all, exist and hamper even upscale women and blacks. Class-based affirmative action would permit white men to avoid hiring or promoting blacks or women, of any class, ever again—an option many would surely take. But a deeper logical problem is that it overlooks the fact that class distinctions are what the whole country is about. What is the point of being rich if your child is no more likely to get into Harvard than the child of a coal miner?

And if Harvard was not the gateway to yet more privilege—elite professional schooling, old-boy-and-girl networks, upper-class polish and prestige—what would be the point of it?

April 24, 1995

IS MARRIAGE LIKE A
BRAN MUFFIN?

Why did you get married? Was it to boost your savings rate? Lengthen your life span? Protect yourself against risky behaviors like driving too fast and getting into fistfights? If you're like me, you probably can't give a coherent account of your decision to marry. You may even be paying a therapist large sums of money, thus lowering your savings rate rather drastically, to explain yourself to you. But now, thanks to Linda J. Waite, professor of sociology at the University of Chicago, you can put that checkbook away. "Does Marriage Matter?," her paper at the Population Association of America's annual conference, sets out the benefits of wedlock with such enthusiasm that it won't be her fault—or that of the media, which have trumpeted her findings coast to coast—if the nation's aisles aren't trampled beneath the stampeding hooves of brides and grooms.

Marriage, Professor Waite has discovered, is good for you. Married people have more money, more sex, more satisfaction and, as previously noted, longer lives than singles or cohabitants (actually, her tables show cohabitants have the most sex, but her text elides this inconvenient datum). Married people live in safer neighborhoods, "experience an orderly lifestyle" and have children who are less likely to drop out of school.

None of this is exactly news. After all, if marriage didn't hold out powerful advantages, why would anyone wed? Certainly we don't need sociology to tell us that two people pooling their resources and facing life together can reap benefits closed to those who are single or who live together but keep their resources separate. This would probably be true in any society, but is particularly the case in America, where for millions of people, marriage is the only social-welfare system: It is how they obtain health insurance and pensions, get help with the kids and keep a roof over their heads. From the legal system to Thanksgiving at Grandma's, Americans shower approval on marriage. As any advocate of gay marriage could tell you, Waite's big revelation is actually a buried tautology: Marriage confers upon John and Jane the advantages society accords to married people.

Everyone understands this. That's why, despite oceans of social change, the rate of white women who've never married has hardly budged from around 20 percent since 1950—a fact Waite obscures by stressing the rising proportion of never-married black women, a tiny percentage of the adult female population, whose never-married status is largely a function of declining numbers of marriageable black men. So who, exactly, does Professor Waite think needs to be sold on marriage in the same urgent spirit in which doctors campaign for exercise and against smoking?

She writes as if the nation were teeming with antimarriage zealots, women (naturally) who "see the traditional family, balanced on the monogamous couple, as fundamentally incompatible with women's well-being." But, in fact, the people fleeing marriage are the people who've tried it. And it's a funny thing, Waite's own statistics suggest there's something in that feminist critique: The benefits of marriage are notably skewed. Men report greater physical satisfaction in sex within marriage; for women, marital status makes no difference. Unmarried and divorced *men* are the ones with the noticeably increased risks of heavy drinking, and it is men who derive an income "premium" from marriage or cohabitation. For women, the negative health effects of nonmarriage are fairly trivial, and marriage, which boosts men's earnings, lowers theirs (unless, interestingly, they're black). The downside of the "specialization" of roles Waite calls a plus to the married couple is the wife's second shift: housework, child care, husband-mothering.

For a scholarly paper, "Does Marriage Matter?" uses some rather odd data. Chart 5, for example, "Being Unmarried Is More Dangerous Than Heart Disease," comes from a 1979 article in *Health Physics* by the physicists Bernard L. Cohen and I-Sing Lee, who included unmarriedness in a whimsical list of ordinary life conditions that were more dangerous than nuclear radiation, about which they felt people were foolishly concerned. The home of this factoid, then, lies somewhere between humor and propaganda. I enjoyed Cohen and Lee's proposed remedy for fatal singlehood, though: government-run computer dating services. Perhaps, as an added inducement, Newt Gingrich could come across with some of those honeymoons in space he likes to talk about.

The truth is, social science is not much help to the individual trying to chart a course through life. The categories are too crude, the numbers too big, the causal connections too suspect. You might indeed be healthier, wealthier and wiser if you married—but what if your suitor was O.J. Simpson or Al D'Amato? Instead of touting marriage's practical advantages, Professor Waite might more usefully have asked why nearly half of all married people nonetheless forgo them in favor of studio apartments and an early grave. Waite lists the usual reasons for the "decline" of marriage—women working, changing attitudes toward nonmarital sex and so on—but these explain only why divorce and cohabitation are possible, not why people embrace them. Could it be that the prospect of spending the rest of your life with someone you don't love, maybe don't even like, is so painful that plump investments and balanced meals pale by comparison?

The troubadours, who argued that love and marriage were incompatible, since marriage was an economic and social arrangement and love was adoration and passion, would have had no problem understanding the marital instability Professor Waite finds so perplexing. To her Ben Franklinish case for marriage as a matter of prudence, prosperity, health and convenience, they would reply, *The world is ablaze with possibility and—mon Dieu!—you speak of savings rates? Of someone to nag you about your smoking?* I don't know about you, but I'm with Bernart de Ventadorn.

May 8, 1995

1945

For the past several years we've been living through a period thickly strewn with anniversaries and commemorations. Last year it was Normandy; the other day, the death of Roosevelt; now, of course, V-E Day. It's a strange way of trying to come to grips with history, because—as we all learned when Ronald Reagan went to Bitburg to lay a wreath on the graves of SS men—the script is written in advance, around the uplifting themes of our civic religion: reconciliation, patriotism, self-sacrifice, the bond of leader and little guy, nostalgia for what is inevitably called "a simpler time." These themes explain why all the emphasis this month is on 1945 and not on the fall of Saigon, which is harder to fit into the uplift-and-nostalgia program. Although, in another thirty years, who knows? After all, we have lived to see the Holocaust routinely depicted as a triumph of the human spirit and an opportunity for personal growth, so who can say what testimonials will adorn the My Lai massacre and the carpet-bombing of Cambodia by the time their fiftieth birthdays roll around?

But it's really the present that anniversaries and commemorations are mostly about, so I ask myself: What do people miss in the world of today that causes them to look back at 1945? My answer comes to me in a flood of clichés: men in hats and women in flowered cotton dresses; families gathered by the radio for a message from a leader whose sex life was not in the news; a sense of collective purpose behind the scrimping and saving and making do; the notion of "the good war," which we did, after all, win. A feeling of energy, bustle, seriousness, danger—but not danger as in Europe or Asia, where all the fighting and mass murder and wholesale destruction of cities was. A sense of hope, of faith in big shaggy ideas like Democracy, Family, Socialism, the People, Progress, Government, Science.

If you overlook the part about millions of people dying, most of them civilians, the war era can look pretty exciting—so exciting, indeed, that even those left out of the official history are now energetically reading themselves back in. Feminists claim Rosie the Riveter; gays and lesbians, the military bar culture. Black soldiers, we're told, helped liberate the death camps, effecting the symbolic brotherhood of blacks and Jews that has proved so elusive today. It's identity politics with a hat, a flowered dress and a happy face.

And after the war—the peace. But not the real, historical peace that included firing Rosie the Riveter and giving her job to a man, suburbs and segregation, McCarthyism, the smashing of militant labor unions and the start of the cold war. No, in 1945, the peace was all hope—for the New Deal promises that had been put on hold during the war, for the comity of nations envisioned in the U.N. Charter. Of course, these hopes were never fulfilled, and unless you believe that the course of history would have been radically altered had F.D.R. lived out his fourth term, the only reason can be that they were illusions in the first place. Today's nostalgia for 1945 turns out to be, like most nostalgia, not the longing for an *actual* past but for the illusions that it was still possible, back then, to maintain. When we miss 1945 what we miss is the dream of a hopeful future, the dream of modernism.

That's understandable, but isn't it time to acknowledge that it can be good to get rid of one's illusions? Sometimes people stop believing in something because they realize it isn't true. We hear a great deal today, for example, about how terrible it is that blacks, women, gays and other social groups want both equality and the right to self-definition. Why, goes the plaintive cry, can't we all just be plain Americans? And here flashes through my mind another wartime cliché: the platoon from countless old movies, with its Italian, its Southern farm boy, its German, its Jew. The answer to the question, of course, is that we are *not* all "just plain Americans" but are complexly embedded in overlapping hierarchies of gender, race, ethnicity, class. Why should it be impermissible to acknowledge this openly, and to make politics on the basis of this truth?

Take another example: suspicion of, and reluctance to bend to, authority figures. On the whole, this seems to me an *excellent* idea. Wasn't the search for a secular savior, a strong man on a white horse, what got Germany and Italy into trouble back in the thirties? A healthy skepticism toward officials, experts, men and women of the clergy, the military, the police and such, seems to me to be justified by events on practically a daily basis.

And why all the moaning these days about how sad it is that "America" can no longer find heroes among sports figures? Sure, it's unfortunate that so many athletes beat (and maybe kill) their wives, take drugs, sleep with teenage girls with and without their permission, place illegal bets and so forth—but was it better before, when these things went on but the public didn't know, and when the perpetual wish of Americans to remain children for life persuaded millions that being able to hit or throw a ball made a man a moral exemplar? Aren't we better off *not* looking to sports figures for moral guidance? What some call cynicism, to be combated with various forms of religious and secular revivalism, can also be called realism and egalitarianism. Would we want to put wife-beating and incest and child abuse and the other horrors of family life back with those hats and flowered dresses in the closet that, in 1945, was still firmly closed?

No, I think we have to admit that the world symbolized by 1945 is over now. Those big shaggy ideas did not solve our problems then, and cannot do so now. In a way, this is too bad—the way it's too bad that smoking causes lung cancer, another piece of bad news of which 1945 was blissfully unaware. But it's also a very good thing, because the death of those false hopes means we can start looking around for some hopes better grounded in reality, and in the circumstances of our own time. After all, that is where, like it or not, we live.

May 22, 1995

Of Grass and Guns

I was feeling pretty burned up at the government the other day, so I loaded a truck full of marijuana and parked it in front of my local federal office building, waited for the parents to drop off their toddlers at the day-care center and got the heck out of there as fast as I could. Do you know what happened? Nothing! Once again, it appears that I had been misled by media pundits, who in the wake of the Oklahoma City bombing have rushed to blame the nineties right on the sixties left. "An Unlikely Legacy of the 60s: The Violent Right," a *New York Times* front-page rumination by Peter Applebome, quoted assorted academics on the "libertarian strain" connecting Vietnam-era hippies and peaceniks with today's bandoliered militiamen. "To the 60s left it might have meant the right to smoke pot, while to the 90s right it might mean the right to own guns, but the instinct is similar."

Oh, really? My own pot-smoking instinct, albeit not a driving passion, has never raised in me the slightest urge to own a gun. This equation of left and right is political science at the high school honor-code level, in which all infractions are treated as more or less equally grave, regardless of intent or consequence or scale, because the real infraction is rule-breaking itself. "What happened in the

1960s was that the government was successfully 'delegitimated,' " the sociologist Gerald Marwell said to the *Times*. "We were told in the 1960s that the emperor has no clothes and people shouldn't accept what they're told." I like that "we were told," as if nothing actually happened in the sixties except mass brainwashing from some unspecified source—Country Joe and the Fish? The way I remember it, the government delegitimated itself, with phony body counts, lights at the end of ever-lengthening tunnels, destroying villages in order to save them, children in flames on the evening news and so on—not to speak of the F.B.I. harassment of Martin Luther King Jr. and sundry other semi-criminal domestic activities. Doesn't the question of whether people should "accept what they're told" depend on what's being said? Resisting an unjust war that even Robert McNamara has finally publicly admitted was misconceived and deceptively presented doesn't strike me as bearing a close resemblance to organizing a private army of fellow gun nuts to fight the Antichrist and its earthly representatives in the Clinton administration and the British royal family.

Timothy McVeigh is not some libertarian free spirit gone astray. He felt at home in the army, hardly a countercultural outpost, and wanted to be a career soldier; he won medals for his Gulf War service, in which his main task was to bury Iraqi soldiers alive. If we're seriously interested in understanding how a young man could blow up a building full of hundreds of people, why not start by acknowledging that the state he now claims to oppose gave him his first lessons in killing?

When it comes to understanding American history, those in charge of its official version are like Hera, who renewed her virginity each year by bathing in a magic spring. Because they are committed to a vision of America as forever young, innocent, fresh off the farm in what politicians and editorial writers love, repellently, to call "the heartland," the existence in our economic and cultural structures of conflict, alienation and violence—both freelance and organized—comes as a perpetual surprise. But why reach for the left to explain the far right? The far right's been around forever. It has quite a history of its own. Why not talk, for example, about the

Ku Klux Klan—a violent paramilitary anti-federal-government organization that's been murdering innocent people for more than a hundred years? As for the personal antiauthoritarianism exemplified by the sixties pot smokers, the obvious historical analogy is Prohibition, another unrealistic legal interference with private pleasure that was openly mocked and flouted by millions of otherwise solid citizens. Indeed, one could argue that the "libertarian strain" of American culture would not exist without the Puritan strain, for which we are equally famous.

I'm still waiting for someone besides Frank Rich and *The Nation* to point out that the Oklahoma City bombing, which seemed so out of key with American values that Islamic terrorists were immediately blamed for it, in actual fact coincides with an ongoing wave of homegrown violence against abortion clinics: bombings, arson, death threats, murders. No real political will has been applied to combating this outrage—"Christian terrorism"?—or to probing its possible connection with the far-right militias. Curiously, the F.B.I., which has dragged its feet on clinic violence, nonetheless, according to documents released May 15 by the Center for Constitutional Rights, has been closely following the doings of ACT UP and other AIDS and gay groups. The bureau claims it was worried that activists would throw AIDS-infected blood at people.

Now *that's* paranoid!

June 5, 1995

SWISH, THWACK, BOO

There ought to be a rule that bold proposals for the social and political betterment of mankind be accompanied by explanations of how these ideas will be brought to reality and why, if they're so brilliant and beneficial as all that, they haven't already been implemented. I figure this requirement would put most pundits out of business within weeks, which would be all to the good. Imagine, for example, if the many who facilely advocate adoption over abortion actually had to explain how it would work: where the millions of would-be parents would come from; how women with unplanned pregnancies, who overwhelmingly reject adoption no matter how desperate their circumstances, will be brought to embrace it; how mass adoption will sit with current notions of genetic determinism, father's rights, cultural and racial identity. Are Tennessee Baptists really prepared to see their grandchildren shipped off to be raised by New York Jews—or vice versa? To spell out what it would really involve is to make clear what a crackpot idea it is—which is, of course, why its advocates tend to move right along to the next "thought experiment," like orphanages over A.F.D.C.

But why criticize the right alone? Our own pages are full of visionary schemes. Let's tell Clinton to abolish the C.I.A.! Let's permit noncitizens to vote! Let's raise children to be noncompetitive! Missing is a serious discussion of what organized interests are served by the status quo, how those interests are to be defeated and by whom. Lots of good ideas have no constituency in a position to bring them about: Think of all those Op-Ed articles that crop up every four years advocating the abolition of the Electoral College.

Well, I'm no better than the next columnist, so here's my big idea: Let's get rid of sports. Baseball, basketball, football, boxing—*especially* boxing—tennis, gymnastics, Little League, high school, college, professional, Olympic, the whole schmear. Away with them!

Fans say athletics promote values, and so they do—the wrong values, like the childish confusion of physical prowess with "character" that is such a salient feature of the O.J. Simpson trial. Sports pervert education, draining dollars from academic programs and fostering anti-intellectualism. They skew the priorities of the young, especially the poor, black young, by offering them the illusory hope of wealth and fame. Sports scholarships, often touted as a poor kid's only chance, just mean less money available to other poor kids, like girls, and ones with O.K. grades and no trophies. Besides, without the will-o'-the-wisp incentive of a scholarship, physically gifted kids might not be so ready to blow off their schoolwork. Why not give scholarships for art or music instead?

Although women are becoming more involved in sports, it's still a male world, which actively encourages and protects the worst forms of male privilege and jerkiness. Athletes are disproportionately represented in reported campus sex crimes, and the pros' reputation for violence, against women or otherwise, is legendary. Without sports, we never would have heard of Ty Cobb, O.J. Simpson, Mike Tyson, Billy Martin, Darryl Strawberry.

Being a sports fan is even worse than being an actual athlete, since instead of getting all that exercise, one simply watches TV, punches the chair and curses. But for both fans and players, sports are about creating a world from which women are absent. Men who follow sports, which means most men, have a realm of conversation that allows them to bond across classes effortlessly but superficially. Lefty sports advocates like to tout this cross-class appeal as a virtue—How about those Knicks?—but, even setting aside the fact that it's based on the exclusion of women, why would a leftist think it's good for class divisions to be smoothed over?

Sports fandom trains the young in group identification, passivity, spectatorship and celebrity-worship. I know men whose entire lives are mediated through sports, like my cousin who brings a little TV to family gatherings to catch The Game, or my writing student whose efforts at autobiography consisted entirely of play-by-play of long-ago Little League tournaments. Maybe once, sports functioned as a family, communal activity—the whole town out at the ballpark for a good time. Now it's just another form of isolation: every man in his own living room, staring at the screen. Women who object to pornography should be even more upset about sports. After all, whatever else porn may do, it does encourage sexual interest, which is why couples rent those videos. But sports are basically a way for men to avoid the claims of other people. That's one of several reasons why David ("Fatherless America") Blankenhorn's idea of promoting fatherhood by getting athletes to endorse it is such a joke: A man who spends half the year on the road with the team pitches family life to men who are watching him expressly because he symbolizes the footloose and fancy-free life.

But what about the game, you cry, the thwack of ball against bat, the arc of football on its way to touchdown, the swish of ball into net? O.K., let's keep sports—but let's have only women play. Women can thwack and throw and swish too, after all. Turning sports over to women would change their meaning—you can't have bimbo cheerleaders if the athletes are women too—and instead of promoting the worst qualities of men, they'd counteract the worst qualities of women, like defining themselves through men and wearing three-inch fake fingernails.

I know what you're thinking: Sports is a billion-dollar industry, deeply woven into the fabric of American life, avidly followed by millions who would go berserk if deprived. Besides, all-female football wouldn't *be* football. Right. Forget the whole thing. I don't know what came over me. And the next time a pundit comes up with a big idea—Let's bring back shame! Let's not let parents divorce!—you can probably forget that too.

July 17/24, 1995

FACTS AND PUNDITS

"Facts are stubborn things," said Lenin, which only goes to show how wrong a guy can be. Maybe facts are stubborn if you're that surgeon who cut away at the healthy half of his patient's brain instead of the half with the fatal cancer, or if you're one of the 12,000 employees slated to lose their jobs in the merger of Chemical and Chase. But if you're in the opinion business, facts are about as stubborn as wilted lettuce. You can say just about anything, however absurd or self-contradictory, and die of old age in bed before a fact hits you squarely on the head.

Take, for example, the belief that education is the solution to the loss of jobs overseas. A few years ago, with manufacturers decamping en masse for the Third World, Robert Reich made a big splash by arguing that the United States could become the world capital of high tech and "symbolic analysis." Education and retraining would bleach blue collars white—as if what prevented I.B.M. from opening offices in Trenton or Detroit were the paucity of locals who'd mastered WordPerfect. Now it's become clear that white-collar jobs are following manufacturing overseas. The information-age technology that was supposed to rescue the economy by turning us all into technocrats has in fact helped to subvert it by turning the residents of Bangalore and other Third World enclaves into technocrats—at one-twelfth U.S. wages. Turns out people go to college all over the world now. Who knew?

These facts were laid out in all their gloomy splendor by Lester Thurow, M.I.T. economist and talking head, on the Op-Ed page of *The New York Times* on September 3. "The old remedy for lower wages—more education—no longer works," Thurow states flatly. What to do? Well, "The remedies lie in major public and private investments in research and development and in creating skilled workers to insure that tomorrow's high-wage brain-power industries generate much of their employment in the United States." In other words . . . more education!

Again on the *Times* Op-Ed page, this one from August 22, we find Danielle Crittenden, editor of *The Women's Quarterly*, organ of the ultraconservative Independent Women's Forum, arguing that mothers earn less not because of discrimination or the failure of workplaces—or families—to adapt to their needs but because of "nature," the genetically based desire of mothers to get off the career fast track. Her sole example: herself. It seems that in 1991, the year her first baby was born, Crittenden earned only $800, and thereby "contributed to the depressing Census Bureau statistic that women earn 76 percent of what men do." Crittenden's case actually disproves her thesis—after all, in 1991 no one had ever heard of her and now she's a well-known right-wing antifeminist and, according to the I.W.F.'s *Media Directory: Women Experts*, an authority on "Children & Family, Family Leave & Child Care, Feminist Ideology, Health: Women's, Affirmative Action & Equal Opportunity, Glass Ceiling, Sexual Harassment." I'd say Crittenden's $800 years are behind her. Her own case is also irrelevant to the 76 percent statistic, which represents the relative income of women employed full-time and year-round. Thus, she presents no evidence for her argument that women's lower earnings are the product of the voluntary withdrawal of baby-besotted moms from the workforce. That she puts it forward, even as mothers of tiny children move into the workforce in historically unprecedented numbers, betrays a striking indifference to reality.

Speaking of indifference to reality, Camille Paglia, in a *Times* Op-Ed piece on September 1, hit what is surely a new low even for her—this is the woman who told a TV reporter that the Spur Posse was "beautiful" and who charged that the women's movement had replaced Betty Friedan with Gloria Steinem because of its anti-Semitism (P.S.: Steinem is Jewish). Based on her textual analysis of the press kit and other documents, Paglia criticized the Beijing conference on women as dominated by white First World liberals who are insufficiently attentive to the problems and charms of . . . men. "Men are never depicted as devoted friends," complains the celebrated proponent of the innate hostility between the sexes. She was particularly upset by the citation of statistics showing that "75 percent of refugees and 'displaced persons' are women and children . . . blotting out the men who, dead or imprisoned after fighting for their family and land, did not have the luxury of flight." To speak of "the luxury of flight" to describe, say, the plight of Afghan women, parked for over a decade now in broiling camps under the eyes of fanatical mullahs while the menfolk duke it out for theological supremacy at home, is possible only to someone who knows nothing and cares nothing about the Third World except as a stick with which to beat American feminists.

The Last Marxist likes to say that these kinds of self-contradictions and bloopers are an inherent part of punditry. If Lester Thurow or Robert Reich were to admit to himself that education will not produce jobs, or Danielle Crittenden were to acknowledge that women are economically disadvantaged, or Camille Paglia were to see the world as anything but a screen for the projection of her own personality, they couldn't occupy the delightful social positions they now hold. That seems awfully cynical, I know. But maybe we need some sort of scorekeeper for these bouts of punditry, someone to keep everyone honest, on their toes and answerable for all the silly things they said last year—or last paragraph—that they've conveniently dropped without ever admitting they were wrong.

Not very likely. After all, Francis Fukuyama made himself a famous young man by arguing that the triumph of bourgeois democracy over communism would mean "the end of history." History went right on happening, but Fukuyama is still a major hot-air artist, having shifted his interests to "civil society" as the key to national well-being—an idea impervious to facts one way or another. Perfect!

September 25, 1995

THE O.J. VERDICT:
WHILE YOU WERE SLEEPING

Of the many people, black and white, who think the O.J. Simpson verdict was the right one, I wonder how many believe he is indeed innocent. To lawyers, I realize, factual innocence does not have a particularly interesting connection with what a verdict ought to be. Given the adversarial system of justice, and the crucial role of the defense bar in checking the overwhelming power of the state, that's appropriate. But what about regular people, the millions across the races and up and down the income scale who've spent the past 478 days acquiring a Talmudic knowledge of the case and its many players? Are there women and waiters in Los Angeles looking fearfully over their shoulders because the "real killer" is still at large? O.J. has vowed to spend the rest of his life tracking down whoever killed his ex-wife, as well as raising his two children in the way he and Nicole "had always planned." If O.J. is innocent, we must all support him in his custody fight and cheer his intention, announced by one lawyer at the press conference, to put a lot of money "on the street" to lure informants. It seems strange to me that O.J. hadn't done that earlier, but, as you've probably guessed, I always thought O.J. was guilty, and I always thought he would be acquitted.

By now the issue of race has so thoroughly shaped the way we talk about the trial and its verdict that it's hard to see either in another light, to remember that before O.J. became the heroic black Everyman persecuted by a lawless racist police force whose depredations against the Constitution were condoned by the local judiciary, he was the celebrity wife-beater whom that same police force had fawned over and whom that same judiciary, in deference to his busy showbiz career, had allowed to become the nation's only court-ordered telephone counselee.

Channel-surfing Tuesday night I heard an astonishing amount of high-level discussion of virtually every legal and racial angle of the case, not just from the many buffed and polished lawyers who are now national media stars—Peter Arenella, Milton Grimes, Gerry Spence in his trademark fringed jacket—but also from callers and interviewees, none of whom needed a definition of "reasonable doubt" or "search and seizure." Doubtless there were some I missed, but the only people I caught talking in a serious, analytical way about domestic violence were Nicole's sister Denise Brown and Westchester County district attorney Jeanine Pirro, who noted that her office was getting calls from women whose abusers were boasting that like O.J. they could kill and beat the rap. But then, if O.J. is innocent, domestic violence is just a red herring, part of what dismissed juror Michael Knox called the "ups and downs with spouse and girlfriends" and Johnnie Cochran called part of being "human." Sure, it was depressing to hear one commentator dismiss O.J.'s well-substantiated career as a violent husband as "an incident in '89," but then, five or six or ten million dollars buys a lot of spin.

For me, the O.J. trial was always about domestic violence, and it still is. Americans don't want to believe that respectable men, much less beloved sports heroes, assault and even kill girlfriends and wives. The contortions that juries put themselves through to acquit these men are truly amazing. "Hey, men and women fight," commented one Queens juror after last May's acquittal of Karamchand Singh, who stabbed his former girlfriend twelve times and smashed her head with a four-pound piece of cable. Self-defense, said Mr. Singh; besides, she was a slut. Even his lawyer was stunned that the jury bought it. If O.J. were white, we would have heard even more about what a slut/gold-digger/drug user/shrew Nicole Simpson was, and about O.J. as the abused husband he claimed—in his best-selling, tell-nothing book—to be. That, I seem to remember, was indeed the Dream Team's original strategy.

The O.J. trial was supposed to be educational—"better than a year at Harvard!" one cabdriver told me. But what was the lesson? O.J.'s wealth bought what some call justice and others "rich man's justice." Either way, it will be hard to argue now that rich and poor get equal treatment in the courts. But who ever believed they did? The trial put into play a staggering number of American preoccupations: race, class, gender, sex, money, violence, sports, drugs, celebrity, cops—even dogs. But it remained a spectacle. You got from it what you brought to it. Camille Paglia told *Playboy* that Nicole's frantic 911 call proved she was a tease who enjoyed playing sadomasochistic games. On NPR, Scott Simon drew from the hate-spewing Fuhrman tapes a wistful meditation on the policeman's lot. Polls showed the same racial divide at the end as at the beginning.

The trial's cultural significance will doubtless replace transgender studies as a hot academic subdiscipline. Its political significance, though, is about zero. How many of O.J.'s black supporters know about the impending cuts in legal aid, which will affect countless black defendants? How many whites who see him as a vicious abuser have thought about the ways in which budget cuts, "welfare reform" and proposals to forbid legal-services lawyers from taking divorce cases will trap countless women in violent homes?

What if, instead of devoting the past sixteen months to a hopelessly distorted symbolic representation of our current predicaments, those millions of O.J. watchers had paid some attention to Congress, busily dismantling sixty years of progressive legislation in every area of life? What if the millions of blacks who thought O.J. was being railroaded took up the case of Mumia Abu-Jamal, who really did have an unfair trial, or mobilized against the crime bill, or the death penalty? What if the millions appalled by Nicole's beaten face had joined last spring's march on Washington to oppose violence against women?

What if, instead of talk-show politics, we had politics?

October 23, 1995

MILLION MAN MIRAGE

There's dignity in working for $3 an hour, said Louis Farrakhan at the Million Man March. Whoops, sorry—that was Phil Gramm. Farrakhan calls on government to "not cede manufacturing to 'Third World' countries, but to the Black community." Nor did Farrakhan call Congress "Israeli-occupied territory," or write a book of paranoid religious ravings involving a worldwide Jewish banking conspiracy. The responsible parties there were, respectively, Pat Buchanan and Pat Robertson. Farrakhan called Jews, along with Palestinians, Koreans and Vietnamese, "bloodsuckers" of the black "nation." And it wasn't even Farrakhan who said that women couldn't be combat soldiers because they're prone to "infections" every thirty days or so. That was Newt Gingrich. Farrakhan said that women should stay home and pray.

There was a lot of talk on the day of the march and after about not confusing the messenger with the message. It's a valid point. The hundreds of thousands of black men, with a sprinkling of women and at least one much-interviewed white teenage boy, may have been summoned to Washington by Farrakhan, but they were there for their own reasons: to claim political space, to bear witness, to make a statement about the need to do *something* about the poverty, violence and despair that have overwhelmed so many black communities. What the statement was may have been hard to pin down: atone for abuse and neglect of women and children or show the world that black men have family values too? In any case, Jesse Jackson was surely right when he quipped that Clarence Thomas had organized the march. What he didn't say was that Clarence Thomas was leading it too.

If Louis Farrakhan were a white superpatriot instead of a black nationalist, if he led a weird Christian sect instead of a weird off-shoot of Islam, the Republican Party would be rolling out the red carpet for him. Shorn of the Masonic folklore and flights of numerological fancy that dotted his speech, his basic message was Gingrichism: family values, entrepreneurship, self-reliance, volunteerism, God. Farrakhan even shares Gingrich's pie-eyed globalism. One of the afternoon's stranger moments had him making the crowd promise in one breath not to sexually abuse children and in the next to engage in international trade. The much-noted hateful aspects of Farrakhan's ideology—homophobia, sexism, anti-Semitism, bigotry, vigilantism—inform the Republican right as well. There's even the same appeal to militarism and top-down authority—the Fruit of Islam guarding the bulletproof speaker's podium in their paramilitary uniforms—a yearning for discipline and order one finds also in the muddled middle that looks to Gen. Colin Powell.

Like Gingrich, Farrakhan likes to talk about individual initiative while refusing to confront, or even to mention, the true implications of global capitalism for U.S. workers, black and white. When Farrakhan calls for unprofitable industries to relocate in black America instead of the Third World, he is calling on blacks to join the race to the bottom with Chinese and Salvadoran garment slaves. If the safety net is replaced by the sweatshop, what will the ghetto have gained? I didn't hear anyone call for raising the minimum wage.

The audiences for Gingrich and Farrakhan are also not so different. Mostly these are people to whom other modes of political expression are not available, who do not belong to the chattering classes and who, when a rare chance at visibility comes along, have every reason in the world to overlook the personal shenanigans and offensive remarks that so obsess the media. Unfortunately, seizing that momentary escape from alienation often sends them into the arms of opportunistic "leaders." Farrakhan was hardly the only one of that sort heading the march. There was Marion Barry, fresh from signing a measure that bans increased payments to women who have babies while on welfare; Ben Chavis, whose vainglory and womanizing practically destroyed the N.A.A.C.P.; the recently baptized Rev. Al Sharpton, who was once an F.B.I. informer. And then there was Cornel West, who in a particularly incoherent *New York Times* Op-Ed piece proclaimed himself a "radical democrat" and "Christian freedom fighter in the King legacy" while embracing Farrakhan in the name of "black operational unity."

Farrakhan's doing fine now, and so are the other march leaders. But what about the million men? The message of the day—personal responsibility, civic activism—is good, so far as it goes. I wish a million white men—*ten* million—would throng the Washington Mall to apologize to women and children. As long as they included sexism in the list of sins, I'd gladly stay at home and watch on CNN. But—and I think Cornel West, at least, knows this, since in addition to calling himself a radical democrat and a Christian freedom fighter he also claims to be a socialist—the economic and social crisis of black America cannot be resolved by eschewing gangsta rap and starting more bean-pie bakeries. What is the point of "operational unity" that rallies people around a chimerical program, that fills the much-discussed leadership vacuum by increasing the power of shysters?

Actually, I don't believe in this leadership vacuum business. It seems to me the political scene positively teems with leaders, who leap out of bed each morning full of plans and projects. What's missing—for all the lip service paid to self-help—is ordinary people taking action on their own behalf. The million men, and the million women, could do all sorts of things: organize mass protests against inner-city hospital closings, monitor the courtrooms of racist judges, stage sit-downs at the Board of Ed until every black child has new textbooks, clean schools, committed teachers. They could vow to unseat any politician who takes a single cent from poor mothers and children.

But then they couldn't vote for Marion Barry, could they? Which is why no leader will ever tell them to look to themselves instead of to the man on the bulletproof podium.

November 6, 1995

WHERE ARE THE WOMEN
WE VOTED FOR?

Remember the Year of the Woman? In 1992 record numbers of Democratic women ran for federal office vowing to fight for a more "caring" domestic agenda and such mainstream feminist goals as reproductive rights and child care. Women in power would stand up for women, we were told. Was not the ordeal of Anita Hill the direct result of the absence of estrogen in the Senate Judiciary Committee, whose members, in a famous catch phrase, "just didn't get it"? We heard an awful lot about how women politicians were more altruistic and civic-minded than their male counterparts, how, as "outsiders" to the system, they would resist the wheeling-and-dealing culture of Congress. On the strength of these appeals, EMILY's List and other PACs extracted vast amounts of energy, time, enthusiasm and, most important, money from justifiably fed-up women voters, including me, and, sure enough, more women won election to Congress than ever before.

Now flash forward to September 19, as four out of five Democratic women senators voted for the Republican-backed welfare bill that would abolish the sixty-year federal safety net for poor children in favor of a jerry-built scheme of block grants to the states that not only provides less money to the poor but sends to the trashbin of history the principle that every poor child is entitled to assistance. Under the Senate version of welfare reform—supported by President Clinton and now folded into a compromise bill that's even worse—states can cut their own contributions to welfare by 20 percent right away. They can use their block grants pretty much at whim, setting up a network of Newt Gingrich Homes for Orphans With Living Parents if they like. Five-year lifetime limits on benefits, green lights for family caps and teen exclusions, the commonsense certainty (now confirmed by two major studies, including one that the Clinton administration tried to squelch) that the Senate bill would plunge over one million more children into poverty and deepen the destitution of those now worst off—all this was just fine with our fearless fighters for women and children, those resisters of the backroom-deal Barbara ("Politics is social work with power") Mikulski, Dianne Feinstein, Barbara Boxer and Patty ("Mom in tennis shoes") Murray. Only Carol Moseley-Braun joined the ten Democratic men who said no.

"They didn't want to be marginalized, they wanted to be at the table, and they wanted Bill Clinton to like them," said one longtime feminist lobbyist who, like the other Washington-based activists I interviewed for this column, took herself off the record before plunging into a long and explicit aria of anger, disappointment and bewilderment. "There's an assumption that if you get involved in a bill and win concessions—more money for child care, even if it's just on paper—you'll vote for the final bill." So what really matters is horse trading with your colleagues and helping Bill Clinton keep his election promise to "end welfare as we know it," even if hundreds of thousands of children go hungry and their mothers end up on the streets. No wonder welfare-rights lobbyists who visited Congress in early November described Patty Murray as "squirming" and "uncomfortable." Those tennis shoes must be pinching pretty hard.

Well, as I find myself saying more and more these days, it's good to lose your illusions. The fact is, congressional women have been pretty disappointing in the Age of Newt. During the Hundred Days I heard Barney Frank speak out wittily, trenchantly, mockingly *every day* against the Contract With America. Where were Maxine Waters, Pat Schroeder and Carolyn Maloney as Republicans likened welfare mothers to alligators and wolves? In the Senate it's Daniel Patrick Moynihan—who started the whole anti-single-mother policy ball rolling with his famous 1965 critique of black "pathology"—who "gets it" about what welfare reform will do to women and children. Not Barbara ("Anyone who goes into politics or life wanting power is not a good person") Boxer.

The truth is, except on a few high-profile issues—abortion rights, sexual harassment, violence against women—electoral feminism is a pretty pallid affair: a little more money for breast cancer research here, a boost for women business owners there. The main job of the women is the same as that of the men: playing toward the center, amassing campaign funds, keeping business and big donors happy, and currying favor with the leadership in hopes of receiving plums. To her credit, Carol Moseley-Braun voted against welfare reform, but mostly what she does is carry water for Glaxo-Wellcome, the world's biggest drug company, which gives her large sums of money to fight the generic-drug industry. That women and children—black women and children, poor women and children—would benefit from lower drug prices doesn't come into it.

In a recent *Los Angeles Times* column, Robert Scheer accused the women's movement of standing by as Congress savages poor women and children. That isn't entirely fair: NOW, for instance, has worked hard on this issue, despite being totally ignored by the media. It would be more accurate to say that, like other social-justice movements, organized feminism is caught in a co-dependent relationship with electoral politics: No matter how often and how blatantly our hopes are betrayed, we keep coming back, begging to have our illusions rewoven for another bout at the polls.

Why not try something different for a change?

December 4, 1995

KEPT ILLUSIONS

"We keep trying to get a meeting with President Clinton to spell out for him what welfare reform will do to poor women and children," a Washington-based antipoverty expert told me a few weeks ago. Her explanation for the chilliness of the presidential shoulder? "With Joycelyn Elders gone, we don't have any women in this administration who are willing to speak up forcefully on behalf of poor women." The President, she continued, is now entirely surrounded by cynical white male yuppies like George Stephanopoulos and Dick Morris, whose sole concern is mining immediate political advantage out of the day's headlines, no matter what ensues—so long as it ensues after Election Day.

"Gee," I said, "do you really think President Clinton hasn't heard your arguments already?" It was his own Department of Health and Human Services, after all, that produced the notoriously deep-sixed study calculating that the Senate welfare bill, which Clinton supports, would push over a million more children into poverty. And even the loony right, which thinks the President murdered Vincent Foster to cover up the Satanic ritual child abuse taking place in Hillary's secret love nest, will concede if pressed that the man is reasonably well informed. No, in seeking to blame the President's indifference to the plight of the poor on his insulating advisers, my interviewee was succumbing to the Bad Boyar theory of politics: If only the czar knew! If only the people could get past the evil cabal of nobles and viziers who have him locked up in that Fabergé egg of a palace! Surely the Little Father would hear the people's cry.

Right. Now, my interviewee knew that she was grasping at straws, and who can blame her? Here's a woman who cannot get Senator Moynihan's office to return her calls, even as he gives meaty quotes to the press about the nonexistence of people like her. (This is a good place to mention the Women's Committee of 100, a network of academics, activists and journalists dedicated to fighting welfare "reform," whose valiant efforts, most recently a November 15 vigil at the White House, have been studiously ignored by the media.) But she's hardly alone in her desire to believe, despite everything she knows and sees and feels and understands, that what's keeping the President from doing the right thing is lack of information, bad advice and bad company.

It's the *déformation professionelle* of the policy/media/academic classes—the think tankers, lobbyists, pundits, columnists, foundationeers—to imagine that the gimlet-eyed frauds who run the country look to them for guidance. Is there a liberal journalist in America who hasn't written his "How Clinton Can Still Redeem Himself" think piece, his "Run, Bill, Run—as a Populist" Op-Ed? I almost feel sorry for the man. It must be tough sitting in the Oval Office when *Mother Jones* has all the brains. An enormous amount of shrewdness and strategizing is on display in the liberal press (what's left of it), but what is the point of this endless giving of excellent advice? President Clinton shows no signs of taking it, and never has. Why not talk about that fact, and its implications for the liberal-pundit biz?

Ordinary Americans understand perfectly well that politicians are paid by corporations and other organized interests to do their bidding; that's why most people don't vote. But even when liberal crusaders argue the same, bemoaning the domination of politics by big money and big lobbies, they shrink from the logical conclusion, which is that their bright ideas and clever suggestions, not to mention their frequent summonses to morality and meaningfulness, are destined for the circular file. Even if Clinton *were* the unhappy captive of the Democratic Leadership Council, as many disappointed fans believe, and not one of its founding members, as is actually the case; even if he had those good intentions and instincts and impulses with which those fans are still so eager to credit him—so what? He's not going to start acting differently just because liberals tell him to. It would make a lot more sense to devote all that strategic cunning and policy brilliance to building some kind of movement that's more than an address list and a fax machine.

The fact is, lack of information rarely explains why people, and not just presidents, fail to do the right thing. Ignorance cannot explain why the United States has so many children living in appalling poverty, and is about to have still more. The exposé of lower-class squalor and the appeal to conscience on behalf of its victims has been a thriving literary genre ever since Jacob Riis wrote *How the Other Half Lives* in 1890. Think of the many fine books of Jonathan Kozol and Susan Sheehan, Alex Kotlowitz's *There Are No Children Here,* the documentary *Hoop Dreams*—all major mainstream successes. Every season seems to bring its crop of heartbreaking eyewitness accounts by teachers, doctors, youth workers and sometimes even children themselves telling more or less the same story of terrific kids abandoned by the larger society. Yet all this informing, documenting, narrating, explaining, has little effect on the ongoing, tidal withdrawal of middle-class engagement with the inner city. After such knowledge, what forgiveness indeed?

The problem isn't ignorance; there are no Bad Boyars. If he's smart, the President will take some meetings with antipoverty lobbyists and let them know he feels their pain. So far, that's worked pretty well to keep potential dissidents in the fold. After all, as Gloria Steinem told this month's *Mother Jones,* "If we lose the presidency, there's nothing to stop all of the regressive legislation they have in mind."

Our President, Ourselves? To understand that "we"—whom it includes and whom it writes off—is to understand how a liberal Democratic President can dismantle the welfare state and *still* get the nation's leading feminist to see him as the only bulwark against reaction.

December 18, 1995

The Violence of
Ordinary Life

Not since Lisa Steinberg, beaten to death in 1987 by her cocaine-crazed adoptive father, crooked lawyer Joel Steinberg, has the press focused on a fatal child-abuse case the way it's zeroed in on the story of six-year-old Elisa Izquierdo, beaten to death, allegedly by her crack-crazed mother, Awilda Lopez, after months, perhaps years, of bizarre torture. Between those two killings, both of which took place in New York, approximately seven hundred children in the city have died as a result of abuse or neglect, and it's almost always a one-day, if not a one-paragraph, story. Why did Elisa get headlines? One talk-radio caller suggested the story broke on a slow news day, Thanksgiving Eve. Then too, she was an exceptionally pretty and charming little girl. Would *Time* have put on its cover a child-abuse victim who was retarded, unattractive, fat?

Perhaps most important, though, Elisa's story, unlike that of many child victims, had a plot. Yes, neighbors in Manhattan's grim Rutgers Houses ignored her screams and pleadings; yes, Awilda Lopez's sisters, now loud in denunciation, pretty much let things drift. But unlike Lisa Steinberg, Elisa had would-be rescuers too: her father, who had custody until he died, when Elisa was four, and then his cousin; teachers and school administrators; even, in one of those "only in New York" twists the tabloids love, Prince Michael of Greece. Authorities were warned of Elisa's situation no less than eight times. Each time they dropped the ball.

It's a horrible story that needs to be told, but I'm sure I'm not the only person repelled by the weeklong orgy of child-death pornography: innocent "princess" versus "animal" mother; lurid replays of Awilda Lopez's many acts of sadism, which while officially intended to spur outrage also pander to the reader's sadomasochism. The pictures of Elisa lying in a coffin in her First Communion dress and surrounded by teddy bears recall Victorian corpse photography. They remind me too of the funerary cult of dead children in the *favelas* of Brazil as described by Nancy Scheper-Hughes in *Death Without Weeping:* an elaborate folk poetry of little-angels-going-back-to-Heaven which enforces fatalism even as it consoles.

On the surface, fatalism does not seem to be the dominant note in the Elisa postmortem. Quite the contrary. Names are being named, memos leaked, reports issued at a furious pace. The ongoing scandal that is the city's Child Welfare Administration is in the spotlight: the badly trained and overextended caseworkers, the lack of supervision and follow-up, the red tape, the Kafkaesque rules of confidentiality. So obvious is it that the ferocious cutbacks of the Dinkins and Giuliani administrations have shredded the agency's ability to protect children, or even remember where it puts them, that no less an antigovernment conservative than columnist Mona Charen is calling for an infusion of funds. This has not prevented Mayor Giuliani from demanding deeper cuts—while also engineering $14 million in raises for himself and other city pols.

At the policy level Elisa's case has reopened debate over child welfare's eternal triangle: family reunification vs. foster care vs. institutions. Awilda Lopez won custody—despite strong indications that she was abusing Elisa on weekend visits—because of the biological tie. The child's death thus lends resonance to the "don't call them orphanages, call them boarding schools" arguments, such as put forth by Richard Rhodes in an eloquent Op-Ed piece for *The New York Times.* But the Andrew Drumm Institute, which rescued Rhodes from his demented stepmother and prepared him for Yale, costs $25,000 annually per child. A society that is unwilling to pay for caseworkers is not going to shell out Harvard-size tuitions for any but a lucky handful of abused kids. The last time New York City put group care at the center of its child welfare policy, in the late 1980s, we had the boarder-baby scandal: newborns removed from drug-using mothers and crowded into filthy, unsafe, poorly staffed facilities. Many sickened; a few died. Foster care, another overwhelmed and disorganized system, has produced its own scandals. Maybe family reunification has gone too far, but there's a reason for that. Mom may be on and off drugs, out of her mind, living with a violent partner (Awilda Lopez's husband once stabbed her seventeen times), but even with drug treatment and parenting classes, she's cheap.

There's a certain weariness to the whole Elisa discussion. It's almost a cliché now to say that we only pretend to care about children, so obvious has become our vast social neglect. But even if we were to decide to invest in protecting children from outright abuse—hiring enough caseworkers, training them well, not stashing active case files away in closets and so forth—where would we be? An ideal child-welfare bureaucracy could save more children from dying like Elisa. But the real fatalism here is that no one questions that millions of children have to live like her.

Although brutality exists in every social class, the kind of abuse Elisa suffered is disproportionately an aspect of poverty, which produces in great quantities addiction, mental illness, domestic violence, social isolation and household chaos. That government can simultaneously deprive poor families of the wherewithal to survive while stopping child abuse is a fantasy; unfortunately, it is the animating idea behind Governor Pataki's budget proposals, which call for radical reductions in virtually every benefit a poor person might receive in New York State, while offering to restore $80 million of last year's $90 million cut in child protection services.

The left is often criticized for insisting that solving social problems requires larger social change. This used to be called unrealistic; now it's called amoral—denying personal responsibility, right and wrong, the existence of Evil. But if poverty produces violence against children, fighting social inequality is the *realistic* program—that is, the one that will actually work. Certainly that approach to child abuse is preferable to the conventional one, in which sentimentality alternates with cynicism and indifference, so that children like Elisa get to be princesses for a day—after they're dead.

January 1, 1996

No God, No Master

When people complain about the secularization of America, and the naked public square, and the banishment of religion from civic debate, as Stephen L. Carter does in his *Culture of Disbelief* and Harvey Cox did recently in *The Atlantic* and *The Nation,* I always want to ask, What on earth are you talking about? Show me a modern, prosperous industrialized Western country where religion plays a bigger part in public life than it does in the United States. Could a politician be elected if he admitted to being a nonbeliever? Would a jury find credible a witness who refused to swear to God? Even to get into the public square requires that one tip one's hat to the corner church or risk the hairy eyeball—which is why you rarely hear people call themselves atheists, the way people identify themselves as Methodists or Catholics. Indeed, when I happened to mention on *Crossfire* that I didn't believe in God, the Freedom From Religion Foundation was so delighted it made me its Freethought Heroine of 1995.

Of course, I wasn't heroic at all; what did I have to lose? It was the foundation's Freethinker of the Year who was the true heroine: young Beverly Harris, whose challenge of commencement prayers at her Idaho high school resulted in death threats, ostracism and the murder of her cat. I had a wonderful time at the F.F.R.F. convention in Denver, singing "Die Gedanken Sind Frei" with my new secularist friends and catching up on the F.F.R.F.'s various lawsuits, like the one against the statue of the Ten Commandments in the apparently not-so-naked public square below the Colorado State Capitol. I also enjoy and recommend their journal, *Freethought Today.* Its coverage of "black-collar crime" puts the *National Enquirer* to shame: pages and pages of rapes, child abuse, fraud and other bad deeds committed by men and women of the cloth. It's like a direct pipeline into the fantasy life of Diderot ("Mother Superior Fondles Nun?" "Priest's Victim Now Prostitute?"), except for its ecumenical scope and the fact that it's all real.

No, the whole country's drenched in religion, and that goes for the so-called left as well. That wonderful old anarchist slogan *Ni Dieu ni maître* seems to stir few hearts today. Think of the big black voices: Jesse Jackson, Cornel West, Michael Eric Dyson are Protestant divines; bell hooks is a Buddhist; Marian Wright Edelman just published a book of prayers. Among whites, Michael Lerner has a whole magazine devoted to his peculiar view of Judaism as a hybrid of socialism and psychobabble. On a higher plane of seriousness, Jonathan Kozol sees religious activism as the hope of the poor. Feminism? The divinity schools would be bankrupt without feminist theology and the women students it draws. And don't forget Goddess worship and Wicca; they're religions too.

Is the American left hostile to religion, as Cox charged? I wish! So far as I know, there are only a handful of true anticlerics active on our end of the spectrum, and three of them have columns in *The Nation.* Reluctant to enter into coalitions with religious groups? Hardly. The organized fragments most people mean when they speak of "the left" work with churches and synagogues on a wide range of issues: Third World solidarity, human rights, union activism, voter registration among the poor, community organizing, immigrants' rights, campaigns for a livable wage. NOW has teamed up with the Conference of Catholic Bishops to oppose "family caps" and other punitive aspects of welfare reform. Clergy are active in the A.C.L.U. and other groups that are fighting to keep church and state separate.

In fact, clergy are important supporters of abortion rights. Many mainstream Protestant denominations, as well as both Reform and Conservative branches of Judaism, favor them—although you'd never know it from pro-lifers, who go on as if they'd just got off the phone with God. Indeed, churches were essential in the struggle for legal abortion. Prominent Baptist ministers like Howard Moody in New York and Harris Wilson in Chicago arranged illegal abortions for hundreds of women, at considerable personal risk. How come we never hear about them when Martin Luther King's name is invoked to lend luster to the antiabortion cause?

The left has, in short, no trouble making common cause with religion, sometimes even when it means opportunistically abandoning its own philosophy and constituents. Consider the widespread compulsion to "dialogue" with Louis Farrakhan, embrace the Pope or find something nice to say about the Promise Keepers. But what is it, exactly, that the secular, or semi-secular, left could fruitfully discuss with the Christian Coalition, as Cox suggests? It doesn't matter that Sister Helen Prejean opposes the death penalty from a somewhat different perspective than the A.C.L.U.; they're both working for the same concrete goal. But there isn't *anything*, even on the most inclusive left or liberal shopping list, that is on the C.C.'s agenda. So what would we talk about? Whether school breakfast programs undermine the family? Whether Judgment Day is coming sooner rather than later? Given that there are no common goals, the fact that there is also no common agreement about what constitutes a relevant argument becomes important. If you're not a Christian, it doesn't matter whether Ralph Reed or Harvey Cox has the better grasp of biblical morality. Whatever public policies flow from their interpretations will have to be justified, in the public square, on other grounds. It is only in theocracies that "God says so" carries the day.

As to Cox's argument that the left should cozy up to religion because 90 percent of Americans believe in God, you might as well say it should engage with astrology, which is almost as popular. People believe all sorts of things—a 1991 Gallup poll, for instance, found that 45 percent believe in ghosts and 29 percent believe in witches. I'd rather see the believers debating each other: The Pentecostal tongues-speakers beloved of Reverend Cox could duke it out with the Last Marxist's students, a hefty fraction of whom think Stonehenge was built by space aliens. They'd probably find a lot of common ground.

January 22, 1996

VILLAGE IDIOCY

"Saint or Sinner?" asks the cover of *Newsweek* about Hillary Clinton. On *The New York Times* Op-Ed page, Maureen Dowd calls her a hybrid of Earth Mother and Mommie Dearest. I must say, I don't see what all the fuss is about. Don't countless politicians (and their relatives) use their positions to make profitable contacts and advance their friends? And don't they all talk about family, morals, responsibility, children and God? Even if the First Lady is guilty of the worst that is alleged against her—and if you can explain exactly what that is, you've probably been up to no good yourself—there's nothing new or exceptional about it: See the careers of Newt Gingrich, Al D'Amato, Bob Dole et al. This is what politics is all about, especially in places like Arkansas, aka The Heartland. "The people you read about in the papers? They all live next door to each other," an Italian journalist told me after a visit to Little Rock. "It's just like Italy!"

Well, there is one new thing: the gender issue. A lot of people still expect the wives of politicians to concentrate on the *Kinder-Kirche-Küche* side of life, while their husbands go after the bright lights and boodle. H.R.C. has failed to observe this division of labor in her own marriage, for which tradition-minded folk like William

Safire cannot forgive her. Now the First Lady has written a book, *It Takes a Village—And Other Lessons Children Teach Us*, only to land herself in more hot water. In yet another column criticizing H.R.C., Maureen Dowd took her to task for not acknowledging the ghostly pen of Barbara Feinman, a former researcher and editor for Ben Bradlee, Bob Woodward and Sally Quinn, all now apparently up in arms at this slight to their beloved assistant. Between Whitewater, Madison Guaranty, Travelgate and now Thankyougate, H.R.C. isn't likely to get much time to talk about her book, and since I know how painful that can be, I sat down and read the whole thing. Who knows? I may be the only columnist in America who can make that claim.

The ostensible thesis of *It Takes a Village* is that the well-being of children depends on the whole society. The real message is that H.R.C. is for family values. She prays a lot, alone and *en famille*. She's a good mom. She thinks young people should abstain from sex until they are twenty-one. She opposes divorce: "My strong feelings about divorce and its effects on children have caused me to bite my tongue more than a few times during my own marriage"— I'll bet—"and to think instead about what I could do to be a better wife and partner. My husband has done the same."

I know I'm not supposed to take these notions seriously, any more than I'm meant to gag at the weirdly Pollyannaish tone of the prose, or wonder if Sunday school could really have been her formative intellectual experience, as she claims. Like her disapproval of television talk shows—thanks to which "we are saturated with stories about priests who molest children" and have become "skeptical of organized religion"—they're just campaign theater, nods to the cultural conservatives that are balanced by other nods, to flexible gender roles, legal abortion (a very small nod), a "modest" rise in the minimum wage. There's no attempt to think anything through: the damage to organized religion versus the damage to children left at risk of molestation, for example, or the kinds of social pressures that would be necessary to produce that bumper crop of twenty-one-year-old virgins. Her opposition to divorce is left characteristically vague: She's "ambivalent" about no-fault divorce (the pet peeve of former White House aide and communitarian William Galston, who proposed abolishing it for couples with children on the *Times* Op-Ed page), but she says nothing about what it would really mean to return to the old system, in which spouses, lawyers and judges colluded in perjury, and wives who strayed could be denied custody and support. It's easy for her to talk: Her husband has obligingly provided her with grounds that would withstand even the most Savonarolaesque reforms.

What else? The First Lady is for sex ed that has both an abstinence and, for those youths determined to ruin their lives, a birth-control component; a free market that's also socially responsible; government that's both smaller and more social-worky. For every problem she identifies, a study, a foundation, a church, a business or a government-funded pilot project is already on the case: teaching poor young mothers how to improve their babies' cognitive abilities, encouraging fathers to spend time with their families, involving parents in their children's school. Some of these programs sound terrific, but none of them is on remotely the same scale as the problems it confronts. If parents are too poor to afford school uniforms, they've got troubles much graver than the community recycling of hand-me-downs can solve. The First Lady is thus a kind of center-liberal version of Arianna Huffington, who claims that "spirituality" and volunteerism can replace the welfare state. For H.R.C. the state itself becomes a kind of pilot project, full of innovation but short on cash, and ever on the lookout for spongers.

The real irony, of course, is that at the same time H.R.C. is conceptualizing society as a "village" united in its concern for and responsibility toward children, her husband is panting to sign the original Senate welfare bill, which his own administration's figures say would plunge 1.2 million more children into poverty and render more desperate the condition of those already poor. How can a self-described child advocate, who goes on and on about the importance of providing children with enriched parental attention and quality care from their earliest moments of life, square herself with policies that would force low-skilled mothers of small children into full-time subminimum-wage jobs, with warehouse care for their kids? Exactly how will permitting states to deny benefits to children born on welfare further those kids' development?

After the media figure out Whitewater and ensure proper recognition of Ms. Feinman's labors, some enterprising reporter might consider asking the First Lady about that.

February 5, 1996

FRENCH LESSONS

Quick! Name the big news stories of 1995. Let's see—Bosnia, O.J., Oklahoma City, Million Man March, Rabin assassination, O.J., Gingrich Revolution, Chechnya, Windows 95, Tokyo subway gassings, Rwanda and—whoops, I almost forgot: O.J. The usual panorama, in other words, of reaction, madness, mayhem and drift, with feel-good accents provided by techno-business and religio-racial hype. We're constantly told how apathetic and boobish the ordinary citizens of this country are, but just in case any showed signs of emerging from stupor, those end-of-the-year news roundups that are a journalistic New Year's Eve staple are guaranteed to make them cross "be more politically active" off their list of resolutions. In the immortal words of R. Crumb's despairing TV addict: Why bother?

Yet 1995 was a year when something amazing happened: the French general strike. Here was a three-and-a-half-week mass action by hundreds of thousands of workers and students that brought the country to a standstill, held the sympathy of the majority of the population—truly remarkable, given the genuine inconvenience entailed by the transportation stoppages—and actually succeeded in forcing the government to back off planned cuts in social benefits. Talk about a man-bites-dog story! You'd think the press, which often bemoans its bias toward the startling, would have been all over it. But no—coverage was low-key and superficial, full of the usual American jocular provincialism toward the Gallic, which probably comes from having been made to watch *Mr. Hulot's Holiday* once too often in high school. We heard a lot about baguettes, bicycles, Cartesian logic, cuisine and fashion chic. "Zut Alors! Parisians Pick Survival Over Chanel," as *The Christian Science Monitor* put it. We heard too about the dangers to all those beloved institutions—not to mention European unity—posed by "coddled" public-sector workers (*Time*) unwilling to make "sacrifices" (*The New York Times*) of their "luxuriant" benefits (*Newsweek*) and "cushy social programs" (*Business Week*) in the cause of "improving competitiveness" (*The New York Times*). Must be something in the Perrier.

The brush-off from the media is as nothing, though, to the silence from the public realm. Or did I miss the speech in which Labor Secretary Robert Reich saluted the French public-sector unions for defying the government cutbacks, and the one in which A.F.L.-C.I.O. head John Sweeney congratulated French workers for exceeding those unions in militance? French students have been subject to the same sort of cutbacks we're seeing in our own state university systems—overcrowded classrooms, canceled courses, insufficient resources. Have any Democratic politicians—any of the hatful of contenders for the job of New York City mayor, for example—urged American students to follow the French example and fight for their education, except, of course, by voting for them?

A while ago, in this space, I noted that the Democratic women elected to the House and Senate to defend women's rights were not exactly mounting the barricades to fight welfare "reform." I suggested that electoral politics had its limits, and maybe we should try something else for a change. A number of people wrote wondering what on earth I was talking about. A good question—I too find it hard to imagine a politics that does not revolve around Washington, election cycles, leaders, fund-raising, polling, the whole elaborate apparatus of opinion management that assumes—

in fact, relies on—the essential passivity of almost all the citizenry, almost all the time.

The French strike, though, shows what can happen when people refuse to accept the parameters of the debate as defined for them by the political class. The Juppé government used the same arguments that both Republicans and Democrats agree on here: the bloated public sector that the nation can no longer afford; the need to get lean and mean to win in the global marketplace. It even tried the "family values" ploy, although—lacking our centuries-long marination in punitive Protestantism—the French so far seem unpersuaded that single motherhood is the cause of unemployment.

Interestingly, the liberal end of the political spectrum has also been rather quiet about the French events, despite their direct bearing on our own predicament. Who talks about slashing the defense budget? Who asks why payrolls, and not profits, should be lean and mean? If the search for "underclass" scapegoats defines right-wing and centrist ideology, the appeal to benign authority defines left-wing-of-the-Democratic-Party liberals: Let's all share the pain and sacrifice together in the service of "the economy." These liberals speak the same language as their adversaries, the language of the bottom line, in which every social good from prenatal care to funding for the arts has to be justified on economic grounds. Worse, they actually believe what the right only pretends to: that America is essentially a classless society, in which it's un-American for the bottom 80 percent of the country to fight social service cutbacks and downsizing by saying, "I don't care where you get the money, it's not my problem." That's what the French strikers said—and curiously enough, the money was found.

The strikes in France had an interesting side effect not much noted here: marginalizing xenophobic neofascist Le Pen and his National Front. Apparently, given something concrete to do, the Archie Bunkers of France lost interest in blaming their troubles on Algerian immigrants. That makes me wonder about the high hot-air and paranoia quotient of our own political moment. It certainly seems as if huge numbers of people are obsessed with chimerical cure-alls: prayer in schools, the death penalty, abolishing affirmative action and building that double-link fence on the Mexican border that Pat Buchanan likes to talk about. At this very moment, otherwise intelligent people are busily persuading themselves of the magical properties of the flat tax, no doubt preparing the way for next year's proposal to do away with the middleman and pay tithes directly to the richest 1 percent. Could it be, though, that the ugly conservative mood liberals love to lament is not the cause of our political stagnation but the result? Maybe it's time to brush up on our French.

February 19, 1996

Sweet Swan of Avon

If there's a dead white male alive today, it's William Shakespeare. He's on screen—Laurence Fishburne's Othello, Ian McKellen's Richard III (a startlingly inventive setting of the play in 1930s Britain, with Richard as a fascist royal—don't miss it). He's on cable—just last month, Bravo did five evenings of nonstop classic Shakespeare films. He's on stage—hands down the most often produced playwright in the land. He's in the bookstore—supporting a huge critical industry and occupying thirty-four feet of shelves at my local Barnes & Noble. And, although you'd never know it from campus conservatives, who talk as though Romeo and Juliet have long since been banished in favor of Homi Bhabha and Queen Latifah, he's in the classroom too—far and away the most-assigned writer in high school and college.

No, the Bard's all right: Not even being forced to read *Julius Caesar* in tenth grade can ruin him, and his plays belong to the rather small selection of school texts that stand a chance of being opened after graduation. So I'm not going to join Maureen Dowd and others in the ongoing journalistic frownfest over Georgetown University's reorganization of its English major, which will render optional courses in Shakespeare, Chaucer and Milton, of whom students now have to take two out of three. In the deregulated English-department economy, the Bard will do fine.

It's Chaucer and Milton who stand to lose customers in the free market: A staggering percentage of their readers—who knows, maybe *all* their readers—come to their verses under duress. Not only do they have a much lower profile than Shakespeare in nonacademic culture—although, come to think of it, why not radio readings from *Paradise Lost,* a *Canterbury Tales* miniseries on PBS?— they're also less inviting to the unaided reader. Chaucer's English is practically another language until you get used to it; *Paradise Lost* is long and theological. But you don't hear pundits thundering that a nation unfamiliar with The Nun's Priest's Tale or *Samson Agonistes* is a nation that has lost its cultural marbles. It is only too clear, alas, that life can be fully lived without benefit of either; most Americans, including most pundits, do so every day.

Defending the canon in the popular press is a tricky business: After all, if people were as sensitive to language, as attuned to history and high-mindedness as canonical literature supposedly makes them, why would they be reading *The Washington Times,* the ultra-right Moonie-owned lowbrow paper that started the Georgetown flap? You have to place yourself carefully: If you get too specific— mourning the undergraduate indifference to *Astrophel and Stella* or *The Golden Bowl*—you risk losing readers who have painful memories of forced marches over those particular bits of literary turf, as well as those who've never heard of them and feel perfectly civilized anyway, thanks very much. You don't want to sound too, well, literary when defending the canon in a nation that's made Stephen King a zillionaire. Best keep things general—excellence, common culture, Western civ, shared values, all that—and talk as though the only thing keeping young Susie from majoring in Queer Studies is compulsory vaccination with *Measure for Measure* and *The Tempest.*

I don't mean to sound flippant: Actually, I tend to prefer old books to new. The truth is, though, the canon wars are over, the anticanon camp has won, and the fear-mongering around Shakespeare proves it: He's one of a handful of classic writers like Austen, Dickens, Blake, the Brontës, Keats and Whitman who still have some sort of living presence in our culture.

For those who love the classics, this cultural shift is sad, but it's also only natural: We are none of us what we were in the 1950s, so how can one expect that we would read the same books—and read them in the same way—any more than we look at the same pictures or eat the same food? To see the threat to the canon as an artifact of "the left"—feminism, multiculturalism—is much too simple, and ignores the important role "the left" has had in revitalizing some areas of literary study, including Shakespeare: *Othello* is a much more interesting play today, viewed through the lens of race, than it was in the days when it was taught as the undoing of a noble simpleton by a Machiavellian villain.

The real danger to Shakespeare is not that he will cease to be compulsory at elite colleges like Georgetown but that he will cease to be made available and accessible to a broad range of students. The Bard's popularity is not entirely due to his own fabulousness, after all: A rather elaborate network of educational and community resources has ensured that hundreds of thousands of students in secondary school are introduced to the plays in an exciting, intelligent way. Around the country, though, these programs—the teacher-training projects of Massachusetts's Shakespeare & Company and the Folger Shakespeare Library, which also runs a celebrated monthlong summer Teaching Shakespeare Institute; the school performances of Washington's Shakespeare Theatre—are struggling under federal and state cutbacks, including major slashings at the National Endowment for the Humanities and the Department of Education.

These federal agencies are held in horror, of course, by canon defenders, who fought long and hard and apparently successfully to delegitimize them in the public eye. Defund the left—remember that slogan?—by defunding education? Talk about destroying the village in order to save it! But who points out that Lynne Cheney and other canon conservatives are depriving students of the ability to appreciate the very literature they claim to care about?

It's a poor literary culture that values the classics only as discipline, not as pleasure. But that's the way things seem to be going these days—and not just with Shakespeare.

March 4, 1996

TAKE BACK THE RIGHT

Raise your hand if you voted for Bill Clinton because he was pro-choice. I thought so. Me too. When Clinton was elected, a lot of smart people thought abortion rights were safe. Activism plummeted and contributions to groups like NARAL dropped off as the President eliminated the infamous gag rule, made Joycelyn Elders surgeon general, nominated Ruth Bader Ginsburg to the Supreme Court and directed states to pay for Medicaid abortions in cases of rape, incest and life endangerment.

But it's not for nothing that they call Bill Clinton the Great Triangulator. Since the 1994 elections, he has signed legislation with riders that bar military hospitals from performing abortions even if women pay for them with their own money; that deny abortion coverage in health insurance for federal workers; that ban research on embryos; that gut foreign-aid funds for family planning. Joycelyn Elders is long gone, and every time I open the paper the President is telling another church group that there are "too many" abortions. My point is not to blame the President. To criticize him for backbonelessness is like blaming a cloud for not being made of granite: The man is what he is. If Clinton finds himself able to trade away reproductive freedom, it's because we're not exerting enough of the right kinds of pressure to his left.

When, for example, was the last time you read a defense of abortion in positive terms? Not as a tragic necessity, or to limit the damage already done to a desperate victim of rape or incest, or to save a pregnant woman's life, health or fertility? In their media campaigns and fund-raising appeals, pro-choice organizations stress these situations—the so-called hard cases—and you can see why: They reveal the pro-lifers' blanket moral language as unnuanced and callow, and replace the image of feckless yuppies having "convenience abortions" with that of "innocent victims." While this kind of rhetoric has been successful—polls show most Americans favor legal abortion for the "hard cases"—it concedes a lot of ground too: What about the vast majority of abortion-seeking women, who had sex willingly, perhaps even carelessly, who could give birth healthily and either raise the child themselves, or—the latest trend in "abortion compromise" thinking—give it up for adoption?

Pro-choicers need to start talking again about abortion as an essential part of women's right to self-determination: to sexual expression, to schooling and jobs and youth, to choose when and if they become mothers. We need to say it's all right for a woman to put her life first, *not* to pay with childbirth for the "sin" of sex. When we are accused of "individualism" we can point out that women, staggering numbers of whom have had abortions, do about 99.44 percent of the child-raising in this country and, besides, how would society be better off with more teenage mothers, more overburdened single moms and flown-the-coop fathers, more sad "birth mothers," more hastily formed, economically marginal families? To speak of abortion as anguish—the current pro-choice rhetoric—is true or partly so for some women, but what about the many who feel nothing but relief?

Failure to articulate in practical, concrete language what's positive about abortion has allowed pro-life romantic moralism to shape the public discourse: *The Village Voice* has Nat Hentoff, *The Nation* has Christopher Hitchens. In *The Atlantic Monthly,* George McKenna compares abortion to slavery, with pregnant women, presumably, in the Simon Legree role; in *The New Republic,* Naomi Wolf writes of her pregnancy-inspired discovery that women are vessels, embryos are babies and many abortions, like those of her friends in high school, frivolous; she looks forward to the day when, "the patriarchy" having finished "crumbling in spite of itself," feminists can sponsor candlelight vigils for dead fetuses. (Since that article, Wolf has made headlines for advising President Clinton to energize the disaffected women's vote by presenting himself as "The Good Father." Our votes belong to Daddy? About that crumbling patriarchy . . .)

In addition to seizing the discourse, pro-choicers need to seize the day. Even our major grassroots activity, clinic defense, is a reaction rather than an initiative. Laura Kaplan's *The Story of Jane: The Legendary Underground Feminist Abortion Service* reminded me that the root of abortion rights lay in direct action by ordinary women and men. While we wouldn't want to imitate such popular anti-choice tactics as murder, arson, death threats and stalking, there's a lot that people can do. Conduct information pickets at pro-life "pregnancy centers." Write a leaflet explaining what abortion is, debunking myths and listing reputable abortion clinics; print five hundred copies, distribute in front of your local high school. Send money to The National Network of Abortion Funds, which pays for poor women's abortions in states with no Medicaid funding.

If you've had an abortion, go public. Tell your gynecologist you think abortion is part of normal medical practice and would stand by him if he performed them in the office. If he looks horrified, find another doctor. Get your church or synagogue involved: Why should pro-lifers have a monopoly on God? Or on TV? Next time you catch one of those repellent antiabortion and antisex ads ("Life. What a beautiful choice"; "You're worth waiting for") produced by the fundamentalist megabucks De Moss Foundation, pick up the phone and demand equal time for birth control ads and the spots ("Choice. What a beautiful life") produced by NARAL. If you're really feeling ambitious, plan a network to transport, house and befriend women marooned far from clinics and girls who live in parental-notification states.

If you've got a phone and a friend, a fax machine and a lunch hour, you can be an abortion activist. The way things are going, you won't be a moment too soon.

March 18, 1996

For Whom the Ball Rolls

The only things I like about bowling are the shoes and the beer. Maybe that's why I can't get excited about Robert Putnam, the Harvard political scientist whose slender article "Bowling Alone: America's Declining Social Capital," in the January 1995 *Journal of Democracy*, has spawned more commentary than *Hamlet*, including a profile in *People*; it even brought him tête-à-tête with President Clinton, whose State of the Union address he helped inspire. Putnam argues that declining membership in such venerable civic institutions as bowling leagues, the P.T.A., the League of Women Voters, the Boy Scouts, the Elks and the Shriners is an index of a weakened "civil society," the zone of social engagement between the family and the state. Why should you care about the leagues? Because, says Putnam, they bowl for thee: A weak civil society means less "trust" in each other, and that means a less vigorous democracy, as evidenced in declining electoral turnouts.

It's the sort of thesis academics and pundits adore, a big woolly argument that's been prereduced to a sound bite of genius. Bowling alone—it's wistful, comical, nostalgic, sad, a tiny haiku of post-industrial loneliness. Right-wingers like Francis Fukuyama and George Will like it because it can be twisted to support their absurd contention that philanthropy has been strangled by big government. Clintonians and communitarians like it because it moralizes a middle-class, apolitical civic-mindedness that recognizes no hard class or race inequalities shaping individual choice: We are all equally able to volunteer for the Red Cross, as we are all equally able to vote. Putnam's prime culprit in the decline of civic America—television—is similarly beyond the reach of structural change. It's as though America were all one big leafy suburb, in which the glad-handers and do-gooders have been bewitched by the evil blue light of *Seinfeld* and *Friends*.

At least Putnam doesn't blame working mothers. Still, the discussion around "Bowling Alone" is peculiar in a number of ways. How many of those who praise its thesis fit either half of his theory, I wonder: Is Bill Bradley a Shriner? Does *The Washington Post*'s David Broder bake cookies for the P.T.A.? If not, is the boob tube to blame? As Theda Skocpol noted in her politely devastating rejoinder to Putnam's follow-up article, "The Strange Disappearance of Civic America," in *The American Prospect* (Winter 1996), Putnam seems to place both the burden of civic engagement and responsibility for its collapse on the nonelite classes. Tenured professors may be too busy to sing in a choir (Putnam's former avocation): The rest of us are just couch potatoes.

Although Putnam is careful to disclaim nostalgia for the fifties, his picture of healthy civic life is remarkably, well, square. I've been a woman all my life, but I've never heard of the Federation of Women's Clubs. If membership is down in the League of Women Voters, maybe it's because politically engaged women are volunteering with newer, more partisan organizations: Planned Parenthood or NOW or Concerned Women of America. It's probably going too far to argue that the decline of the Boy Scouts is directly related to its barring of gay and nonbelieving lads. But should it really surprise us that such a stodgy organization has a hard time finding volunteers?

Or take those bowling leagues. Putnam treats these as if they arose merely from the appetite of individuals for fellowship and tenpins. But in fact they came out of specific forms of working-class and lower-middle-class life: stable blue-collar or office employment that fostered group solidarity (businesses and unions often started and sponsored teams), a marital ethos that permitted husbands plenty of boys' nights out, a lack of cultural and entertainment alternatives. It would be amazing if league bowling survived the passing of the way of life that brought it into being, nor am I so sure we need mourn it. People still bowl, after all. In fact they bowl more than ever, although they consume less beer and pizza, which is why league decline bothers the owners of bowling alleys. And despite Putnam's title, they don't bowl alone. They bowl with friends, on dates, with their kids, with other families. The bowling story could be told as one of happy progress: from a drink-sodden night of spouse avoidance with the same old faces from work to temperate and spontaneous fun with one's intimate friends and relations.

No, the whole theory is seriously out of touch with the complexities of contemporary life. If church membership is down (good news in my book), it's hardly because people are staying home to watch TV. More likely, organized religion doesn't speak to their spiritual needs the way (for example) self-help programs do. Putnam dismisses the twelve-step movement much too quickly. At the very least, its popularity calls the TV-time-drain theory into question. I know people who've gone to A.A. every day, for years. As for building social capital, my own brief experience with Alanon more than fifteen years ago is still my touchstone of ordinary human decency and kindness. What's that if not "trust"? My membership in the P.T.A., by contrast, is motivated mostly by mistrust: As another parent put it, we join the P.T.A. to keep our kids from being shafted by the school system.

Putnam's theory may not explain much about the way we live now, but its warm reception speaks volumes. The bigfoot journalists and academic superstars, opinion manufacturers and wise men of both parties are worried, and it isn't about bowling or Boy Scouts. It's about the loss of "trust," a continuum that begins with one's neighbor and ends with the two parties, government, authority. It makes sense for the political and opinion elites to feel this trust—

for them, the system works. It's made them rich and famous. But how much faith can a rational and disinterested person have in the setup that's produced our current crop of leaders?

Love your neighbor if you can, but forget civic trust. What we need is more civic skepticism. Especially about people who want you to do their bowling for them.

April 15, 1996

GAY MARRIAGE?
DON'T SAY I DIDN'T WARN YOU

When gay friends argue in favor of same-sex marriage, I always agree and offer them the one my husband and I are leaving. Why should straights be the only ones to have their unenforceable promise to love, honor and cherish trap them like houseflies in the web of law? Marriage will not only open up to gay men and lesbians whole new vistas of guilt, frustration, claustrophobia, bewilderment, unfairness and sorrow, it will offer them the opportunity to prolong this misery by tormenting each other in court. I know one pair of exes who spent in legal fees the entire value of the property in dispute, and another who took five years and six lawyers to untie the knot. Had these couples merely lived together they would have thrown each other's record collections out the window and called it a day. Clearly something about marriage drives a lot of people round the bend. Why shouldn't some of those people be gay?

Legalizing gay marriage would be a good idea even if all it did was to chasten conservative enthusiasts like Andrew Sullivan and Bruce Bawer, who imagine that wedlock would do for gays what it is less and less able to do for straights—encourage monogamy, sobriety and settled habits. Gay conservatives are quick to criticize heterosexual offenders against the sociomarital order, like divorced and single parents and poor women who nonetheless have children. Legalizing gay marriage will do a lot to open these men's eyes: Soon they'll be divorcing, single parenting and bankrupting each other like the rest of us. Maybe we'll hear less about restoring the stigma of "illegitimacy" and divorce over at *The New Republic* when gay men find themselves raising kids with no help from a deadbeat co-dad.

I'm for same-sex marriage because I'd be a hypocrite not to be: I married, after all, for reasons that apply to gay couples—a mix of love, convention and a practical concern for safeguarding children, property, my husband and myself from unforeseen circumstances and strange legal quirks. I don't see why gays shouldn't be able to make the same choice, and I've yet to see an argument on the other side that doesn't dissolve into bias and prejudice and thinly disguised religious folderol. In a recent *New York Times* Op-Ed, former Quayle speechwriter Lisa Schiffren attacked the idea of gay marriage by defining marriage as about procreation, with the many nonprocreating couples—infertile, voluntarily childless, middle-aged and elderly—included out of politeness. (It was a banner weekend for Schiffren at the *Times*—the very next day the *Magazine* published her essay claiming that the legalization of abortion explains why no one offered her a subway seat when she was pregnant.) In a particularly overwrought 1991 *Commonweal* essay, Jean Bethke Elshtain depicted gay marriage as "antinatal—hostile to the regenerative female body." Haven't these writers ever heard of Heather's two mommies and Daddy's roommate? *Lots* of gay and lesbian couples are raising children together these days. Interestingly, neither of these defenders of the hearth mentions love—maybe gays are the last romantics, after all.

For social conservatives like Elshtain and Schiffren, opposition to gay marriage is more than homophobia: It's a move in a larger, high-stakes policy struggle over the family. The kernel of truth grasped by anti-gay-marriage conservatives is that same-sex wedlock is part of the modern transformation of marriage: What used to be a hierarchical, gender-polarized relationship whose perma-

nence was enforced by God, law, family and community is becoming a more equal, fluid and optional relationship whose perma-
nence depends on the mutual wishes of the partners. Whatever its
conservative champions think, gay marriage could never have become a realistic political issue, with considerable popular support
from straights, without the breakdown of traditional family values—widespread divorce, nonmarital births, cohabitation, blended
families, double-income couples, interracial and interfaith and no-
faith unions, abortion, feminism. When it becomes legal, as I believe it will, same-sex marriage will be the result, not the cause, of
a change in the meaning of marriage. The reason arguments
against it sound so prudish and dated and irrational is that they are.

Proponents of same-sex marriage make much of the unfairness
of denying gay couples the many rights and privileges awarded
husbands and wives—health insurance, survivors' rights, mutual
custody of children, job protection under the Family and Medical
Leave Act and so on. Far be it from me to pooh-pooh as a motive for
marriage a system that has saved me literally thousands of dollars
in dental bills. But even as we support legalizing same-sex unions,
we might ask whether we want to distribute these rights and privileges according to marital status. Why should access to health care
be a by-product of a legalized sexual connection, gay or straight?
Wouldn't it make more sense to give everyone his or her own health
insurance? Similarly, gays and lesbians rightly resent the ways in
which their inability to marry leaves them vulnerable to parental
interference: The case of Sharon Kowalski, whose parents took custody after she suffered brain damage in a crash and for many years
denied visitation to her lover, is a notorious example but hardly
unique; the annals of the AIDS crisis are full of parents who cut
their child's lover off from contact, participation in medical decisions and property—including shared property. But all unmarrieds
are potentially subject to this kind of hostile takeover, not just gays.
What's wrong is the legal mind-set that regards unmarried forty-
year-olds as the wards of Mom and Dad.

The truth is, we are moving toward a society in which the old
forms of human relationships are being disrupted and reshaped,

and sooner or later the law must accommodate that reality. Legalizing gay marriage is part of the process, but so is diminishing the increasingly outmoded privileged status of marriage and sharing out its benefits along different, more egalitarian lines. Andrew Sullivan and Bruce Bawer may have more in common with single mothers than they would like to think.

April 29, 1996

POMOLOTOV COCKTAIL

You've got to hand it to Alan Sokal, the New York University physicist who tricked *Social Text*, the cultural studies journal, into publishing in its special "Science Wars" issue—as a straight academic article—his over-the-top parody of postmodern science critique. "Transgressing the Boundaries: Toward a Transformative Hermeneutics of Quantum Gravity" is a hilarious compilation of pomo gibberish, studded with worshipful quotations from all the trendy thinkers—Derrida, Lacan, Lyotard, Irigaray, *Social Text* board member Stanley Aronowitz (cited thirteen times) and issue editor Andrew Ross (four times). Its thesis, barely discernible through the smoke and fog of jargon, is that the theory of quantum gravity has important affinities with assorted New Age and postmodern ideas; it concludes with a call for "emancipatory mathematics." The whole production was rigged so that anyone who knew physics would realize how preposterous it was. I tried it out on the Last Marxist and had to leave the room, he was laughing so hard. To judge by the gleeful e-mail that's been zipping around academia since Sokal revealed his prank in the current issue of *Lingua Franca*, the L.M. is far from alone.

When one has been duped so incontrovertibly and so publicly

there's only one thing to say: Is my face red! Instead, Ross has circulated an editorial response that stakes out some very dubious turf, much of it seeded with land mines. "A breach of professional ethics"? Talk about the transgressor transgressed! A "hokey" article, "not really our cup of tea"? And yet they published it. *Social Text* not a peer-reviewed journal? Maybe it should be.

Certainly Ross's well-known claim that people need no expertise in science to direct its social uses has been done no favors by this rather spectacular display of credulity. And surely it does not help matters to impugn Sokal's motives, as Ross did when I spoke with him—to insist that this self-described leftist and feminist who taught math in Nicaragua under the Sandinistas is not on the level. Equally foolish is his attempt to play the gender card—calling the parody a "boy stunt" and urging responses from "women's voices, since this affair, at least as it has been presented in the press so far, has been a boy debate." It's chicks up front all over again.

It's hard not to enjoy the way this incident has made certain humanities profs look self-infatuated and silly—most recently, Stanley Fish, who defended *Social Text* on the *Times* Op-Ed page by comparing scientific laws to the rules of baseball. Sokal's demonstration of the high hot-air quotient in cultural studies—how it combines covert slavishness to authority with the most outlandish radical posturing—is, if anything, long overdue. Unfortunately, another effect of his prank will be to feed the anti-intellectualism of the media and the public. Now people who have been doing brilliant, useful work for years in the social construction of science—some of whom (Dorothy Nelkin, Hilary Rose, Ruth Hubbard) are represented in that same issue of *Social Text*—will have to suffer, for a while, the slings and arrows of journalists like the *Times*'s Janny Scott, who thinks "epistemological" is a funny word, and who portrays the debate over science studies as being between "conservatives" who "have argued that there is truth, or at least an approach to truth, and that scholars have a responsibility to pursue it" and academic leftists who, since they believe nothing is real, can just make up any old damn thing. No light can come from a discussion whose premises are so fundamentally misconstrued (including by Sokal, who in his *Lingua Franca* piece cites as ridiculous postmodern "dogma" the argument that the world is real but unknowable, a position put forward by Kant in 1781, and that I have to say exactly accords with my everyday experience).

And the biggest misconstruction, of course, is that "the academic left," aka postmodernists and deconstructionists, is the left, even on campus. When I think of scholars who are doing important and valuable intellectual work on the left I think of Noam Chomsky and Adolph Reed, of historians like Linda Gordon and Eric Foner and Rickie Solinger and Natalie Zemon Davis; I think of scientists like Richard C. Lewontin and Stephen Jay Gould; feminists like Ann Snitow and Susan Bordo. None of these people—and the many others like them—dismiss reason, logic, evidence and other Enlightenment watchwords. All write clearly, some extremely well. All build carefully on previous scholarly work—the sociology and history of science, for example, goes back to the 1930s—to approach that "truth" that has somehow become the right's possession. As if Charles Murray is a disinterested scholar!

How "the left" came to be identified as the pomo left would make an interesting Ph.D. thesis. I suspect it has something to do with the decline of actual left-wing movements outside academia, with the development in the 1980s of an academic celebrity system that meshes in funny, glitzy ways with the worlds of art and entertainment, with careerism—the need for graduate students, in today's miserable job market, to defer to their advisers' penchant for bad puns and multiple parentheses, as well as their stranger and less investigated notions. What results is a pseudo-politics, in which everything is claimed in the name of revolution and democracy and equality and antiauthoritarianism, and nothing is risked, nothing, except maybe a bit of harmless cross-dressing, is even expected to happen outside the classroom.

How else explain how pomo leftists can talk constantly about the need to democratize knowledge and write in a way that excludes all but the initiated few? Indeed, the comedy of the Sokal incident is that it suggests that even the postmodernists don't really understand one another's writing and make their way through the text by moving from one familiar name or notion to the next like a frog jumping across a murky pond by way of lily pads. Lacan . . . performativity . . . Judith Butler . . . scandal . . . (en)gendering (w)holeness . . . Lunch!

June 10, 1996

ADOPTION FANTASY

Bill Clinton loves it. Bob Dole too. Newt Gingrich thinks it's so terrific he wanted to mass-produce it through the Personal Responsibility Act. Hillary Clinton told *Time* she dreamed of trying it herself. As the family-values/teen-sex/abortion debate winds on with no end in sight, adoption is being touted as a rare area of consensus: the way to discourage "illegitimacy" while providing poor children with stable homes, the peace pipe in the abortion wars. Whatever may be the difficulties and conflicts of actual people involved in the adoption triangle, at the political level, it's all win-win: adoption and apple pie.

Whenever I question the facile promotion of adoption as a solution to the problem du jour I get angry letters from adoptive parents. So I want to be clear: *Of course* adoption can be a wonderful thing; *of course* the ties between adoptive parents and children are as profound as those between biological ones. But can't one both rejoice in the happiness adoption can bring to individuals *and* ask hard questions about the social functions it is being asked to fill? I can't be the only person who has noticed that the same administration that supports the family cap—the denial of a modest benefit increase to women who conceive an additional child while on welfare—is about to bestow on all but the richest families a $5,000 tax credit to defray the costs of adoption. Thus, the New Jersey baby who is deemed unworthy of $64 a month, or $768 a year, in government support if he stays in his family of origin immediately becomes six times more valuable once he joins a supposedly better-ordered household. Maybe unwed mothers should trade kids.

Last year, mass adoption was supposed to rescue innocent babies from the effects of defunding their guilty teenage mothers—a bizarre brainstorm of Charles Murray that has fortunately faded for now. This year, adoption is back in a more accustomed role, as an "alternative" to abortion—a notion long supported by abortion-rights opponents from Ralph Reed to Christopher Hitchens, and recently picked up by some pro-choicers too. The wrong women insisting on their right to have children, the right women refusing to—it's hard to avoid the conclusion that adoption is being pushed as public policy as a way of avoiding hard questions about class and sex. After all, if poverty is the problem, we could enable mothers and children to live decently, as is done throughout Western Europe. If teenage pregnancy is the problem, we could insist on contraception, sex education and health care—the approach that has also worked very well in Western Europe, where teens are about as sexually active as they are in this country, but where rates of teen pregnancy range from half of ours (England and Wales) to one-tenth (the Netherlands).

How much sense does adoption make as a large-scale alternative to abortion? Journalists constantly cite the National Council for Adoption's claim that one to two million Americans wish to adopt—which would make between twenty and forty potential adopters for every one of the 50,000 or so nonkin adoptions formalized in a typical year. But what is this estimate based on? According to the N.C.A., it's a rough extrapolation from figures on infertility, and includes anyone who makes any gesture in the direction of adoption—even a phone call—which means they are counting most of my women friends, some of the men and, who knows, maybe Hillary Clinton too. The number of serious, viable candidates is bound to be much smaller: For all the publicity surrounding their tragic circumstances, last year Americans adopted only 2,193 Chinese baby girls. Even if there were no other objections, the adoption and abortion numbers are too incommensurate for the former to be a real "alternative" to the latter.

But of course, there are other objections. There are good reasons why only 3 percent of pregnant white girls and 1 percent of pregnant black girls choose adoption. Maybe more would do so if adoption were more fluid and open, a kind of open-ended "guardianship" arrangement, but that would surely discourage potential adoptive parents. The glory days of white-baby relinquishment in the 1950s and 1960s depended on coercion—the illegality of abortion, the sexual double standard and the stigma of unwed motherhood, enforced by family, neighbors, school, social work, medicine, church, law. Those girls gave up their babies because they had no choice—that's why we are now hearing from so many sad and furious fifty-year-old birth mothers. Do we really want to create a new generation of them by applying the guilt and pressure tactics that a behavior change of such magnitude would require?

Right now, pregnant girls and women are free to make an adoption plan, and for some it may indeed be the right choice. But why persuade more to—unless one espouses the anti-choice philosophy that even the fertilized egg has a right to be born, and that terminating a pregnancy is "selfish"? I'm not belittling the longings of would-be adoptive parents, but theirs is not a problem a teenager should be asked to solve. Pregnancy and childbirth are immense events, physically, emotionally, socially, with lifelong effects; it isn't selfish to say no to them.

Promoting adoption instead of abortion sounds life-affirming, but it's actually physically dangerous, cruel and punitive. That's why the political and media figures now supporting it wouldn't dream of urging it on their own daughters. Can you imagine the Clintons putting Chelsea through such an ordeal? Hillary Clinton is entitled to her adoption fantasy, but maybe she ought to think a little more about the girls who are already here. They have a right to put themselves first.

July 8, 1996

UTOPIA, LIMITED

How on earth, I wonder, do conservatives manage to put themselves across as hardheaded realists? I confess I used to feel this way about them myself sometimes. At least right-wingers understand that wishes aren't horses, I'd mutter a little enviously after reading some starry-eyed left-liberal appeal to the better angels of our nature. But I was wrong: That wishes are horses is exactly what they think. Beneath those Brooks Brothers shirtfronts beat hearts that thrill, perversely, to the wildest Utopian fantasies.

You would think, for example, that the right would by now be used to the presence of married women and mothers in the workforce. After all, their numbers have been increasing for decades. The decline of homemaking as a full-time occupation is so closely tied to so many other features of modernity—urbanization, secularization, low birth and high divorce rates, increased education for women—you'd pretty much have to repeal the twentieth century to get women to stay home.

So, asks David Gelernter in "Why Mothers Should Stay Home" (*Commentary*, February), wouldn't it be nice if moms quit their jobs? Not just nice for children, whose bad grades, drug use, suicide and violence Gelernter blames squarely on maternal employ-

ment, but also for "us," that useful pronoun whose precise refer-
ent—potential victims of violent youth? society as a whole, minus
would-be working moms? readers of *Commentary*?—need never be
specified.

Why have working mothers become the norm? Not because of
economic need, Gelernter argues: After all, most Americans are
much better off than they were in 1935, when far fewer mothers
worked. What was good enough for Grandma in the Great Depression should be good enough today. (I must say, this is a bit much coming from a man who teaches at Yale, where annual fees are $29,528.)
No, moms take jobs because they've been indoctrinated by feminism. Not a word about declining male wages; not a nod to the positive aspects of having a working mother, to which I, and many other
working women's children, can attest; only scorn for the notion that
in an age of long lives, tiny families and Chinese takeout the homemaker role is simply not an adequate life project anymore. Even
more scorn in the June letters page, responding to Amy Wax's reminder that many women find stay-at-home motherhood lonely and
boring and financial dependence on their husbands "irksome and
humiliating." Mothers work because of a mistaken idea; therefore—
maybe—a different idea could get them to quit. It's that simple.

The Weekly Standard's William Tucker also wants mom back in
the kitchen, but at least he admits that her family needs her paycheck. His big idea ("A Return to the 'Family Wage,' " May 13) is to
bring back the system, fought for by unions and underwritten by
management, whereby (white) men were paid enough to support a
stay-at-home wife and kids. A great plan, spoiled in 1963 by Betty
Friedan, who, bitter at losing her job after giving birth, went off and
published That Book. Tucker wants to bring back a gender-neutral
version of the family wage: Every couple would choose one mate to
be the primary worker, sort of like a designated driver, whom employers could legally favor, and one to be the secondary worker,
whom employers could legally discriminate against. How gender-
neutral this system would be in practice can be judged by the enthusiastic response of Phyllis Schlafly, who wrote in to say she had
the same idea in 1977.

It's interesting that neither writer suggests that both parents work part-time and share a family wage. Nor do they consider that society could encourage mothers (or fathers) to stay home with small children through generous parental leave policies and child-care benefits rather than by lecturing and short-changing them. Not only are these policies associated with Scandinavia, Italy, France and other socialistic dragon's nests but they put money directly in the hands of women. That's the tip-off that what's really at stake for Tucker and Gelernter is not children—for kids, the amply funded social-welfare state works very well, as many studies comparing European and U.S. children confirm. It's restoring the "traditional" family, in which wives depend financially on their husbands.

The family wage, as Tucker points out, is a venerable idea with many leftist proponents. It also has a long history in Catholic teaching; it was reasserted in 1981 by Pope John Paul II, who dispensed with the gender neutrality, as you might expect, and placed it squarely on the table, along with direct payments to mothers, as a way of keeping women home. But the historical campaign for the family wage called on workers to make demands on government and industry. The Pope can appeal to Divine Providence. To whom do right-wing family-wagers address themselves? Not to the state—that would intrude on the free market—and certainly not to capital (after all, Tucker is opposed to raising the minimum wage). As with Gelernter's call for downwardly mobile domesticity, there is no way to make the family wage happen, and no constituency for it either, except of course our old friends "we" and "us."

Well, it's all nonsense, isn't it? We'd need to turn back not just the clock but the global economy too, in which, far from a smaller workforce earning double wages, a doubled workforce is barely keeping pace. The real question is why these highly intelligent fellows are denying such a prominent piece of reality—even as Congress is forced by popular demand to raise the minimum wage and Chief Justice Rehnquist, hardly a brainwashed disciple of Betty Friedan, joins Ruth Bader Ginsburg in compelling the Virginia Military Institute to admit women.

On the other hand, magazines need copy, pundits need subjects. And if right-wingers were really to confront what unrestrained capitalism is doing to children and to families, what on earth could they say?

July 29/August 5, 1996

THE STRANGE DEATH OF
LIBERAL AMERICA

I woke up this morning to the voice of Linda Chavez-Thompson—first and only female, first and only minority executive vice president of the supposedly revitalized, supposedly reprogressified A.F.L.-C.I.O.—telling National Public Radio how thrilled she was with the Democratic Party platform. That's the one that claims as a party triumph the Republican-authored welfare bill that will push countless children into poverty, deprive legal immigrants of a wide array of benefits and force millions of poor mothers into minimum- or even subminimum-wage jobs that do not, so far as we know, exist. "I love this platform!" announced Dennis Archer, mayor of Detroit, where 67 percent of children are on public assistance. Did I mention that the platform this year omits the usual lip service to the ongoing urban crisis?

The passage of the welfare reform bill signifies more than the end of welfare as we know it; it signifies the end of a certain kind of liberalism too. Plenty of solid liberal Democrats voted for the act in the Senate: Russell Feingold, Bob Graham and Barbara Mikulski, who wasn't even up for reelection. The House vote included yeas from Nita Lowey, who is co-chair of the Congressional Caucus for Women's Issues; Elizabeth Furse; Jane Harmon and Lynn Rivers.

I'm ashamed to say I actually contributed to the campaigns of some of these people, through EMILY's List and other supposedly feminist PACs. Maybe you did too.

"Sometimes you're in a position in which you have to make a decision," Representative Lowey told me. "The system is so broken." Is it? Lowey asserted that 25 percent of those on welfare are third-generation recipients, a figure she revised later in our talk as 25 percent on welfare for ten years or more—"that's two generations." Maybe she was thinking of *horses* on welfare? (Actually, only about 6.7 percent of recipients have been on welfare continuously for that long, and only 9 percent grew up in households that frequently received welfare.) It was unnerving but strangely enlightening to hear the head of the congressional women's caucus defending her vote with numbers plucked out of the air and Orwellian tributes to "the dignity of work," while simultaneously professing herself "concerned" about the actual content of the bill—the free hand given to states with atrocious records, the cutoffs of legal immigrants, food stamp limits, and so on. When the Democrats retake Congress we'll be monitoring those things, she assured me. So now we're supposed to vote for the Democrats so they can undo their own votes! Talk about triangulation.

Well, why single out Nita Lowey? Elizabeth Furse's press aide wanted me to believe that Furse voted for the bill in order to protect Oregon's "wonderful" programs. (Hello? There are forty-nine other states out here? Full of women you asked for campaign contributions?) The picture from the world of Beltway advocacy is not much brighter. Marian Wright Edelman threw away the last, best chance to organize popular resistance to punitive welfare reform and convened a giant Stand for Children that attracted 200,000 people to . . . stand for children. A.F.S.C.M.E. finally decided to use its phone banks to organize callers to urge a White House veto—on the very day Clinton announced he would sign the bill. NOW (which, to its credit, is refusing to endorse or support legislators who voted for the bill) is mounting a daily vigil at the White House with a coalition of progressive groups. Patricia Ireland and other NOW staffers are on a hunger strike.

All this is good, but why so little? Why so late? This bill has been moving toward passage for months, and welfare reform has been a major political issue for four years. It's because these liberal groups are caught up in mainstream electoral politics, which in practice means clinging to Clinton and the Democratic Party, waiting and hoping and beseeching, working on the inside, faxing and phoning and producing yet another study or poll. Meanwhile they preach the gospel of the lesser of two evils, that ever-downward spiral that has brought us to this pass and that will doubtless end with liberals in hell organizing votes for Satan because Beelzebub would be even worse—think of the Supreme Court!

They really didn't think he'd sign it, one welfare expert told me when I asked why protests were so lackluster as the bill moved toward passage. That was a miscalculation that goes way beyond the President's character—it applies to a whole mode of political action. Liberalism is the idea that the good people close to power can solve the problems of those beneath them in the social order. Its tools are studies and sermons and campaign contributions and press conferences. The trouble is, the political forces they call on are not interested anymore—and this is true not just in the United States. In country after country, social benefits are being slashed and the working class's standard of living lowered, and the major parties, including the ones that call themselves Labor or Socialist or Democratic, accept this process as a given. Of course, there will always be a few noble oddballs like Paul Wellstone, the only Democratic senator up for reelection who voted against the welfare bill. But the general direction of government in the age of globalized corporate power is clear.

Advocacy politics can't turn this around, because advocacy is based on speaking for people rather than those people acting on their own behalf. Enormous demonstrations around the country, with strikes by S.E.I.U. and A.F.S.C.M.E., sit-downs in welfare offices and 100,000 homeless people camping out on the capital Mall might have affected the debate. Marian Wright Edelman issuing a press release no longer can. Indeed, the media didn't even pick up the most recent one, eloquent as it was.

The Women's Committee of 100 is suggesting that people return fund-raising letters from party organizations, PACs and anti-welfare politicians with a note saying that you're now sending your disposable dollars to social welfare organizations. Why not take it a step further and fund activism? All over the country, there are groups with great politics and no money. The Democratic Party cannot make the same claim.

August 26/September 2, 1996

OF TOES AND MEN

Revelations that Mephistophelean Clinton political consultant and family values strategist Dick Morris paid a call girl named Sherry Rowlands for kinky sex had me sympathizing with the man for the first time. Imagine a forty-eight-year-old mover and shaker who pays $200 an hour to caress the feet of and receive some well-deserved discipline from a woman whose age was first reported as forty-two! What, not a teenager in one of those fetching school uniforms he and the President are so keen on? Not a twentysomething policy analyst with a thing for married men? A man who loves the company of women his own age so much he will pay for the privilege of sucking their toes—who daydreams, says Rowlands, of trysts with mature Hillary Clinton!—this is not a man to hound from public life so quickly. Unfortunately, the early report must have been a typo, because according to the *Star*, which is publishing Ms. Rowlands's "love diaries," she is actually a mere thirty-seven. So the heck with him, I say. Let the tabs do their worst.

You'd think by now politicians would realize that promoting family values is like wearing a Kick Me sign on your back. Two years ago John Major's Back to Basics campaign foundered amid gales of laughter as Tory after supposedly straight-arrow Tory turned out to have a mistress or a love child or more fetishes than the Museum of Natural History. (It wasn't all so funny, actually: One political wife committed suicide; Tory wunderkind Stephen Milligan died under bizarre circumstances that may have included autoerotic asphyxiation.) Here in the States, recent years have brought us Gennifer Flowers and Paula Jones, the Packwood diaries, Enid and Joe Waldholtz, the jailing of Mel Reynolds for having sex with a minor, the outing of Jim Kolbe as gay after he voted for the Defense of Marriage Act and revelations of Newt's callous ditching of his first wife and failure to pay child support. Joe Conason in *The New York Observer* and Karen Houppert in *The Village Voice* charge Bob Dole with similarly caddish behavior in his first marriage; after twenty-three years of devotion, Phyllis Dole—the woman who put Dole back together from that war wound that seems to constitute his entire political platform—found herself replaced by a nontyping girlfriend-on-the-payroll and divorced with lightning speed in proceedings so rushed no records exist. Both the judge and her lawyer were Dole cronies, which may explain why he got the house and she got the furniture plus $18,000 a year on his salary of $115,000 and no child support. I guess right-wing antifeminist Danielle Crittenden hadn't heard about that when she contributed an item to *The Wall Street Journal*'s "Does Character Count?" forum praising Dole for his "old-fashioned uptightness" and likening his convention speech to the words of a "wise grandfather," "a tough reminder of what good character is, and what the enduring truths of nationhood are." Maybe the Defense of Marriage Act should have been called the Defense of Remarriage Act.

For obvious reasons, male pundits are quick to adopt a *sub specie aeternitatis* attitude to what they like to call "peccadilloes." Thus, in that same *W.S.J.* forum, Gary Hart (of all people!) blames "sensationalized journalism" for the low quality of today's political leaders. Female commentators have less incentive to take the lofty view. For one thing, women are still more likely to be the ones asked to play the suffer-in-silence role. For another, the old public-private distinction, now in tatters, never covered them, and still doesn't. Women in public life are judged twenty-four hours a day on matters much more trivial than illicit foot fondling: their hair, their clothes, their voices (shrill? strident?), their weight, their cookie-baking and their record of attendance at Little League. When you consider the contortions demanded of women, who must contrive to combine, or appear to combine, attractiveness and asexuality, brains and deference, zeal for work and absence of ambition, it doesn't seem much to ask that men in politics live by the family values they are eager to enforce on the rest of us.

Actually, the Morris scandal suggests an answer to one of life's great mysteries: How will those three-million-plus mothers to be thrown off welfare support themselves? Family values don't seem to generate much work. Government-funded public service jobs, the current pipe dream of the liberal intelligentsia, cost a fortune and lead nowhere. No, as the President reminds us in his convention speech, the solution lies with private enterprise.

Welfare moms should take a leaf from struggling single mother Sherry Rowlands. They should become dominatrixes. Here is a lucrative profession with flexible hours that combine well with child-rearing, which, indeed, it resembles in many ways. Most moms already possess many of the required skills—spanking, diapering, playing unbelievably boring games of make-believe—obviating costly training. Simply rework your usual mommyspeak ("Walk the dog now, or no TV") into the argot of your new career ("Bark like a dog *now*, you miserable worm, or I'm talking to Fox TV"). You get to wear great clothes, and the risk of sexually transmitted diseases is practically nonexistent.

We hear constantly that poor black women, deformed by the "welfare culture," are too bossy and man-hating for marriage. Moreover, a recent *New York Times* article suggests that single mothers, black and white, accustomed to wielding authority at home, take poorly to the subservience demanded by employers. For these women, the dominatrix business is perfect: Dissing your boss is your job. Unlike government-funded leaf-raking, it offers too the promise of economic growth: Ms. Rowlands now runs a cleaning service called "A Woman's Touch," giving needed employment to others. Psychologists tell us that men who go for this kink tend to be rich, powerful, domineering types—like Morris. Too much pressure at work (according to the *Star,* his sessions with Rowlands helped Morris "relax") or just a guilty conscience? Whatever. As anyone who follows politics knows, there's a vast untapped customer pool out there.

Single mothers, discarded housewives and other family-values victims: Forget the elections. Vote with your feet!

September 23, 1996

WE WERE WRONG:
WHY I'M NOT VOTING
FOR CLINTON

In 1992, I voted for Bill Clinton. Despite Rickey Ray Rector, the brain-damaged prisoner whose execution Clinton left the campaign trail to supervise. Despite the demagogic pledge to "end welfare as we know it." Despite Sister Souljah. Despite his by no means progressive record as governor of Arkansas, a state run, as we all now know, as a kind of business-elite fiefdom. I voted for Clinton because, even though he represented the right wing of the Democratic Party, he was better than George Bush: on reproductive rights, AIDS, gay rights, Haitian immigrants (remember them?). He didn't tell mothers not to work, or insist that the Endangered Species Act had us all up to our necks in spotted owls, or blather about points of light. If Clinton won, I thought, the political discourse, set so long by the right, would surely move left; although he was no progressive, his presidency would enlarge the space for progressive politics both inside and outside government. Maybe you had the same thought when you cast your vote four years ago.

We were wrong. In 1996 we can say with some certainty that Clinton has more than fulfilled the fears of critics, including the ones at this magazine, who received a great deal of grief in the early years of the new administration for being too "negative" and "carping." Michael Kazin and Maurice Isserman's 1994 *Nation* article urging leftists to give Clinton a break looks positively quaint today. Among his accomplishments they list the "affirmative action" appointments of Mike Espy, Ron Brown and Janet Reno, three big disappointments; a "sexually explicit" anti-AIDS campaign (what?); an expanded definition of homelessness (with expanded actual homelessness soon to come) and access and jobs for our side (plus the chance to quit on principle). Yes, in a few high-profile areas Clinton has been less bad than Bush would have been: the Supreme Court (but not the lower courts), abortion rights, the largely symbolic assault weapons ban and the Family and Medical Leave Act, the Violence Against Women Act. But it's a short, narrowly tailored list. On many of the great issues before government he's continued Bush's policies—the crime bill, the neglect of the cities, the erosion of civil liberties and privacy, NAFTA. On some—welfare, food stamps—he's arguably been worse.

Liberal defenders of Clinton blame the 1994 Republican victories for his current conservative stands, particularly on welfare. But it was Clinton himself who made welfare a burning issue. His original welfare proposal, which Gloria Steinem and other feminists now portray as benevolent, included many of the punitive features of the bill he eventually signed—cutoffs, time limits, forced work. Donna Shalala herself (whose tenure as secretary of H.H.S. is hardly an argument for getting "liberal to radical activists" into government service) admitted that under the Clinton plan some mothers would lose their children.

Besides misreading the actual chronology of events, blaming Gingrich for Clinton takes much too narrow a view of politics. Clinton and Gingrich are part of the same worldwide phenomenon: the slashing of the welfare state, the lowering of the working class's standard of living and the upward transfer of wealth. You can plausibly argue that Clinton prepared Gingrich's way by accepting Republican terms of debate.

Of course, we cannot know what a second Bush administration would have brought. We can safely say, though, that we would not see Bernie Sanders voting for more prisons and Carol Moseley-

Braun advocating trying thirteen-year-olds as adults. We would not have Barbara Mikulski and Tom Harkin voting to abolish the federal entitlement to welfare, or Nita Lowey supporting abstinence-only sex education. We would have an opposition in Congress—and out of it too. If Bush had proposed the Clinton health plan, single-payer activists would never have signed on to flack it. If Bush had suggested hooking up to the Internet schools that don't have enough desks he would have been ridiculed as a clueless showboater. And if a bill cutting $54 billion out of public assistance had come up during his tenure, Marian Wright Edelman, Jesse Jackson and Gloria Steinem would have been out in the streets. Who knows, Donna Shalala might have been there too.

Clinton supporters like Steinem argue that progressives are to blame for the failures of the Clinton administration because "we" didn't make a strong enough movement. She's right in a sense, though it's hardly an argument in favor of voting for Clinton. But it leaves out the fact that the weakness of the movement is directly related to its fantasy of access and influence: to the siphoning off of energies into wishy-washy "advocacy," Beltway schmooze and fund-raising for "moderate" Democrats who happen to be women or minorities. The motor-voter bill is all very well, but in real life you can't organize poor people by urging them to vote for the man who's taking away their food stamps.

One thing that has always struck me about the relation of the so-called left to Clinton is how profoundly progressives want to believe he's one of us. We must be the only people in America who ever believed he feels our pain. It's always someone else who thwarts his good intentions: the Democratic Leadership Council, Congress, Dick Morris, Al Gore. *Ms.* editor in chief Marcia Gillespie even blames herself: If only she'd called the White House comment line more often! Up until the minute Clinton signed the welfare bill a lot of liberals thought he'd veto it. Now this same naïveté has them believing that he'll "fix" it when a second term allows him to come out as a liberal. Unfortunately for this theory, the United States is not a medieval kingdom where laws can be annulled with a stroke of the royal pen. Nor does the hard business of party politics evaporate after Election Day: There are favors to repay and scores to settle, an organization to be preserved, a successor—Al Gore?—to be promoted.

Vote for Clinton *again*? As Voltaire is said to have replied when the Marquis de Sade invited him to a second orgy, since he'd enjoyed the first one so much: "No, thanks. Once is philosophy, twice is perversion."

October 7, 1996

FIRST WIVES, LAST LAUGH

My daughter, Sophie, who is nine, thought *The First Wives Club* was great. "You'll like it, Mom," she insisted. "The women get revenge!" Personally, I think fourth grade is a little early for a slapstick comedy about acrimonious divorces and what rats men are, and I would have expressed myself in even stronger terms to the mom whose curious idea of a playdate this was, except that when I called my friend Katherine for moral support for daring to criticize another mother's judgment it turned out she'd taken *her* nine-year-old daughter to the same showing. As Goldie Hawn says, It's the nineties.

Journalistic ethics compel me to admit that I didn't happen to see *The First Wives Club* at one of the many theaters around the country crammed with cheering women, who have put the film at number one on the charts and landed Hawn, Bette Midler and Diane Keaton on the cover of *Time*. At the discount matinee I attended on Upper Broadway, there were four other people in the audience, all over seventy—but they were indeed all women, and they were all smiling broadly when the lights came up.

I smiled too, even though it's not a very well made movie. The three heroines are cartoons, the gender analysis is about as subtle as a subpoena and, apparently fearful of an excess of "feminism," the movie devolves into uplift at the end. Having resolved their various personal issues (food and frumpiness for Midler, drink for Hawn, wimpiness for Keaton), driven away their husbands' "Pop-Tarts" and extracted fair recompense for their years of child-raising, household management, career-boosting and ego-massage, the trio renounce vengeance in favor of good works and open a "women's crisis center." That's fine—but can't Hollywood let women be mad, just once, for a whole movie, without giving them a lecture about the threat anger poses to their souls? After all, the frank acknowl-edgment that women have ample grounds for fury is what's made the movie a hit.

But then, Hollywood's so-called women's pictures usually ex-emplify on one level the sexism they critique on another. In *Thelma & Louise* the heroines' determination not to be victimized blinds them to their need for the chivalrous protection of Harvey Keitel. In *Waiting to Exhale*, the women embrace self-reliance and find . . . better boyfriends. *The First Wives Club* mines both laughs and pathos from the unfairness of the way women are seen as over the hill while their male coevals are still desirable, but the fact is, Hawn and Keaton actually do look quite a bit older than their mates (and all three look older than real-life forty-six-year-olds too, which isn't surprising, since they probably are: Keaton, featured this year on the cover of *Modern Maturity*, is fifty). In the same way, Hawn's character is mocked for her multiple plastic surgeries, but she's the one who finds a new lover, while the best that dowdy Midler can manage is to get her chastened crook of a husband back—after she slims down.

Still, confused and contradictory as it is, *The First Wives Club* demonstrates the superior realism of even mediocre pop culture over the official political discourse. In the movie, the husbands cheat and replace their wives because they are men: frivolous and exploitative and socially dominant. Their wives are doormats who feel, and are, socially marginal. Hawn plays a fading movie star and Keaton an Upper East Side homebody; Midler was her husband's unpaid assistant. What has produced these divorces, in other words, is the same thing that reduced the vital, eager college girls of the opening flashback to the miserable, insecure fortysomethings of today—gender inequality in and out of marriage. The moral for women: Don't put all your eggs in your husband's basket. It's a tough world.

Compare this down-to-earth view of marriage with that put forward by our current mavens of virtue, who blame divorce for all the evils of modern life not caused by unwed motherhood and who think marriage can be shored up by making it more "traditional," and harder to get out of. Midler and Keaton actually had traditional marriages, which prevented them, but not their husbands, from walking. Would the husbands have stayed if faced with such popular think-tank nostrums as fault divorce or mandatory counseling? Hardly—as the antidivorce crowd always forgets to mention, New York already has fault divorce, which hasn't stopped the city from being Gomorrah-on-the-Hudson. As for therapy, which cultural conservatives seem to believe works miracles in this area alone, the movie takes a properly skeptical view; Keaton's couples counselor, a best-selling fraud who tells her she must "grow from love," steals her husband.

Of course, *The First Wives Club* is a fantasy. Everyone's rich, healthy, attractive and lives in a beautiful apartment. Since the husbands are creeps and the cuties are morons, the first wives don't have to sit around blaming themselves, like real women. There's nothing to envy in their exes' shallow new relationships—no adorable new baby, no second wife with her own admirable qualities, no beautiful new country house, no love.

Still, next to, say, the Promise Keepers or the Million Men, or Irving Kristol's hymns to family values on the Op-Ed page of *The Wall Street Journal*, the movie seems so sane. It knows this *is* the nineties; that marriages die and sometimes ought to; that divorce is sad but that life moves on; and that women, though arrived at the geriatric age of forty-six, can make something of even an unsought independence. Nobody proposes to save her marriage by finding Jesus or submitting to her husband's "leadership." Nobody blames feminism or homosexuality—in fact, the movie has a nice, relaxed attitude toward Keaton's gay daughter, and there's a hilarious scene in a lesbian bar. There are no calls for the restoration of Victorian values. No one suggests that couples simply give up on happiness and trudge on toward the grave together—the one-size-fits-all marital advice of gloomy virtuecrat David Blankenhorn.

A movie that assumes there's a constituency for feminism might not seem like much. But with Cornel West and Jack Kemp united in admiration of Louis Farrakhan and the official women's movement turning blander and more corporate by the minute, it's more than worth the price of a ticket and a box of popcorn.

October 21, 1996

KISSING AND TELLING

When I was enrolled in what would now be called family day care, presented by its bored-out-of-her-mind-at-home psychologist director as the latest in progressive pre-preschooling, a very large little boy named Seth hit me on the head with his cap pistol. Nothing happened: The director did not take Seth's gun away, or make him apologize. When I was ten and eleven, an inseparable trio of older boys, Mongoose, Chuck and Tweetie, made summers at Camp Woodland a misery of teasing and insults. After ignoring the situation as long as he could, the head counselor took me aside and suggested that by talking back I was "encouraging" them.

I felt these injustices keenly at the time—in fact, I still do. Chuck's stupid, flaccid face and self-satisfied smile, the eyes of Mongoose and Tweetie sparkling with malice, even the whiny, galumphing four-year-old Seth—I'd recognize my old enemies on the street tomorrow, and when from time to time I hear rumors that one or another has come to no good, my heart blazes with triumph. Take that, Mrs. Phony Progressive Psychologist Doyenne of the Brooklyn Socialist Freudians, although you are long dead. And you too, Mr. Old Left Boys Will Be Boys Sexist Coward, although you are probably dead too. *Now* do you see that you should have stuck up for me?

Well! I didn't sit down to write about this. I sat down to write a piece in which, like every other columnist in America, I deplore and mock the nutty excesses of school administrators who in two separate, by now world-famous, incidents suspended six-year-old Johnathan Prevette of Lexington, North Carolina, and seven-year-old De'Andre Dearinge of Queens for "sexual harassment"— Johnathan kissed a girl in his class; De'Andre kissed a girl and tore a button from her skirt. I was going to wonder out loud how it happened that the first thing that comes to the mind of all too many people these days when they hear the word "feminism" is this sort of obsessive policing of daily life. I was going to bemoan school administrations, and bureaucrats generally, and grown-ups who impose outlandishly excessive punishments on small, bewildered children.

That's all true—consider it bemoaned. But the real story here is the media frenzy. Children are suspended every day, but Johnathan's missed ice-cream party was an international scandal; De'Andre's whole family was famous, until they stopped returning reporters' calls after he punched and bit a teacher. Only some of the interest in these two children has to do with a commendable devotion to mildness and common sense. There's also the wish to paint sexual harassment as the paranoid fantasy of joyless prudes. Two cases involving serious harassment got much less attention: In California, a jury awarded Tianna Ugarte $500,000 because her school failed to act when she was menaced daily (including death threats) in sixth grade; meanwhile, the Supreme Court refused to hear the case of two Texas eighth-graders who were regularly groped and called whores by boys on their school bus.

The truth is, nobody—least of all the talk-show anti-P.C. brigade that has made these little boys celebrities—really believes that children's behavior should go uncorrected or that it has no connection to the adults they will become. These are the people, after all, who are usually calling for more discipline. If Jonathan and De'Andre had kissed other *boys*, I doubt columnist John Leo would have found them so adorable. So, the issue is, What behavior gets taken seriously, and what is dismissed as child's play?

These stories are sensations because they take a real problem—sexual aggression and violence—and turn it into a joke. In the formulaic way the media have packaged the story, it becomes impossible to ask some important questions, like, Isn't there a connection between childhood and adult aggression? And how can we raise children to respect one another's limits at thirteen—and thirty—if we think it's cute when they don't? And what *about* those little girls? Don't their feelings count?

Please note that I am not defending overkill punishments or the use of the term "sexual harassment" to describe these incidents. But a valuable teaching opportunity is being missed—and not one about God and Country, as Robert Coles harrumphed in a *New York Times* Op-Ed, as if these sorts of incidents, and worse, were unknown to Eisenhower's America. Imagine if instead of shipping the kissing bandits home, their teachers had led pupils in a talk about boys and girls and what kisses mean—and also about kindness and respect and all those old-fashioned values the anti-P.C. crowd claims are enough to ensure good behavior without bringing nasty old feminism into it. Interestingly, the anti-P.C.-ers were curiously quiet about the week's other school news—the suspension of assorted junior high school girls for taking over-the-counter pain relievers without the permission of the school nurse. Part Just-Say-No hysteria, part anti-litigation insurance, part hostility to teenagers, this might have been a moment to note that sometimes a Midol is just a Midol.

I don't know if my young tormentors would count as sexual harassers today. Certainly there was some sort of gender content—but even when there isn't, why condemn children to one another's not-so-tender mercies? My daughter spent much of third grade in tears because a girl she adored made fun of her clothes and small size and existence on earth. Wasn't it a good thing that the teacher didn't say "girls will be girls" but confronted the culprit and helped my child develop self-reliance?

If adults had listened to me and defended me and helped me defend myself instead of treating my struggles as unimportant, those bullying boys would have learned an important lesson, and I would have shed a lot fewer tears. Certainly, I would not be sitting here with graying hair amazed to find myself wishing that I could tell Seth, Mongoose, Tweetie and especially the detestable Chuck, at great and satisfying length, how hateful they were and how often and heartily I have fantasized their destruction. After which, they would stammer and blush and utter those beautiful words: I'm sorry.

If I thought they meant it, I might even let them live.

November 4, 1996

No Vote for Clinton?

Readers Bite Back

Lots of mail about my column on not voting for Clinton—and not very nice mail either. A high proportion of handwritten notes on lined loose-leaf paper, always a bad sign. Much use of laborious sarcasm—words like "whining" and "mini-Jeremiad," a congratulatory postcard ("Atta-girl!") signed "Bob" and "Newt." H. John Rogers of Martinsville, West Virginia, challenged my disparagement of Clinton's appointments to the federal bench—he says the six who are friends of his are great. (My source for the rough equivalence of the appointees of Clinton and his predecessors was Neil Lewis's August 1 article in *The New York Times*, "In Selecting Federal Judges, Clinton Has Not Tried to Reverse Republicans"; see also John Nichols's excellent analysis in the September *Progressive* and Nat Hentoff's column in the October 29 *Village Voice*. Almost nothing on the topic in this magazine.) Mr. Rogers also thinks political writers should have to make at least one run for office. Interesting proposal—I wonder how far he'd take it. All medical reporters have to perform at least one coronary bypass? All lawyers should be defendants in at least one trial?

Two major themes emerge from the mailbag: the Lesser of Two Evils and the Fetishizing of Voting. Some think I undersell President Clinton—that is, I am too cynical; others mock me as the victim of naïve hopes—that is, I am not cynical enough. But all agree: However narrow his edge over Dole—and I did not deny the differences between them, for example on reproductive rights—it's sufficient to earn the progressive vote in what Peter Connolly of Washington, D.C., calls "the grimy world of actually existing American politics." The important thing, according to many letter writers and also this magazine's own nonendorsement editorial, is to put the kibosh on the militias and the Christian Coalition, whose tool, in this version of reality, President Dole would be.

Here we see the dangers of believing one's own propaganda. While the far right fundamentalists and gun nuts have some power in some states, what the Dole campaign shows is that the national market for those politics is very small indeed. That's why Dole is courting soccer moms and women small-business owners, even as the jilted true believers threaten to punish him on Election Day; that's why neither candidate says much about the "social issues" (abortion, divorce, school prayer, affirmative action, etc.) that pundits in 1994 predicted would be driving the electorate totally round the bend by now. *Où sont les angry white men d'antan?*

Even if Dole *were* the captive robot of the mad Christians, though, and Ella May Ablahat of Naples, Florida, were right to foresee a Dole victory unleashing the Promise Keepers to descend on American women with Taliban-like ferocity, the fact is he's not going to win. Clinton is going to win. And Clinton will win even if every single *Nation* reader votes Vegetarian or not at all. So the real question to ask is why would a person who abhors what Clinton has been up to for the past four years (as most of you say you do) feel this strange compulsion to add his or her tiny mite to Clinton's electoral hoard? Sheer masochism? Bad historical analogies? John Attlee of Silver Spring, Maryland, compares arguments against voting for Clinton to "the acrimonious political debates in Germany . . . which split the left and brought Hitler to power." One could argue that the German left's mistake was to think voting for *anyone* was the way to stop Hitler, a man with no such illusions and a private army too. But in any case, I don't see how the drifting and doomed Bob Dole, from whom his own party is fleeing in horror, bears much resemblance to the highly popular Führer. If ever there was an election in which you can safely act on your principles, this is it!

Once you resign yourself to the fact that you are not going to cast the heroic deciding ballot against the Nazis, you can see your vote in a number of different ways. In twenty-one states you can vote for Nader, despite his weird campaign, and officially register your existence to Clinton's left (something a vote for Clinton obscures). Or, like nearly 50 percent of the voting age population in a typical presidential election, you can withhold your vote. This too is a political act; it's even an electoral-political act, a vote of no confidence in the choices offered—and thus actually expresses what many of you letter-writing reluctant Clinton voters claim to feel. Think about it: You won't have to spend the next four years tied up in knots of guilt and shock as your President, the man you voted for, turns the safety net into a safety doily. You'll have a head start on lesser-evilism 2000, which is sure to be even less lesser. You may even find that you start thinking about politics in a different way, more as collective action and less as a wistful search for, to quote William I. Bernell of San Francisco, "at least one true progressive, a person with courage, vision and leadership."

For the hypereducated middle-class model citizens who make up the *Nation* "family," not to vote is kind of scary—I'm not even sure I can do it myself (Nader is my fallback position). It means giving up a certain view of oneself as an important individual actor on the stage of politics, able to command governments and shape history by pulling the levers that connect one with power. "I would vote for the brutal Henry VIII against Tamerlane (who built pyramids of skulls) or for Franco against Hitler," writes Thomas Robbins of Rochester, Minnesota. "To refuse to make this choice is not to really care about those piled-up skulls." It's hard to imagine the circumstances, outside a dream, under which such choices could be made: Henry and Tamerlane lived in different centuries and countries, and neither of them was big on holding elections; Hitler and Franco also belonged to different nations, and Franco didn't bother with the ballot either, as I recall. But surely, had he run for office in some imaginary Hispano-German state, he would have been on Hitler's side, the way he was in the real Europe. The strain of justifying that Clinton vote must really be getting to Mr. Robbins.

Do you want to spend the next four years lying awake at night calculating how many lives you can save by voting for Henry VIII? Why not take a leaf from the soon-to-be-forgotten campaign of Bob Dole? Just Don't Do It.

November 18, 1996

LET THEM EAT NUMBERS

As the *Social Text* affair earlier this year so vividly demonstrated, the foibles of the academic left offer an irresistible source of mirth to the mainstream press. I've always considered raillery a small price to pay for the many delights of academic employment: A certain amount of ridicule has always been directed at the humanities in America, after all—as you might expect of a nation that invented the business school, the sports scholarship and the communications major. But if you are a professor who is tired of explaining why Jean Baudrillard's celebrated claim that the Gulf War happened only on television doesn't mean that thousands of Iraqi soldiers aren't actually dead, there's something you can do and still keep both your academic status and your right to say whatever pops into your head: Forget cultural studies. Become an economist.

For the past few weeks the news has been full of articles marveling over the report of the Boskin commission, which argues that annual inflation is about 1.1 percent lower than the 3 percent claimed by the Bureau of Labor Statistics. This means that Social Security benefits can be adjusted so you get less, and taxes can be adjusted so you pay more—and *presto!* the deficit is busted without anyone actually having to cast an unpopular vote. As pensioners flail their canes in letters to the editor, the press looks wryly on: Imagine, all that time we thought our living standards were stagnating or deteriorating, they were actually going up!

The Boskin findings are postmodernism in action, a perfect assertion of the supremacy of discourse over "the real world," but you don't see the commissioners being harrumphed off the stage as ivory-tower obscurantists by pundits eager to champion the commonsensical wisdom of the average Joe, do you? No, this time Joe's the problem, victim of the economic-stagnation "myth" (Robert J. Samuelson in *The Washington Post*) fueled by leftists, unions, Robert Reich (*The Wall Street Journal*) and "whiner-anecdote journalism" (*The Kansas City Star*). Except for *The Nation*'s Doug Henwood, what commentator has pointed out that all five Boskin commissioners, supposedly neutral inquirers into the accuracy of the Consumer Price Index, had previously given congressional testimony that the C.P.I. was too high? Apparently it's only professors of English who can't have an ax to grind.

What makes this generalized murmur of approval so interesting is that the Boskin commission's three major arguments are so tendentious that even I can see through them. Take the first one: They claim the C.P.I. overstates the cost of living because if the price of a product goes up, people often buy something cheaper. So they do, but switching to cheaper products is what having a lowered standard of living *is*. *Time*'s George Church obscures this by using the example of asparagus versus broccoli—a gourmet treat versus an equally delicious if slightly less chic vegetable; Boskin's beef-versus-chicken is another loaded example, since chicken is healthier than beef and many people like it better. How about chicken versus a baloney sandwich? A one-bedroom apartment versus a studio? A taxi versus waiting for the bus in the rain? A night at the movies versus a night of TV?

In the real world, when I choose the cheaper item I am not cleverly maintaining my standard of living by being a smart shopper; I am simply living less well. Even if I have a car and can offset price increases by using discount stores, which the Boskin commission cites along with ordering from catalogues (have they actually tried this?) as a second example of inflation-mitigating behavior, I am still living less well: Now I'm spending time, energy and gas hunting for bargains. Of course, it may be true, as the third argument goes, that some of the rise in prices is due to improvements in products—but why is that relevant? I still have the same amount of money to spend, so the improved product just moves out of my reach.

It isn't just Social Security and taxes that are affected by these numbers. Millions of people receive cost-of-living adjustments: union members, veterans, pensioners, divorcées awarded maintenance and moms who get child support. You could almost say that COLAs are part of what defines a payment as merited and respectable rather than a grudging handout: Welfare has not kept up with inflation, and in fact has lost more than half its value since 1970. Or not: As Dean Baker of the Economic Policy Institute kindly explained to me, taking the Boskin numbers seriously means recalculating a lot more than COLAs. Apparently those "constant dollars" used to compare wages and prices over time should be lower too. Baker faxed me a tongue-in-cheek sheet of "policy implications of Boskin commission findings," including the remarkable discovery that in 1960 nearly half the population was poor, but by 2030 we will all be rolling in money. And so the American story once again resumes its familiar outlines as a master narrative of rags to riches.

What was going on elsewhere while the Boskin commission was telling us that downward mobility was a fiction and summoning up visions of greedy geezers pocketing unmerited cash? In France, home of M. Baudrillard, truck drivers brought the country, and much of Europe, to a standstill to win the right to retire at full pay at fifty-five instead of sixty. They had the support of three-fourths of the population, and they won. In Germany, hundreds of thousands of metalworkers organized walkouts against proposed sick-pay cuts that would still have left them way ahead of most U.S. workers. They won too. (Meanwhile, *The New York Observer* notes that even supposedly liberal Upper West Siders can't be bothered to honor the picket line at Citarella, the elegant food shop with a basement full of Latino workers earning minimum wage or less.)

When are Americans going to grasp the fact that budget cuts—invariably presented as ways of "saving" their hard-earned money from this or that undeserving element—are actually ways of lowering the general standard of living? Before the progression of beef to chicken to sandwich ends up with soup and crackers? Or only then?

December 30, 1996

BORN AGAIN VS. PORN AGAIN

The Last Marxist and I had a good time at Milos Forman's new movie, *The People vs. Larry Flynt.* Great performances by Woody Harrelson as *Hustler* publisher and First Amendment fan Flynt and by Courtney Love as Althea Leasure, his funny, lewd, exotic-dancer-turned-copublisher-turned-AIDS-afflicted-junkie wife. Fine work from Edward Norton as Alan Isaacman, Flynt's droll, long-suffering lawyer, and from a bevy of real-life notables—Burt Neuborne, James Carville, Donna Hanover (Mrs. Rudy Giuliani), Flynt himself as a basset-faced Southern judge. Even the L.M., who is something of a civil-liberties skeptic on the grounds that when the ruling class is truly threatened they do what they want whatever the Constitution says, teared up when Flynt, by now a paralyzed widower, gets the news that the Supreme Court has unanimously recognized his right to make scabrous fun of the Rev. Jerry Falwell. You've got to admire a filmmaker who lets his hero say he doesn't believe in God and doesn't make him die rescuing a hijacked busload of parochial school kids.

But honestly. What is the point of making a film about the founder of *Hustler* that airbrushes both him and his magazine? *The People vs. Larry Flynt* is constructed around a group of stock characters: the cuddly male rebel, the sailor-mouthed but golden-hearted stripper girlfriend, the noble crusading lawyer, the hypocritical Christian crusader (Falwell, Charles Keating, Ruth Carter Stapleton). Its themes are familiar as well: the redemptive power of marriage (albeit not monogamous marriage), the open field for upward mobility capitalism offers the shrewd and energetic however lowly their origins (the prologue shows Larry and his brother as prepubescent moonshiners in the Kentucky backwoods). Most of all, and like all courtroom dramas, the movie celebrates the salvific nature of our legal institutions, especially the Supreme Court, which in the movies always corrects, and never upholds, unjust and bigoted lower-court decisions—which is why *The Bowers v. Hardwick Story* won't be coming to a theater near you anytime soon. There's even the customary I-Love-the-Law conversion speech ("If the First Amendment will protect a scumbag like me," says Flynt, previously seen throwing oranges at the judge and wearing an American flag diaper, "then it will protect all of you"). In other words, the system works, its ability to tolerate gadflies like Flynt is the proof and America is the best country. Not for nothing did Frank Rich call Forman's movie "the most patriotic movie of the year."

In real life, as Gloria Steinem among others has pointed out, Larry Flynt is a more problematic figure than the endearing con artist and loving husband Harrelson portrays (for one thing, he was married three times before Althea and has a daughter who now claims he abused her). And *Hustler* is a weirder, darker, more free-floatingly hostile magazine than comes through in the film, which presents it as a cheerful populist alternative to snooty *Playboy*. We learn about Flynt's insistence on showing models' pubic hair, an industry first; about the nude photos of Jackie O; the cartoon of Santa Claus with a big erection; and the feature showing Dorothy having group sex with the Tin Man, the Scarecrow and the Cowardly Lion. Pretty tame by 1996 standards, and that allows viewers to feel broad-minded and mature, superior both to Flynt and to Falwell ("*Dorothy?*" breathes one scandalized Christian). It's hard to see what the fuss was about.

But then, what can you expect given that Forman has said that he's never read *Hustler*? This to me is truly strange, a kind of willful refusal to engage his subject. Wasn't he curious? Ever the intrepid reporter, I sent the L.M. out into the night in search of a copy (not easy to find even here on the Upper West Side of Sodom). The March 1997 issue features no women who violate conventional standards of beauty or hygiene, a *Hustler* specialty—but for the close-ups of their (shaven) genitals, the women would look at home in *Playboy*, well, *Penthouse*. But it does have several racist cartoons, a diatribe against Alanis Morissette ("a sick, twisted, man-hating cow who blames ex-boyfriends for all her problems") and a photo feature titled "How to Know if Your Girlfriend Is a Dog," which shows a naked woman drinking out of a toilet surrounded by puppies. Liberatory? Childish? Misogynous? Nuts?

You don't have to agree with Gloria Steinem, who connects *Hustler* with actual violence against women, or with Laura Kipnis (*Bound and Gagged*), who in *The Village Voice* sees it as "contesting state power," to think of *Hustler*, and pornography generally, as possessing content, meaning and subject matter. I'm all for waving the flag of the First Amendment—but can't we also talk about the material the amendment protects?

As it happens, I don't think either Steinem or Kipnis has it right. On the one hand, any serious discussion of texts that cause real-life harm to women would have to begin with the Bible and the Koran: It isn't porn that drives zealots to firebomb American abortion clinics or slit the throats of Algerian schoolgirls. On the other hand, only a postmodern academic could seriously propose that a skin magazine offers a serious challenge to "state power." How many divisions has Larry Flynt?

What I see in *Hustler* is a convoluted and sometimes contradictory appeal to white male psychosexual anxieties: The suits are jerks, women (especially welfare mothers) have all the power and blacks have all the breaks—and bigger penises too. Sure, it's woman-hating (also woman-enjoying), but the bravado and swagger barely conceal the envy and anxiety. Ask yourself what message about white men is being conveyed by a photo of two gorgeous white women sucking an enormous black dildo.

Forman's movie would have been more thought-provoking—and an even more powerful defense of the First Amendment—if it had forced viewers to confront what Flynt actually produces. But to do so would have risked the dread NC-17 rating and discomfited the middle-class liberals whose political complacencies and horror of vulgarity the film caters to. The result is a movie that celebrates the First Amendment while embodying its limits. It champions the uncensored while blurring its own crotch shots.

February 3, 1997

CAN THIS MARRIAGE
BE SAVED?

In 1960, when about 16 percent of marriages ended in court, we had strict laws regulating divorce and the highest divorce rate in the West. Today, oceans of social and legal change later, with 40 percent of marriages ending in divorce, we're still number one. All fifty states permit couples to divorce by mutual consent (bilateral no-fault divorce); about forty permit one partner to divorce without assigning blame even when the other wants to stay married (unilateral no-fault). In the mid-sixties, about half of Americans told pollsters they thought parents had an obligation to try to stay together for the children's sake; by 1994 only 20 percent held this view. Indeed, so unpopular is the view of marriage as a bond of steel that the Catholic Church itself has had to go into the divorce business, handing out some 60,000 annulments a year—three-quarters of all annulments worldwide.

Given all this, it's beyond me how David Blankenhorn of the Institute for American Values can campaign to make divorce more difficult. Divorce *is* an American value. So is the mélange of beliefs and material conditions, good and bad, that have produced our high divorce rate—separation of church and state, ease of mobility, relative weakness of the extended family, urbanization, sexism, domestic violence, the rising self-confidence and economic independence of women and our deep-seated conviction that marriage is about two people and their love. You can give this mixture a positive spin—America is the land of fresh starts, self-determination, the pursuit of happiness—or a negative one—we're a hedonistic, irresponsible, throwaway society. Either way, divorce is us; just ask family values fans Ronald Reagan, Newt Gingrich, Bob Dole, George Will, Joe Klein, Jean Bethke Elshtain, Eugene Genovese, Amitai Etzioni, Midge Decter and Michael "Politics of Meaning" Lerner (twice).

Undeterred by these considerations, Blankenhorn and other conservative "pro-family" ideologues have joined right-wing Christian groups to push state legislatures to make divorce more difficult to obtain. In Pennsylvania, supporters of a proposal to abolish unilateral no-fault divorce where children are involved argue that the unilateral system has hurt children by encouraging frivolous breakups. They also claim to champion women, particularly housewives in long-standing marriages, who have lost the ability to withhold consent and thereby win financial and custodial concessions from husbands eager to marry again.

How to reform divorce laws to serve women and children is an important question, about which there is lively feminist debate. But the conservative attack on no-fault is not about helping women, even stereotypically "virtuous" homemakers (much less battered wives, who need to make a quick, clean break). The old "fault" system was also cruel to women: Long litigations penalized the poorer spouse, however blameless; alimony was, contrary to myth, rarely awarded and even more rarely collected; most shockingly, a mother could be denied custody of her children because of a single act of extramarital sex. There's nothing in the proposed reforms about ensuring an equal division of property or adequate child support, or compensating wives for their unpaid labor, or allowing the custodial parent to stay in the home rather than sell it as part of the division of assets—although postdivorce moves are a major source of difficulty for children.

But then, the fault-divorce campaign isn't really about helping children, either. Conservative reformers constantly cite *Second Chances,* Judith Wallerstein's study of children's divorce-related problems. But Wallerstein herself rejects the view that preserving a bad marriage helps kids, and she supports no-fault divorce. "A return to the old system would be disastrous for children," she told me. "The last thing they need is to hear their father call their mother a whore." Should kids learn to blame one parent?

The real aim of conservative divorce reform is to enforce a narrow and moralistic vision of marriage by rendering divorce more painful and more punitive. But it's not hard to find empirical evidence that none of the reforms proposed by the divorce reformers would achieve their stated goal, which is to keep couples together. Court-ordered counseling? "We had mandatory conciliation here in New York in the sixties and early seventies," Timothy Tippins, chairman of the New York State Bar Association's family law committee, told me. "Do you know how many marriages it saved? Zero." Abolition of unilateral no-fault? New York doesn't have it. Is the divorce rate lower in New York than in New Jersey or Connecticut? No. Long waiting periods—three years, or even, as former White House domestic policy adviser William Galston proposes, five (!)—will hardly cause partners who hate each other to recommit. ("This never happens," said Wallerstein. "I *told* Bill that.") On the contrary, such strictures on starting over will have the perverse effect of discouraging people from marrying in the first place, and rendering illegitimate the second families separated partners are going to start anyway, regardless of the law, as they do in Ireland and other countries where divorce is hard to get.

The antidivorce campaign may be a nonstarter, legally and practically, but it has an ideological function. As more people are spun off into economic instability as the safety net is shredded, "family values" becomes a way of explaining downward mobility as an individual moral failing: The selfish quest for happiness is what makes women and children poor. (You'll notice the antidivorce crowd never cites unemployment or poverty as a cause of breakup.) Similarly, the effects of economic dislocation on the young—depression, suicide, early pregnancy, high dropout rates—are attributed entirely to their parents' self-indulgence. "A change in attitude toward parenting and marriage would do children far more good than any government program," *Time* airily observed recently. Let them eat wedding rings.

Pennsylvania retained no-fault divorce and it's likely other states will too, if only because state legislators want the freedom to dump their wives, if they haven't already done so. But the arguments have already entered the emerging bipartisan consensus: Your problems—and your children's problems—are your fault.

February 17, 1997

PAULA JONES, CLASS ACT?

The good news is that the mainstream media have discovered their own class prejudice. The bad news is that so far they've managed to find only one victim: Paula Corbin Jones. Spurred by Stuart Taylor's supportive reexamination of Jones's story in *American Lawyer* last fall, *Newsweek*'s Michael Isikoff and Evan Thomas have berated themselves and their colleagues for dismissing Jones as a big-haired bimbo, out for money and trash-TV celebrity. What a difference two years makes: Jones, labeled "one of the worst people on earth" by *Time* in 1994, is now officially salt of the earth, and James Carville, who famously dismissed her charges with the flip "drag a hundred dollars through a trailer park and there's no telling what you'll find," is the faux populist. Indeed, trailer parks—make that "manufactured-home communities"—are in, reevaluated in *The New York Times* as no-fuss housing for the frugal ("Mobile Homes Go Upscale"). Feminists are out, tagged with class bias and liberal hypocrisy for scorning Jones after rallying to Anita Hill.

Well, my conscience is clear. I always thought Jones deserved a respectful hearing, especially from feminists, and said so right here on this page. As it happens I also think she is probably telling more or less the truth. Now certainly, she did herself no favors by placing herself under the aegis of Pat Robertson, Reed Irvine and other hard right-wingers, or by hiring first an Arkansas lawyer with whom she signed a contract to split the proceeds from book and movie deals, and then high-powered conservative litigators Gilbert Davis and Joseph Cammarata. Her No Excuses jeans commercial sits a little oddly too with her claim to have been forced into the public arena to rescue her reputation after her chastity was slandered in *The American Spectator.* These elements don't quite fit Stuart Taylor's portrait of her as a shy provincial homebody, but so what? The people promoting her may have an anti-Clinton agenda, and her motives may be mixed, as motives often are—but none of that makes her a liar.

Still, there are some funny elements in the new spin on Jones. Is it a defense of Jones, or the latest chapter in the continuing attack on Anita Hill? It's true that Jones, who had six corroborating affidavits, has more documentation than Hill, who had four—but Hill wasn't *suing* Clarence Thomas. The question Hill's testimony placed before us was not whether Thomas was guilty of a legally actionable offense (she herself was unsure if his behavior added up to sexual harassment) but whether he belonged on the Supreme Court. And what made many women so furious was not just the charges; it was the way the all-male Senate Judiciary Committee initially agreed across party lines to discount her story and close up shop without hearing her.

Stuart Taylor describes Jones as apolitical, while suggesting several times that Hill "had far stronger ideological disagreements with Thomas than she let on." In a fourteen-page article praised for its meticulous and methodical documentation, he neither proves nor explains this charge. A woman who leaves the Reagan administration for a job at Oral Roberts University doesn't sound like a flaming leftist to me. At moments like this I begin to feel that pro-Paula revisionism is mostly an attack on the women's movement, and indeed, in his long-running debate with Susan Estrich in *Slate,* Taylor, while jovially professing himself a feminist, accuses the women's movement of "victimology"—an antifeminist term of art that seems to contradict his argument that Jones is justified in seeing herself as a victim of a crime.

Has snobbery played a role in the differing receptions given by many feminists to Hill and Jones? It could be, but surely as, or more, important was Hill's personal gravitas—her clear and cogent testimony, her ability to hold up under withering, almost surreal questioning—which made her attackers' allusions to erotomania and pubic hairs in students' exams seem crazy. Working-class women possess these qualities too (let's not forget that Hill is the daughter of Oklahoma sharecroppers), but Jones has yet to display them. On the *700 Club*, she was unable to give a coherent account of her charges and let her husband do most of the talking.

It's true that some feminists have gone after Jones. But is it class or is it Clinton? Susan Estrich pretty much tells Taylor that her main interest is defending the President: "You believe in principle. I believe in politics." But it's also true that NOW's May 6, 1994, press release asserted Jones's right to a hearing: "Every Paula Jones deserves to be heard, no matter how old she is and how long ago the incident occurred, no matter what kind of accent she has or how much money she makes, and no matter who she associates with." According to Patricia Ireland, Jones blew off a meeting with NOW officers to go shopping; her lawyers promised but failed to send over their files and were next heard from two years later, denouncing NOW on the steps of the Supreme Court for being unprincipled and hypocritical. "We were rebuffed in our attempt to get involved," Ireland told me. "I smelled a setup."

What's strange about the media mea culpa is that it treats the coverage of Jones as an exception when in fact it was closer to the rule: Mostly, women who accuse powerful men are portrayed unsympathetically and with suspicion. Patricia Bowman and Desiree Washington too were labeled as sluts who were out for money and "attention," and nobody's apologized to them, although today both lead completely obscure lives. Jones is trashy, Hill ambitious. There's always some way to make a woman look unreliable.

As for class bias, why stop with Paula Jones? The mainstream media have spent the better part of a decade promoting class bias. They have heaped scorn on working-class institutions—unions, urban public colleges—and helped to render suspect the claims on society of just about every kind of economically vulnerable person: the homeless, the long-term unemployed, single mothers, urban youth and now even poor children—tomorrow's "superpredators." They have made Charles Murray—the man who believes that people who live in trailer parks are genetically inferior—a respectable intellectual.

I wish someone would apologize for that.

March 17, 1997

SECRETS AND LIES

Ron Fitzsimmons's dramatic statement that he "lied through his teeth" fifteen months ago when he said, in a never-aired comment for *Nightline,* that only 450 "partial-birth abortions" are performed annually in the United States, always for serious medical reasons, has the press in one of its favorite tizzies. Once again, it's beating its breast for being too liberal, in this case for having followed a pro-choice bias and trusted pro-choice numbers in last year's debate over the procedure. Lazy maybe, forgetful definitely—both *The Washington Post* and *The Bergen Record* carried stories last September suggesting the procedure was performed several thousand times a year, mostly in the late second trimester of pregnancy, and mostly not as a matter of life and death. But biased? If the media are so pro-choice, how come we're all talking about "partial birth" instead of "intact dilation and extraction" (D&X), the proper medical term? It isn't often that the insurgents define the language of the debate: You are not likely to open your *Boston Globe* or your *Time* and find a story about events in "the country that opponents call the 'Zionist entity' but supporters refer to as Israel." As for lies, how come journalists aren't furious over the constantly repeated anti-choice lie that *Roe v. Wade* allows a woman to have an abortion up to the minute she gives birth? Or that five-month-old fetuses are viable?

Actually, the National Coalition of Abortion Providers' executive director, Fitzsimmons (who, for the record, is neither "prominent," as the media sloppily anointed him, nor "an abortion provider," as Katharine Seelye described him in *The New York Times*, but a lobbyist), had it right the first time. D&Xes performed on women carrying theoretically viable fetuses—that is, after twenty-four weeks—are extremely rare and performed only for grave medical cause. The anti-choicers' claim that large numbers of viable fetuses are aborted, almost always for frivolous reasons (such as fitting into a prom dress, as the Catholic bishops claimed), is false. *Roe v. Wade* permits states to criminalize abortion after twenty-four weeks for any reason except the mother's life and health, and forty states and the District of Columbia have done so. New York State, as a matter of fact, does not even have a health exception, and requires a second doctor's attendance on abortions performed after twenty weeks, to provide medical attention to the fetus—both of which strictures are in flagrant violation of *Roe*, not that this seems to matter. In other words, in the third trimester, abortion on demand by any method is *already illegal*—and almost no doctors will perform abortions then, even when they are medically advisable.

The big anti-choice lie was obscured by the consistent merging of third-trimester abortions, which, as I've just said, are already illegal under almost all circumstances, with second-trimester abortions, which are protected by *Roe*, and by then describing both with the brilliant propaganda term "partial birth"—as in live-baby-who-could-survive-if-not-murdered-by-doctor, and also as in, Gross! Much hay was made of the gory details of dilation and extraction—as if the anti-choicers would approve of the other available methods (dismembering the fetus in the womb, for instance, or poisoning it with a saline solution). By banning a procedure, performed at whatever stage of pregnancy, anti-choicers seek to undermine the legality of second-term—that is, previability—abortions, which are constitutionally protected by *Roe*—and undermining *Roe* is what this fight is really about.

In response to this onslaught of propaganda, pro-choice groups made a decision to focus on third-trimester medical tragedies that a ban would only have exacerbated. This was understandable—the anti-choicers claimed their however many thousands of frivolously aborted fetuses were as good as born, so why not challenge them on the numbers and the reasons for these very late abortions that the anti-choicers claimed to be talking about (but really weren't)? But the failure to discuss openly and to defend second-term procedures helped create the circumstances in which Fitzsimmons's "revelation" could do its immense damage.

This whole mess shows that the pro-choice movement needs to reclaim the debate and start aggressively setting its terms. We wouldn't be forced into this ridiculous corner, having to deny that women who are seven and eight months pregnant resort to abortion as a quick weight-loss method, had we not conceded a lot of ground already by failing to defend abortion as an essential—indeed, normal—aspect of women's reproductive lives: every kind of woman, including anti-choice ones, in every social class. Since the anti-choicers talk about abortion as if it were never justified, we've fallen into the trap of talking only about what philosophers call the "hard cases," the extreme situations in which the woman is clearly a tragic figure: a molested child, a rape victim or, as in the debate over intact dilation and extraction, a woman whose much-wanted pregnancy has gone horribly awry. It's right that we insist on those cases, but not in a way that helps to further delegitimize the vast majority of abortions—including, Fitzsimmons reminds us, the majority of previability D&Xes—which are performed for social, economic and personal reasons. We need to defend women's freedom to choose when and if to become mothers—not just the right of women to choose abortion over serious injury or death.

Instead of brushing those second-trimester abortions to the side, we should talk about the women who have them and why they have them so late. We need to talk about sexual ignorance, about shame and denial, about lack of access to good information and consistent health care, about why the United States has the highest rate of teen pregnancy and unwanted pregnancy in the West, about the crippling and cumulative effects of state and local abortion restrictions—those supposedly not-undue burdens permitted by the Supreme Court. We need to talk about poverty and isolation: what it means not to be able to scrape together $250, or a ride to a distant clinic, in time for an early abortion.

Those circumstances—not the use of one particular abortion method—are the real abortion scandal.

March 31, 1997

Go Figure

Why is it that some women are always trying to persuade other women that their troubles are grossly exaggerated? A few years ago we were told that date rape was really "bad sex" and domestic violence a much-overblown—and genderless—problem. More recently, the word was that the barriers to equal participation in electoral politics are down—it's women's lack of confidence and interest that keeps Congress 90 percent male. Now comes the Independent Women's Forum (who else?) under the aegis of the American Enterprise Institute (who else?) to argue that job discrimination against women is a thing of the past, and that statistics and studies indicating otherwise are an attempt to promote "victim status for women."

"Women's Figures" (note the cutesy pun) by Diana Furchtgott-Roth and Christine Stolba is an elegant little booklet—thick, creamy paper, brightly colored graphs, lots of airy white space between the lines, a three-page bibliography and many quotations from I.W.F.'s own Elizabeth Fox-Genovese. It comes with a shiny blue bookmark listing all the A.E.I. phone numbers and homepage address, and it fits right into your purse. Unfortunately it's full of half-truths, non sequiturs, advocacy numbers, unproven assumptions and buried premises—but then, how could it not be, given that what it argues is insane?

According to Furchtgott-Roth, depressing statistics about sticky floors, glass ceilings and women's earnings vis-à-vis those of men—71 cents on the male dollar, up from 59.4 cents in 1970—give a false picture of women's current prospects: Only in recent years have women had the access, education, consistent participation in the workforce and, she suggests, desire to equal men in the job market. To assess the effect of economic discrimination today we need to look at young women, and if we do we find that "National Longitudinal Study of Youth data show that among people ages twenty-seven to thirty-three who have never had a child, women's earnings approach 98 percent of men's earnings." Thus, with a wave of a statistical wand, a twenty-nine-cent wage gap shrinks to a two-cent wage gap. Do you think Furchtgott-Roth could come over and do my taxes?

What's wrong with this statistic? Well, in the first place, young men and women have always had earnings more comparable than those of their elders: Starting salaries are generally low, and do not accurately reflect the advantages that accrue, or fail to accrue, over time as men advance and women stay in place, or as women in mostly female kinds of jobs reach the end of characteristically short career paths. In the second place, the figure applies only to the childless, but by age thirty-three, 76 percent of women are mothers. And, as Heidi Hartmann of the Institute for Women's Policy Research explained to me, childless women and childless men are different: Since children negatively affect women's careers, but have either no effect or a positive effect on men's, young women without children tend to be those most dedicated to their professional advancement, whereas young men without children are more likely to be (I'm just quoting here) misfits. Furchtgott-Roth's simple little statistic turns out to be a veritable gift basket of apples and oranges.

For Furchtgott-Roth, what looks like discrimination is really the result of women's personal choices. Women choose to have children, and make work choices that fit in with domesticity: jobs that make fewer demands, offer flexible hours and require skills that can be easily maintained. (This points to one of those contradictions in right-wing ideology I love so much: Motherhood is simultaneously the very definition of women's existence—rejection of which has caused the country to go to pot—and a free, individual choice, like buying a motorcycle, whose costs the individual must bear alone. I guess if women decided not to bear those costs humanity would just die out.) One might ask why only mothers bear the costs of children, and why Furchtgott-Roth doesn't include money as one of the things working mothers want out of their work. One might also note that some of the biggest mostly female job categories are famously inflexible (nursing) and require constantly updated skills (anything involving computers), and that the twenty-nine-cent wage gap concerns full-time workers, not part-timers on the "mommy track." Besides, childless women also earn less than men as time goes on. But beyond that, why isn't the resistance of the job market and the workplace to working mothers' needs an aspect of economic discrimination against women?

"Women's Figures" makes much of the progress women have made in closing the wage gap, but it does not mention that most of that gain is a statistical artifact produced by stagnant or declining male wages. If men's annual earnings had remained at their 1979 levels, women in 1995 would have earned only 65.3 cents on the male dollar. Not a lot of progress for sixteen years. Similarly, "Women's Figures" trumpets the growth and success of women's businesses, while failing to mention that one of the reasons women start their own businesses is that they get fed up with being discriminated against in the corporate world, and that many women-owned businesses are small and precarious ventures. And what about the poor, who are disproportionately female? Furchtgott-Roth reprints the Cato Institute's discredited table claiming that welfare benefits add up to a pretty good salary: from a lavish $36,400 in Hawaii to a modest but tidy $11,500 in Mississippi. I wonder how Fox-Genovese, who only a few years ago was lambasting the women's movement for abandoning poor and minority women, likes them apples.

As economics, "Women's Figures" is claptrap. However you slice and dice the numbers—by age, education levels, across job categories or within them—women earn less than men, except in a few rare instances (acting in porn movies, for instance). But as ideology it's kind of interesting. Here we see the usefulness of antifeminism to right-wing free-marketeers like the folks at the A.E.I.: Since remedying gender discrimination would require government and other sorts of intervention and regulation, wouldn't it be helpful if gender discrimination could be found not to exist? I choose, you choose, the corporations choose, the right-wing think tanks choose, we all choose together!

April 14, 1997

HEAVEN CAN WAIT

I know, I know, Heaven's Gate was last week—by now, the nation's opiners have left the subject as far behind as Marshall Herff Applewhite and his thirty-eight followers have left their sweatsuited and beNiked "containers"—but I'm still having trouble with the religion-cult distinction. It can't lie in the area of doctrine, since, as many cynics have noted, the belief systems of the major world religions are easily as strange as that of the Heaven's Gaters. Belief in the divinity of Christ wins you a place in Heaven? The Jews are God's chosen people? Papal infallibility? Reincarnation? The big thing the major religions have going for them is that they were codified back when language had weight and dignity and images a preindustrial freshness and simplicity: "loaves and fishes" sounds a lot better than "tuna fish sandwiches." Poor Applewhite, a creature of our own sorry times, had to dress his absurd theology in fake science—U.F.O.s and extraterrestrials and a comet with an ugly name. But it's no more ridiculous than other modern homegrown faiths: Mormonism, which insists that an angel with the unfortunately suggestive name of Moroni gave Joseph Smith golden tablets containing the gospel God had delivered to the Indians, or the Nation of Islam, who believe that white people were created by a mad scientist. Time and success round off such rough edges: Today the Mormons are mainstream and the N.O.I. is becoming more respectable by the minute. And what about the Moonies? From mass-marrying robots to folks next door and proud owners of the right-wing *Washington Times* in barely a single generation!

Stripped of that comical *Star Trek* imagery, the core beliefs of the Heaven's Gaters plainly derive from Christianity—not surprisingly, since Applewhite was the son of a Presbyterian minister and served for a time as a (semi-closeted) choirmaster. A small band of believers will be saved by virtue of their faith from the imminent destruction of the world. Death is the portal to life everlasting. The movements of the heavenly bodies are divine signs and portents. The body, especially in its sexual aspects, is the enemy. Admittedly, Applewhite's male followers went a bit overboard on this last item when they "neutered their vehicles" with castration. But barbarous, humiliating and painful practices are embedded in standard religion too: circumcision (Islam, Judaism), menstrual and childbirth taboos (Judaism, Christianity), self-flagellation (still practiced by some Catholic monks and nuns, also Mexican *penitentes,* Opus Dei, Shiite devotees).

One letter writer to *The New York Times* argued that only cults, not real religions, practiced suicide. I wonder. The early Christians courted martyrdom with such zeal church authorities finally clamped down. Since then assorted saints have drunk pus and kissed lepers in the same spirit. More recently, Iranian theocrats have sent young boys rushing against Iraqi troops with the promise they would go straight to Heaven, and at least one young Indian widow has become a sort of local heroine after she committed suttee, although there are questions about how voluntary her self-immolation was. And what about Jehovah's Witnesses who refuse blood transfusions, or Christian Scientists who refuse life-saving medical attention? Aren't those forms of suicide? Besides, the Heaven's Gate people, in their own minds, weren't committing suicide when they downed their poisoned applesauce and vodka; they were merely moving to the Next Level.

I like the Last Marxist's theory: The difference between religions and cults is that while both hurt many of their members, so far in world history only religions, particularly the more organized and orthodox ones, have inflicted major casualties on people who are outside them, or in the wrong branch of them. All over the world the faithful are committing holy mayhem in the service of the divine: Think of Bosnia, Northern Ireland, Uganda, Sudan, Egypt, Algeria (a brief news item reports ninety-one villagers murdered by Islamic fanatics), Sri Lanka, Kashmir, Afghanistan, not to mention the so-called Holy Land itself.

And what about our own country? In forty-six states, it is legal for parents to deny their children medical aid and rely on faith healing and prayer instead. Thus it is acceptable under law to let your diabetic child go into a coma and die if you happen to believe the Christian Science doctrine that disease does not exist in God's perfect creation, but it is child abuse (or, with luck and a good lawyer, insanity) to do the same if you think you are exorcising him of demons. This seems most unfair to me—why privilege the collective delusion over the individual one? I thought individualism was what America was supposed to be all about.

My favorite reactionary, David Gelernter, has argued that Heaven's Gate and other weird cults are a response to the banishment of religion from public life. Never mind that most of the Heaven's Gaters were over forty, and thus grew up, as did I, in the Golden Age of state-sanctioned religious observance. The truth is, school prayer or no school prayer, America is hardly a secular wasteland: As European travelers loudly marvel, it's by far the most religious country in the West. Thirty-nine percent of the nation goes to church at least once a week—about the same as in 1950. Forty percent of scientists—*scientists!*—believe in a "personal God" who hears and responds to prayer, the same as in 1916.

Are Scandinavian elections enlivened by televangelists? When the Dutch hear voices, do they think it's God telling them to blow up an abortion clinic? Will French village churches take a leaf from the First Baptist Church in Berryville, Arkansas, and close their day-care centers because "God intended for the home to be the center of a mother's world"? Do French churches even have day-care centers, or is it only in America that government pays religious institutions to supply crucial public services?

Fortunately, most members of mainstream religions don't take their faith too seriously—or even, I suspect, know what it is. The Last Marxist's students, who are mostly Catholic, were horrified to learn that when they took Communion they were consuming the body and blood of Christ. "Eew, professor! That's gross!" How many people have killed and been killed over this theological point? A lot more than thirty-nine, that's for sure.

April 28, 1997

WHEN I'M SIXTY-FOUR

For the past two weeks everyone in America has been occupied in writing letters to the editor explaining why the sixty-three-year-old woman who recently had a baby thanks to the wonders of modern science is to be commended or scourged. Try it yourself: Sixty-three-year-old women having babies is *good*, because it (a) maximizes human choices, (b) makes women more equal to men, who have been fathering kids as geezers with younger women since time immemorial to approving smirks, (c) reminds us that postmenopausal women are still sexual beings. Or: Sixty-three-year-old women having babies is *bad*, because it (a) violates the limits of nature and the life cycle, (b) further defines women as having only reproductive value, (c) reminds us that postmenopausal women are still sexual beings.

By now we can all recite the arguments on any side at an instant's notice. Is Miracle Mom selfish? Ahem. For the affirmative: When Miracle Baby is a surly Miracle Teen, mom will be practically eighty, with dad only slightly younger. How will she be able to stand the horrible music that will surely be all the rage among the gilded youth of 2015? What if she's sick, senile, dead? Blah, blah, blah. For the negative: She's got great genes. Plenty of younger parents can't keep up with their kids; tragedy can strike at any age. And what about all those start-over dads? They'll be keeling over by the dozens by the time their kids are out of diapers. Yak, yak, yak.

Let's just cut to the finish line. Of course it's sexist to criticize Miracle Mom while congratulating seventy-seven-year-old Tony Randall or seventy-year-old George Plimpton (whose young brides, interestingly, never seem to make it into the family photo shoot—their role in the media debate is to be on standby for the post-keel-over moment). It's even an illusion to see start-over dads as more natural than postmenopausal moms: Without modern medicine (not to mention Nautilus machines, plastic surgery, money and celebrity) most septuagenarians would be in no condition to attract younger women, much less impregnate them. On the other hand, it's reasonable to wonder if geriatric parenting on the part of either sex is such a great idea for children, although in an era that features as parents anyone from twelve-year-old rape victims to vials of posthumously preserved sperm, why fuss about a few wrinkles?

But the real point is, Who cares? Why are we even talking about this? Postretirement babies are not going to be a popular option, for either sex, any time soon. Most people in their sixties with the necessary cash, leisure and vigor have other plans—playing the slots, driving around the country in R.V.s, writing angry letters to their representatives about attempts to recalculate the consumer price index. If every now and then a woman feels driven to put herself through gynecological hell (according to the *National Enquirer,* Miracle Mom had five in vitros, at a total cost of $32,000), why can't we just add it to the very long list of oddball things people do and leave the whole Miracle Family alone?

The amazing thing about the story is that for all the endless stream of verbiage about it, the important issues it raises still go undiscussed. Just think, for example, about the society that has produced a health care system with the resources to create this baby but that cannot manage to provide prenatal care for one in six women, and that is now congratulating itself over proposals to provide medical insurance for half the ten million children who lack it—never mind the other half, or the rest of the family, either. I'm not attacking Miracle Mom—as long as we have for-profit medicine, why shouldn't she be able to buy a childbirth? But her story certainly illustrates the weird distortions the profit motive has introduced into health care. How come medical ethicists, ever ready with a pious sound bite, don't talk about that?

The truth is, medical ethics, like the media, and like medicine itself, treats individual cases as if they were about personal choices when they really represent masked social decisions. Behind Miracle Mom is a huge medical machinery that we have chosen to render invisible, just as behind the start-over dads is a huge social machinery (not just the young wives but nannies, housekeepers, private schools, wealth) that is similarly unacknowledged and that permits them to limit their fatherhood to its ceremonial aspects.

The Miracle Mom brouhaha obscures another reality too. Like the ongoing sensation of the JonBenet Ramsey murder case, it allows an outlet for self-congratulatory indignation on behalf of children while having almost nothing to do with the conditions in which children actually live. It feels good to fire off a letter about how foolish a late-middle-aged woman is to imagine she can keep up with an active toddler, and how sad it will be for her child to spend her youth caring for aged parents or mourning their deaths. And yet we live placidly in a nation in which thousands upon thousands of poor children are being raised by their grandmothers, under truly grim conditions, and in which, indeed, those grandmothers may be all that stands between those children and the new for-profit foster care businesses permitted under welfare reform. (According to Nina Bernstein's spectacular exposé in *The New York Times,* it was a Democrat, Senator John Breaux of Louisiana, who engineered this coup.)

In the time the nation's spent obsessing over Miracle Mom, how many babies have been born to girls in foster care? To women living in homeless shelters? On the streets? These questions, unlike those of Miracle Mom's longevity and Miracle Baby's future happiness, have answers. Maybe that's why we prefer not to ask them.

May 26, 1997

No Sex, Please.
We're Killers

The whole Kelly Flinn story made sense to me when I saw *Time*'s photo of Marc Zigo, lover and nemesis. He looks just like Oliver North: same shirt-model good looks, unlicensed-therapist eyes, ingratiating little-boy expression of pained insincerity. I had a boyfriend who was a lot like Zigo when I was Kelly Flinn's age. Zigo told Flinn he was legally separated; my swain told me his wife was a lesbian who sent him out for cigarettes during her multigirl orgies. Part of me thought, Really? Your *wife*? The schoolteacher with the dirndl skirt? And another part of me thought, Gee, life's a lot weirder than I ever suspected. There must be some secret training camp where men learn how to make this stuff up, and maybe another camp where women learn how to repress the still, small voice of common sense that points out all those little discrepancies that seem so obvious in retrospect.

So in my book Kelly Flinn is one lucky woman. Not only has she washed Marc Zigo out of her hair, she's washed the air force out as well. Sure, it's embarrassing to have your private life made into a text for a sermonette by every single person, male or female, with access to an Op-Ed page or a bar stool. Let's hope that time and a book-and-movie deal perform their healing work, because the sermons won't let up any time soon. Scandal and steam and spin are the lens through which we Americans in our collective wisdom have decided to view life's great questions, of which relations between men and women are certainly five or six. Thus, one side cries *Remember Tailhook!* and points out that the military has always been a hotbed of sex, consensual and, as we are now learning from the mass trials of drill sergeants at Aberdeen Proving Grounds, otherwise. The other side tries, semi-futilely, to argue that the issue isn't really sex but disobedience and lack of gravitas, and furthermore, what is the world coming to when loose women—or maybe women, period—have access to nuclear weapons? There's an obvious forensic opening here for someone to put in a good word for adultery, but the President is too busy threatening to destroy Paula Jones's reputation to step up to that particular bully pulpit.

When the public debate is cast as thoroughly modern Kelly versus a bunch of puritanical hypocrites, she wins. She's got William Safire, who stood up for Clarence Thomas and Bob Packwood; she's even got Senate majority leader Trent Lott—Trent Lott!—whose memorable words, "I mean, get real," caused William Kristol to fire off a broadside in *The Weekly Standard* accusing the Republican congressional leadership of having "lost its soul." This is the good side of the oft-bemoaned tabloidization of America: The double standard, whether for men versus women or for public versus private citizens, is much harder to maintain when every day seems to bring fresh proof that today's role model is tomorrow's *Enquirer* front page.

When it's feminists versus Man the Hunter, though, the cavemen hold their own, backed up by opinionaters like Anna Simons, UCLA anthropologist, who argued in a *New York Times* Op-Ed that coeducating the military was a bad idea because trash talk about women is how male soldiers bond. On CBS, Republican spokesmodel Laura Ingraham went further: Kelly Flinn was the proof that coeducating the army had compromised our military preparedness. The Russians are coming, the Russians are coming?

Well, I'm all for coeducation. The Vietcong were coed, after all, and they managed pretty well. Besides, as a civilian, my primary identification is with other civilians, like the women and children of the countries we invade, conquer, occupy and inhabit for decades at a time. Recently, a group of 7,000 Japanese opposed to the U.S. military presence in Okinawa ran a full-page ad in *The New York Times* detailing four decades' worth of crimes against women and children committed by Our Boys, of which the horrific 1995 abduction and rape of a twelve-year-old schoolgirl was only the most notorious. I'm hardly a believer in the innate goodness of women, but realistically, the more women in the armed forces, the safer civilian women will be. Our Girls would never have created the flourishing sex industries of Vietnam, the Philippines, South Korea and Thailand, nor would they have left behind throngs of unacknowledged children to live in the streets as ostracized paupers. Around the globe, the exploitation of local women and girls has brought much more discredit upon the armed forces than adultery ever could. But we have yet to see the military bring up anyone on charges of patronizing a brothel, and it continues to evade its duties toward the out-of-wedlock children of U.S. servicemen.

Still, I have trouble seeing the Flinn saga only as a simple case of job discrimination. What's missing from the whole debate is any hint of resistance to the routine militarization of society her story reveals. Back when the women's movement was connected to the peace movement, feminists used to attack both the military budget and the authoritarian and violence-based military culture. Unfortunately, the peace movement turned out to be more a reaction to the cold war, which is over, than to, well, war, which we still have. And so there is no way, without sounding like a hippie-dippy flower-power throwback, to interrogate Kelly Flinn's yearning to fly B-52 bombers, which, amazingly, she has said is the *only* thing she has ever wanted to do. What's the matter with her? I'm all for people fulfilling their dreams, but if she wants to fly a plane, can't she get a job with Delta? If she needs danger and derring-do and the feeling of being part of a tiny elite of swashbucklers, can't she airlift Rwandan orphans out of Congo? Fly humanitarian relief through terrifying mountain passes in Bosnia? Must this particular fantasy involve mass destruction and the possibility of World War III?

Should the last day ever dawn, at least we can all be grateful that the weapons that blow the world to kingdom come were unleashed by a U.S.-government-certified chaste, preferably even virginal, hand. Let him—or her—who is without sin drop the first bomb! The way things are going with sex in the military, that may be our best hope for now.

June 23, 1997

ABOUT RACE:
CAN WE TALK?

I prepped for President Clinton's speech on race by having dinner with a very nice older white gentleman of considerable wealth and impeccable liberal credentials. He explained to me that the reason he and his fellow inner-city-hospital board members had deliberately excluded blacks from their ranks was that any black they appointed would be under such pressure to hand out jobs in the community the hospital would quickly become a patronage mill. What I said: pious drivel about community representation. What I wish I'd said: So does that mean your grandchildren's private school has a board made up of inner-city welfare recipients, because rich white people would be unable to resist pulling strings to get their friends' kids in?

There was no excuse for my lack of a snappy comeback. After all, the previous week I had been discussing public schools with another very nice white person of somewhat less wealth and even better liberal credentials, and she explained to me that the reason Staten Island has the best reading scores in the city is that "they haven't figured out how to cross the Verrazano Bridge yet." *They?* I was so stunned I said nothing, which hasn't happened in years.

We're qualified, they're not. We advance by merit, they need special privileges. We give, they take. When we knock, they're not at home. That's the way it looks to lots of white people, up and down the income spectrum, and on both sides of the political aisle. Liberals still use the *Sesame Street* language of openness and diversity; conservatives portray themselves as color-blind meritocrats deeply immersed in the study of Martin Luther King's sermons. On a questionnaire, in public speeches, the two camps sound very different. But in real life how much difference is there?

I know there are white sixties lefties who have made the integration of their own and their children's lives a big priority; I know there are more biracial couples than ever. But most white people, whatever their politics, move in a segregated world: They live in all-white buildings, send their kids to mostly white schools and camps, socialize mostly or even only with whites and work mostly or even only with whites as equals or superiors. That's how society is set up, and it takes energy and conviction—and maybe curiosity and inner need—to break the mold. Since we are all busy people with multiple plans and projects, it's easy to persuade oneself that one has done all that can reasonably be expected when one has made only a gesture. I know one magazine editor who still counts his unsuccessful attempts to get essays from James Baldwin in 1978 as proof of the difficulty of getting black contributors. You think that's bad? Frederick Douglass didn't even call back.

In his speech at the University of California, San Diego, recently, President Clinton warned against the resegregation of higher education in the wake of California's anti–affirmative action Proposition 209 and a rash of judicial decisions against affirmative action. He said he favored affirmative action, sort of, and called for a national dialogue on race and ethnicity. I would have thought that talk is one thing of which we have no short supply. Yet as so often, what matters is left unsaid: Thus it was left to Jim Cason and David Brooks, U.S. correspondents for *La Jornada*, the Mexican daily, to point out that President Clinton had been silent on Proposition 209 throughout the election season, when his leadership—and his party's money and muscle—might have made a difference.

Here's my contribution to the dialogue. Without equality, meritocracy is basically another form of social privilege: Only his parents would seriously argue that a two-year-old accepted into an elite preschool with a pipeline to an elite private school with a great record of getting students into elite colleges is a genius toddler whom God just happened to place in a prosperous family with a home in the right neighborhood and prominent friends who can put in a word. White liberals of the professional classes should therefore dedicate themselves to a campaign against hereditary privileges—their own. If we can't have socialism, at least let's get rid of feudalism. It's well past time to abolish admissions preference for the children of alumni. This practice, which actually affects more applicants than race-based affirmative action does, is antimeritocratic. It is also racist, since it acts as a kind of grandfather clause, available only to those whose ancestors obtained admission under conditions of virtual segregation. There were, if I remember correctly, nine black women with me in the class of 1971 at Radcliffe. That means my class produced maybe twenty black children out of the, say, thousand kids able to take advantage of an alumni-child admission rate unofficially said to be 40 percent. Princeton didn't even admit blacks until World War II; yet a Princeton alumni child has almost an even chance of admission.

Many have made this point, including me, yet alumni preference shows no signs of disappearing. Colleges have a vested interest in it, because it helps create loyal donors, and alumni adore it for obvious reasons (indeed, the easy ride for our kids was the happy buzz at my twenty-fifth reunion). So here's my question: Would you renounce alumni privilege for your children? Write your college an official letter requesting that your child be evaluated purely on his or her merits? Organize your fellow graduates to pressure your private school, college, professional school to do away with it? Refuse to donate as long as said school practices this insidious form of racial and economic discrimination, thus perpetuating a heredity-based social elite?

Go ahead, surprise me.

July 7, 1997

Get Thee Behind Me,
Disney

The Southern Baptists have been on the wrong side of just about
every issue since their founding in 1845 as a pro-slavery split-off
from the regular Baptists: mixed dancing, racial segregation, equality for women and, my personal favorite, converting the Jews. Ever
since that project was announced last year, I've waited for the mis-
sionary to knock at my door with all the ardor of the spider for the
fly: You'd be surprised how hard it is to get a real theological dispu-
tation going in these ecumenical times. It may be some time before
the Southern Baptists get around to the Upper West Side, though,
because at this year's convention delegates decided to boycott Walt
Disney and all his works—even ESPN, the sports channel, which
must be quite a sacrifice—for being too gay-friendly. Making a
measurable dent in the profit of the Disney corporation is bound to
be even harder than persuading the chosen people to wash in the
blood of the Lamb. This time, though, they don't need to ring my
doorbell. I'm already on their side.

   I tried to like *The Little Mermaid*, which struck me for reasons
that now elude me as less monolithically sexist than *Cinderella* or
Sleeping Beauty, the Disney movies of my youth. I enjoyed bits of
Beauty and the Beast and *Aladdin:* the funny sidekicks and comic show

tunes, the inventive visuals (the fabulous dancing dinner in the Beast's ruined mansion), the amusing repartee. But when you go to these movies with a small child, as I always did, your judgment is skewed by the fact that the alternative is going mad with boredom at the playground or spending a rainy afternoon crouched on the floor playing with plastic horses. With my daughter now nine and off at camp, I went to see *Hercules* by myself. Big mistake.

The ancient Greeks get a lot of criticism these days for being dead white men and all, but you have to give them credit—they knew how to tell a good story. The myth of Hercules may lack a certain grandeur—even the ancients seemed to regard him as a jolly buffoon, and some of those famous twelve labors involved activities that would have been taken as humorously degrading, like cleaning up manure or wearing a dress. But it's still a rich and evocative, if not entirely coherent, tale, with motifs that turn up in stories as apparently different as Gilgamesh (friend seeks to rescue friend from underworld), Christ (child of mortal mother and divine father wins immortality through earthly struggles) and fairy tales (impossible tasks, dragons and giants, enemy stepmother/queen, golden apples, western journey, poisoned shirt). Bits of the Heracles myth appear in writing from Milton to, of all people, Stalin, who saw in the hero's antagonist Antaeus—a giant whose strength depended on remaining in contact with his mother, the Earth—a metaphor for the party cadre's putative connection with the working class.

The myth of Heracles is about a lot of things, I am trying to say, but among the things it is not about is a lonely adopted child who "will go most anywhere to find where I belong," a son with a crush on his powerful benevolent dad, the corrupting influence of celebrity, or the redemptive powers of romantic love. Of course, every generation retells the old stories in new ways—but these particular new ways are already stale, a hyped-up super-glitzy version of a thousand old B-movies. The only truly funny character is Hades, who talks like a Hollywood agent; his sidekicks, the demons Pain and Panic, who talk like stand-up comics, are basically the hyenas from *The Lion King*. The rest are clichés: Hercules' tutor, a satyr named Philoctetes, or Phil, is the tough-talking boxing trainer with a heart of gold; his girlfriend, Megara, or Meg, is the tough-talking "dame" with a heart of gold. The movie is incredibly knowing about show business, its real subject: It mocks both the old Hollywood of film noir and the new world of multimillion-dollar celebrity athlete tie-ins and endorsements (Herc has a theme park, a sandal deal, his picture on a thousand tchotchkes and hordes of screaming fans and would-be groupies). But it offers no alternative to the values of those worlds; the sentimental being-a-good-person-is-what-really-matters conclusion is to the rest of the movie what the Jean Hersholt Humanitarian Award is to the Oscars. In real life *Hercules* merchandise is the new tie-in at McDonald's.

Why do we feed our children this dreck? Why do grown-ups feed themselves this dreck? Over and over, I hear parents complain that their kids don't like to read, that the boys are obsessed with sports and the girls are already superconscious—at eight—of their looks and their weight and their clothes. But where do children get a different message about what's important? In *Hercules*, being strong and destructive is the *summum bonum* for all the men and being beautiful, thin and sexy is the basic requirement for all the female characters, from Hera (Hercules' mother, in this version) and Meg to the Muses, downsized for some reason from the traditional chorus of nine to a black gospel quintet—four glamourpusses and one short, fat frump.

I'm not sure exactly why it's *Hercules* that's brought home to me the totalizing power of the corporate media. Maybe it's the gratuitous know-nothing way Disney puts the myth through a blender, not just free-associating all sorts of story elements (Hera's his *mom?*) but destroying its very essence, which has to do with the testing and acknowledgment of limits, both human and divine. Or maybe it's the mediocre music and dialogue (Thebes is the Big Olive), the long repetitive stretches of rock-hurling and pillar-shattering. Or the general feeling of immense amounts of money and skill expended to impress upon our children that they live in a world entirely processed by the same corporate forces that brought them this movie.

The Southern Baptists will surely lose their fight against Disney. In today's America, the Mouse beats Christ hands down. But if the Baptists, with their intact belief system, their organized and politicized community, their intensely felt (if bigoted) convictions, cannot mount a successful challenge to corporate mass culture, the rest of us clearly have a task ahead worthy of Heracles himself.

July 21, 1997

HONK IF YOU LIKE ART

The other night I came across a television ad encouraging viewers to visit Alabama. It had the customary montage of state attractions. You know, Alabama—the fishing, the football, the beaches, the plantations, the symphony, the ballet. The symphony (with a black conductor, yet)? The *ballet?* The good boosters of Alabama must not have got the word that the arts are elitist, effeminate, blasphemous and obscene. They seem to think they're more like, well, fishing: something you might voluntarily choose to enjoy in that precious sliver of free time, your vacation.

I count this ad as yet another piece of evidence that the right-wing attack on the National Endowment for the Arts is playing to a small, if ferocious, constituency. Contrary to stereotype, Americans *like* the arts, and the more access they have to them, the more they like them. New York City's museums these days are as crowded as Bloomingdale's. Opera—opera! the epitome of long, dull and foreign, the butt of a thousand jokes—is hot, with a whole new audience drawn in over the past few years by the addition of supertitles to live performance and by subtitled PBS broadcasts. Last year Americans spent 50 percent more attending arts than sports events. Even poetry is showing signs of life.

Sure, some of this interest is idle and superficial, an aspect of social climbing and status seeking, the Higher Shopping. The fact remains that more people are seeking out the arts than ever before in American history, which makes this what educators call a teachable moment. If we lived in a civilized country, the government would set itself immediately to expanding and developing and complicating this curiosity and openness to art. It would bring back art and music and drama—aka "frills"—to the public schools, it would hire writers to run classes and book clubs in public libraries, it would make museum-going free again, and subsidize theater tickets (as even the British Tories did) so that going to a play would be more like going to the movies and less like investing your life savings in a high-risk mutual fund. If Oprah Winfrey can get huge numbers of women usually dismissed as romance-reading featherheads to tackle challenging novels by Toni Morrison and Ursula Hegi by talking her audience through them in a warm, enthusiastic, unscary, we're-all-in-this-together way, think what the government could do if it was willing to spend a little money to enlarge our minds and broaden our tastes a bit.

I know, I'm dreaming. The conventional wisdom has it that right-wing Republicans will ultimately fail to shut down the National Endowment for the Arts when it comes to a vote this fall. Even if this proves to be the case, though, the year-in, year-out yahoo-conservative onslaught is having its effect. You see it in the strained attempt of N.E.A. boosters to find a bottom-line rationale for arts funding: Art employs a lot of people, grants for high culture and experimental projects act as "seed money" for eventual pop-cultural blockbusters. To which the right ripostes that funding art as a jobs program is just pork-barreling, which we all detest and despise, and if high culture is R&D for Hollywood, why shouldn't Hollywood pay for it? (Sure—and why not have the A.M.A. finance the National Institutes of Health?) You see the N.E.A. defenders' lack of confidence too in the stress always placed on the paucity of "controversial" grants—*Piss Christ*, the Mapplethorpe exhibition, Karen Finley. Wouldn't it be refreshing to hear an N.E.A. spokesperson speak up in favor of art as, well, art and argue for *more* controversy rather than less? Must everyone like everything?

As an amalgam of high-culture reactionaries, antigovernment

ideologues and faux populists, the anti-N.E.A. phalanx makes a wide variety of mutually contradictory arguments. Thus, *The New Criterion*'s Hilton Kramer attacks the N.E.A. for supporting trendy mediocrity, while Dick Armey attacks it for appropriating the taxpayer's dollar—thirty-eight cents, actually—and giving it to something, anything, that a particular taxpayer might not approve of, presumably including those things Kramer champions, like abstract painting. If the government funds major institutions of unquestioned excellence and magnificence, most of which are located in New York and a few other major cities, that's upper-class urban elitism; if it funds a suburban orchestra in Ohio or a young, unfamous poet in Oregon, that's subsidizing the second-rate. And if it tries to split the difference by underwriting the export of urban high culture to the provinces—say, a production of *Angels in America* in Newt Gingrich's Cobb County, Georgia—that's the invasion of the body snatchers.

Isn't it interesting that none of these arguments are made against, say, the space program? The recent Sojourner Mars extravaganza cost $160 million a day—a little less than twice the proposed *annual* N.E.A. budget, but widely proclaimed an incredible bargain. (NASA will cost $13.7 billion in fiscal year 1997.) Like public arts funding, the space program has lost its cold war rationale but, unlike it, rolls on regardless. It's equally impractical— surely someone would have invented Teflon by now—and at least as "elitist." Representative Sonny Bono says he's never met anyone who benefited from public arts funding; well, I've never met anyone who cares what kind of rocks Mars has. In my opinion, the space program is the obsessive pursuit of trivia, the Higher Stamp-Collecting. Yet despite the fact that I have held this view since Sputnik, I am forced to subsidize NASA with my taxes, while red-meat conservatives like Newt Gingrich exempt space exploration from their condemnation of government programs.

Why should the personal interests of a small band of futurists and technogeeks have a permanent claim on the national treasury, while those of us who enjoy the arts are told to pay full freight? Why isn't Mars a "frill"? Is it because the arts are seen as feminine—worse, gay—but space is all about he-men? I knew there was a feminist angle to this.

I wonder what would happen if arts supporters demanded parity with space fans: They get $13.7 billion, we get $13.7 billion. Or conversely, the N.E.A. goes, and NASA dies as well. Everyone who'd rather go to the ballet in Alabama than watch Martian rock retrieval on TV raise your hand. See? There are more of us than we think.

August 11/18, 1997

THOROUGHLY MODERN DI

Whatever else it may or may not be, the death of Princess Diana was a godsend for pundits. After a summer widely bemoaned as newsless, in which Op-Editorializers were forced to treat the bite Mike Tyson took out of Evander Holyfield's ear with a level of indignation last displayed when Saddam Hussein made similar inroads on Kuwait, and in which they mourned the murder of Gianni Versace as if it were the assassination of Martin Luther King Jr. redux, all of a sudden it's ready, set, write. Diana was the creature and, ultimately, victim of a celebrity-mad age (Jonathan Alter); Diana was the victim of her boyfriend Dodi Fayed's "obsessive urge to race away from prying eyes" (William Safire); Diana was killed trying to escape a photographic sexual assault (Salman Rushdie *and* A. M. Rosenthal); Diana was a vacuous ninny (Maureen Dowd); Diana was a feminist saint who espoused "radical causes" (*The Scotsman*'s Beatrix Campbell); Diana symbolized all that was magical and rarefied, adored because she was beautiful, mysterious, "special" (nearly everyone); Diana was an ordinary woman, whom women identified with because of shared exploitation by men (Francine du Plessix Gray). There's something in all these perspectives, even the description of the princess as a devotee of "radical causes": Her position on land mines, for example, was much more uncompromising than that of the Clinton administration. Similarly, there's some truth in each of the possible positions staked out vis-à-vis the paparazzi who pursued her: They're creepy *but* celebrities use them back *and* people want those photos, *including* the high-end media that scorn them, *although* privacy should count for something *even* for celebrities and *despite* the First Amendment (or not).

But of course, the major radical cause that Diana represented is modernity itself. She may have begun as a nineteenth-century throwback, a barely educated, docile, medically certified virgin waving from a Cinderella glass coach on her way to a "fairy-tale wedding" that was actually a marital transaction as cynical and cold-blooded as any in Henry James. But she ended by symbolizing a new set of values: self-invention, psychotherapy, emotional expressivity, egalitarian marriage and women's right to seek love in and out of wedlock, flamboyant consumerism, public relations, superstardom, the Oprahfication of everything. You can see why women would love her story, which puts a triumphant and glamorous spin on so many themes of contemporary women's lives— eating disorders, depression, chilly husbands, bad marriages, divorce—culminating in near-total victory over the mother of all mothers-in-law from hell. And because these are indeed real issues that in some ways transcend class, those who criticize the princess tend to sound callous, reactionary and misogynous. Imagine, sneered the novelist Fay Weldon last year in an astonishingly venomous and almost incoherent *Times* Op-Ed on the royal divorce, Diana actually believed herself "entitled to a faithful husband"! She wanted to be happy! Stupid girl.

That said, for me, the amazing thing about the Diana story is simply that there *is* a Diana story. It's not just that Britain still has a monarchy, which consumes an enormous amount of money (millions of pounds per annum) and buttresses a still-powerful hereditary aristocracy, and that remarking on this makes one sound like a C.P.A. at the opera. Nor is it that the criticism of the royals provoked by Diana's death seems to come down to complaints that they're too cold, too old-fashioned and too out of it, when what's wanted is a Clintonesque, talk-show-friendly monarchy of high-fashion do-gooders. It's not even just that Tony Blair is trying to save the Windsors' bacon—although what does it mean to be for labor if you're also for kings and queens?

What depresses me about the outpouring of emotion on the death of Diana is what it says about how little so many millions of people expect out of life. It's pathetic, really, all those grown men and women telling reporters how much it meant to them that Diana visited some relative's hospital room, or shook their hand at the opening of a supermarket, or just "meant something" or "made a difference" of some never-exactly-specified nature. It's as if people have abandoned any hope of achieving justice, equality, self-determination, true democracy, and want nothing more than a ruling class with a human face.

Because their deaths so nearly coincided, it was natural to contrast Princess Diana with Mother Teresa. But in some important ways the women were not so different. Both were the flowers of hierarchical, feudal, essentially masculine institutions in which they had no structural power but whose authoritarian natures they obscured and prettified. Both, despite protestations to the contrary, were in the modern mass-market image business. Neither challenged the status quo that produced the social evils they supposedly helped alleviate—in fact, by promoting the illusion that nuns with no medical training, or checks from wealthy donors, or selling your dresses for charity could "make a difference" on a significant scale, they masked those evils (or even, in the case of Mother Teresa's opposition to abortion and birth control, made them worse). Why, after all, should children's hospitals require the fundraising services of Princess Diana instead of receiving adequate support from taxpayers? Why is it thought to be marvelous that the princess took her sons to meet and "love" the homeless, when the whole royal family lives off the system of inequality that produces homelessness? We haven't come very far, it seems, from the medieval view of the poor as a moral opportunity for the rich.

But then, isn't it strange that the two most famous and adored women of the moment are those archetypal medieval figures, a princess and a nun?

September 29, 1997

FREE WILLIE

Can it really be that President Clinton will have to step down from the White House because he had—omigod—extramarital oral sex with an adult human female not his wife? Not rape, not sexual harassment, not child molestation or sleeping with his best friend's wife, nothing painful or kinky or involving drugs or costumes? This in a country where half the kids over fifteen have as many piercings and tattoos as lifers in the gulag and the front cover of this month's *Reader's Digest*, on view in every grocery store, trumpets an article within as "Surprising Health Benefits of Sex!"

I watch the talking-head shows, I listen to the radio and trudge through the endless gray wastes of moaning and harrumphing that fill the daily papers, and I am just astonished. American journalists, who know all there is to know about the routine licentiousness of politicians and are no angels themselves, I might add, seem unable to take the measure of the banal Monica Lewinsky scandal and put it in its place. Clinton-haters like George Will and Maureen Dowd I can understand, but Bob Herbert?

Well, I feel sorry for President Clinton. True, he's a creep and a schmucko, to use Ms. Lewinsky's pet names for him, also a dissembler: I always believed Gennifer Flowers and, most of the time, Paula Jones. Worse, he's a hypocrite, who, as Barbara Ehrenreich points out, has pandered to the right on family values, castigating teens for having sex and women for bearing "illegitimate" children; he signed a welfare bill that, among other cruelties, cuts food stamps while providing millions for classes in abstinence. It's hard to sympathize with a man who's now lying in the straight and narrow bed he helped make for so many others.

Nonetheless, I do sympathize with him. President Clinton executed the brain-damaged Rickey Ray Rector and pushed through a draconian crime bill; he bombed Baghdad and may well do so again. But this love affair is nobody's business but his, his wife's and Ms. Lewinsky's. None of them are complaining, so why should CNN? I don't even care that he may have fibbed in his deposition to Jones's lawyers, or asked Lewinsky to back him up, because they had no right to ask about consensual sex in the first place. Or do we now believe that infidelity is ipso facto suggestive of sexual harassment? It seems to me that the risks of having a philanderer in the White House—whom people have already knowingly elected twice—are far less than the risks of permitting special prosecutors and others to play Savonarola. How would *you* like to be deposed about your sexual partners and practices? If I thought I'd get away with it, I'd lie too.

When it comes to sex, journalists reason like children. We are told that a President can't run the country if, as Gennifer Flowers cleverly put it, "He's thinking with his other head"—but before the scandal broke, nobody charged President Clinton with inattention or stupidity. Or take the view put forward not only by countless right-wing commentators but even by progressive Norman Solomon: Someone who would lie about one thing would lie about others. As a general rule, this is quite false: Most people manage to confine their mendacity to a few subject areas, of which sex is probably number one. Politicians, however, lie all the time, whether or not they sleep around. *That's* what the media should care about, instead of trying to persuade ordinary folk that the President is the national daddy and that the First Family is supposed to enact a pageant of domestic virtue. Thank heaven polls suggest that most people have more sense.

You wait and see, I told the Last Marxist when the Lewinsky story broke. This will all be blamed on feminism. The women's movement will be gleefully mocked as hoist by its own petard, deprived of "Hillary's husband" because it turned all sex into sexual harassment. The L.M. compared me to an old grandma worrying that Woody Allen is bad for the Jews. But the Lewinsky scandal is already being used to make feminists look like special pleaders: Where, assorted male pundits wonder, are the charges that Bill Clinton "doesn't get it," the defense of the much-maligned Flowers and Jones, the warning to the White House not even to think about trashing Monica Lewinsky, whom Clinton has already referred to as That Woman and aides are calling The Stalker? "If Paula Jones is telling the truth," Gloria Steinem told me in a phone interview, "Bill Clinton made a ridiculous gross proposal. She said no, and he accepted it. Clarence Thomas and Bob Packwood did not: The key concept here is respect for women's will."

But then, of course, there are those feminists who see younger women as unable, really, to assert their will with a powerful older man. Some of these commentators are clearly temporary converts seizing a partisan opportunity. It was a bit of a shock to troll through Nexis and find the Independent Women's Forum's Christina Hoff Sommers ("She's only a child") and Rita Simon, who heads the right-wing libertarian Women's Freedom Network, enlisting in the frail-flower brigade. Wouldn't you know that when these doughty opponents of "victimology" found a victim, it would be a woman who, so far as we know, was a volunteer?

Sommers and Simon ought to smoke a peace pipe with Catharine MacKinnon and Brandeis professor Linda Hirshman, with whom I had a friendly chat on the Pacifica Radio show *Democracy Now!* I pointed out that there's no evidence that Monica Lewinsky was bullied or coerced or intimidated into sex and quite a bit of evidence that she was a willing, even eager, participant; that some young women actually like to have sex with powerful older men; that Lewinsky's current troubles spring not from the embraces of the President but from the secret and illegal tapings of her "friend" Linda Tripp. For these mild observations I was likened to Katie

Roiphe, and dismissed as a free-love advocate from the sixties and as someone who supported the "right of powerful men" to take advantage of their subordinates.

"Feminism means respecting the free will of women," said Steinem. "No means no, and yes means yes." In his current predicament, the President could do worse than remind the nation, and its pundits, of that crucial distinction.

February 16, 1998

HELLO, COLUMBUS

Just when it seems like the official media have a total lock on political discourse and nothing will ever again be said except by designated experts in pancake makeup, just when you think the last raw bit of reality has been plastic-wrapped and priced like a slice of processed cheese food—just when, in other words, you are about to consider getting seriously depressed—something wonderful, bizarre and totally unscripted happens.

I am thinking, of course, of the February 18 CNN "Town Meeting" on Iraq at Ohio State University in Columbus, featuring Secretary of State Madeleine Albright, Secretary of Defense William Cohen and National Security Adviser Sandy Berger. Here was an occasion that would seem to have offered about as much chance for the unexpected as a pharaoh's funeral. It was worse than propaganda, it was propaganda privatized: The Clinton Administration manufactures a spectacle of consent by normal red-blooded Americans to the bombing of Iraq, which it offers to a giant news conglomerate. This corporation then twists the already-bent occasion to fit its own commercial needs: banning other news organizations, structuring the discussion around advertising breaks, using the crowds who had come expecting a two-way exchange of views to bolster a false image of robust free speech. Not exactly one of those ideal speech communities Jürgen Habermas talks about! On the floor of the sports arena, carefully chosen likely war supporters— veterans, R.O.T.C. cadets, students enrolled in a military history class. Up in the balcony, barred from even the chance to submit a question for prescreening, everyone else.

Including, through an amazing oversight that White House aides publicly bemoaned for days afterward, some two hundred to three hundred local antiwar activists—old-time peaceniks, students, clergy, anarchists, union people—who proceeded to make an impressive fuss. (Moderator Bernard Shaw's reference to maybe a "dozen" protesters was, of course, inaccurate.) Chanting. Heckling. Interrupting. Unfurling a banner—NO WAR—that one woman had smuggled in under her skirt. The protesters made so much noise that, after seven ejections and one arrest, a CNN producer agreed to let one of them ask a question if they agreed to pipe down. Jon Strange, a twenty-two-year-old substitute teacher (who was, let it be noted, properly dressed and wearing a tie), asked a 64,000-dollar one: "Why bomb Iraq when other countries have committed similar violations?" He mentioned Turkey, which bombs the Kurds; Saudi Arabia, which tortures political and religious dissidents; Indonesia, which has slaughtered hundreds of thousands of East Timorese; Israel, which has been censured by the United Nations for bombing Lebanese civilians and brutalizing the Palestinians; and he could have mentioned many other nations as well.

Down on the floor, Rick Theis, a writer and former O.S.U. student body president, was originally first at the mike but was denied the right to speak when he refused to let CNN prescreen his question and ejected when he protested this censorship. By dint of much vocal protest, he managed to speak at the very end of the evening, and he asked some good questions too. How can you call this a town meeting? How do you sleep at night?

Too much free speech equals a major public relations disaster. In a stunning reversal, the very factors that had given the pro-war discourse the false appearance of monolithic consensus also made it vulnerable. Take conglomeratization: Thanks to CNN's global dominance, the whole world really was watching. How could the Clinton administration persuade foreign governments of a course of action so dubious it couldn't even persuade its own citizens? (Not even Ohio supports the bombing, Egyptian president Hosni Mubarak said a few days later. Why should Egypt?) Take the media near-blackout of weeks and weeks of antiwar actions across the country. Suddenly people with questions about the bombing could see they weren't alone and never had been. "I got phone calls from people all over the country saying our protest gave them courage to do things in their own communities," Strange told me when we spoke by phone. "I think we cut through people's feelings of isolation and hopelessness."

Now if Jon Strange and Rick Theis and their fellow protesters had been, say, first graders suspended for kissing classmates, they would have been on every talk show in the country the next day—like the veteran who wondered at the town meeting if we're "ready and willing to send in the troops." Was this not a news story? Did it not have a hook, an angle, timeliness, human interest, edge and attitude—all those things we leftists are constantly being told we lack when we ask why the mainstream media short-shrift our perspectives and reject our Op-Eds? After he'd had dinner and calmed down, Strange told me, he called *Nightline,* CNN, a newsroom at ABC and the Associated Press. "No one was interested." Only Pacifica's *Democracy Now!* and a few liberal-hosted regional talk shows invited Strange or Theis to be a guest. Theis's well-written and eminently newsworthy account of the evening appeared not in *The New York Times* or *The Washington Post* but in *The Lantern,* O.S.U.'s student paper, where, I must say, I found a level of discussion both of the town meeting and the proposed bombing itself that easily equaled that in the mainstream press.

Columbus wasn't the only protest sidelined in the reporting. An appearance by Albright at Columbia, South Carolina, was met with demonstrators (best placard: CLINTON: MAKE LOVE, NOT WAR). U.N. ambassador Bill Richardson was confronted with such an unruly audience at the University of Minnesota that he left without speaking, a story no major paper saw fit to print.

An interesting clue to the willful media misperception of widespread antiwar feeling lies in the persistent suggestion that the town meeting protesters were members of the famously sectarian and pugnacious Spartacist League. No one I spoke to from Columbus had seen a single Spart. I asked peace activist Mark Stansbery why he thought the press would say such a thing. "Maybe because we were so aggressive," he replied. "People don't expect that of Ohioans."

March 16, 1998

WOMEN AND CHILDREN FIRST

People keep insisting that feminism is over and retro is *de retour*. Virginity is back, white weddings are back, chivalry and cigars are back. The fundamentalist Darwinians think women, or at least their genes, want to be taken care of by older men with thick necks and big incomes. The fundamentalist Christians think women want to be ordered around by dishwashing good old boys. It's been decades now since Hollywood thought about women at all—who cares what they want, as long as they tag along to the movies with their boyfriends?

This background chatter of complacent moralizing and conservative claptrap is what makes the phenomenally popular success of *Titanic* so satisfying. In her *New York Times* review Janet Maslin hesitated to tag James Cameron's epic—a technological marvel and at $200 million in production costs supposedly the most expensive movie ever made—with the dreaded label "women's picture." But it's women, especially teenage girls, whose repeated viewings, often in groups of friends, have made *Titanic* the highest-grossing movie in history.

It *is* a women's picture, although men may like it too (lots of fancy computer imaging, technology, smashed furniture and violent death, plus luscious Kate Winslet). That is, like so many great movies of the thirties and forties, it's a three-hankie romance centered on the female character, with tons of glamour and gorgeous clothes. But unlike any women's picture of recent years I can think of, the heroine does not have to choose between work and love or solitude and compromise. She does not have a violent husband, a fatal illness, a shaved head, a kidnapped child. She is not punished for being sexual—no back-alley abortion, stalker, AIDS, rape. She is not a perky sidekick or a long-suffering, tired-looking wife. We are not asked to believe that she would find Woody Allen attractive or enjoy being a prostitute, even for a night.

As you probably already know, *Titanic* is the story of seventeen-year-old Rose (Winslet), who is being sold into marriage to the very odious, very rich Cal (Billy Zane) by her heartless, snobbish and secretly penniless mother. Returning to America on the fatal ship for her wedding, frantic with boredom and dread, she is rescued from a halfhearted suicide attempt by Jack (Leonardo DiCaprio), a working-class artist and rover. They spend the rest of the movie falling in love, dining in first class and dancing in steerage, evading Cal and his evil manservant (David Warner) and rescuing each other from drowning. We know from the start that Rose survives, because we see her in the present-day framing story as a 101-year-old, still-beautiful bohemian (Gloria Stuart). And, without being told, we know Jack doesn't. It wouldn't be a movie if he did.

Titanic has been criticized for its silly plot, underwritten characters and wooden dialogue ("This is where we first met!" Rose tells Jack dreamily as they cling to the ship's stern, while people all around them slide off screaming into the sea). Also for its many anachronisms (Rose makes penis jokes and gives the finger; wears bright red lipstick day and night; has tête-à-têtes in her negligee with her fiancé. My daughter was sure she glimpsed F.D.R.'s head on a dime in one crucial scene). The 1958 British *A Night to Remember* made much better use of the wealth of knowledge about the liner and its sinking—in particular, the heroic telegraph operators and their desperate attempts to raise any of the several ships nearby. The earlier film gave too a much sharper sense of the various sorts of hubris—class, empire, industry, technology—that led to the disaster. Although my daughter was keen on the water-safety angle ("Don't go on a big boat or you might lose your lover" was her sarcastic version of the movie's message), Cameron's movie is more of a poetic meditation on class and gender and even, in its all-whiteness, race: The sinking of the liner represents the onrushing destruction of the old order, in which a rapacious, cruel and secretly sordid upper class suppresses proletarian and immigrant vigor and sells its own daughters into genteel bondage. It's hokum, of course; Cameron barely individualizes the steerage passengers he champions, and, according to the Nation Institute's Peter Meyer, a serious *Titanic* buff, underplays the disproportionate death toll of steerage passengers and crew members. This is a pro-democracy movie, perhaps, in the sense that Diana was the people's princess.

Still, for millions of women Diana was exactly that, and within the context of Hollywood films, *Titanic* is a feminist movie. DiCaprio and Winslet are far from gender stereotypes. He has a pale, almost androgynous boyish beauty (you can't believe he needs to shave) and a sexiness from which the usual elements of dominance and danger are entirely missing; she exudes a florid vitality, like a pre-Raphaelite angel who's been fed a lot of roast beef. She's flamboyant, even in a way titanic: There's a great scene of her tromping through the rising flood in her wispy gray-and-pink dinner dress, hefting a fire ax to rescue her Jack. She looks like a Valkyrie or a gorgeous fury, wild hair streaming.

Old Rose tells us Jack saved her "in every way that a woman can be saved." Through him she discovers herself as a sexual being and free spirit, and abandons fiancé, mother, class for (bedside photos tell us) a long and exciting life as an actress, aviatrix, traveler, potter, mother. Fifteen hundred people perish in torment, but this is a movie with a happy ending and an optimistic vision of history. The twentieth century, which for so many men is a saga of loss, decline and displacement, has told a different story to women.

So call *Titanic* a women's fantasy—of costless liberation brought to you by a devoted, selfless, charming, funny, incredibly handsome lover. He teaches you to spit, awakens you body and soul, points you toward a long, richly eventful future and dies, beautifully, poetically, tragically—but not before he tells you that freezing to death in a sea full of corpses was worth it because it brought him you. "He had to die," said one friend of mine, "because otherwise he would have disappointed her down the road." I had the same thought: How many happy artists' wives can you think of?

Romantic feminism. It's what women want. See you at the movies.

March 30, 1998

MÄDCHEN IN UNIFORM

The New York City public school system has libraries without books, and 52,000 extra children stuffed into its classrooms. Some kids have to double up on textbooks and can't take them home overnight. Art, music, gym, guidance counselors, nurses—remember school nurses?—have died the death of a thousand cuts. Teachers often lack proper certification, classes are huge, buildings dilapidated—last winter a girl was killed by falling debris at an elementary school in Brooklyn. The boys haven't taken to mowing their classmates down with assault rifles yet, but there's a steady trickle of sexual assaults and rape. Fortunately, a remedy is at hand. Uniforms!

Yes, incredibly, last month the New York City Board of Education voted 7 to 0 to institute a citywide uniform policy in its 660 elementary schools. (Schools can already opt for uniforms, and a number have done so, but now it will be mandatory, with individual schools, and parents, having to opt out.) Proponents of uniforms, like President Clinton and Mayor Giuliani, claim they will produce cohesion, discipline, an atmosphere conducive to learning. They will discourage gangs, fights over brand-name sneakers and the hypersexualization of girls—none of which are problems in elementary schools, which only go up through fifth grade but middle and high school kids are too big, tough and old to be forced to don navy and tartan. The press has treated the whole issue with avuncular chuckles; many Catholic school girls have testified to the ease with which those plaid jumpers can be subtly shortened and accessorized to transmit a variety of erotic signals sure to bewitch the most bashful young Jesuit . . . no, no, sorry, I didn't mean that. I've been spending too much time on the Internet, where plugging "school uniforms" into Alta Vista takes one from the dimmer reaches of the garment business to pedophile heaven in about sixty seconds.

Why are uniforms a bad idea? First of all, as the dirty old men at schoolgirls.com would be the first to admit, for girls, uniforms usually mean skirts. Even when pants are an option, they are ugly and uncomfortable, cut for boys' bodies. Now, skirts have their place—I love wearing them myself—but they are terrible everyday wear for young children, which is why, after the preschool party-dress phase, which, as we all know, is genetically determined and proves that women are programmed to do the housework and throw themselves at Presidents, little girls move into jeans and leggings for the grade-school years. Skirts inhibit girls' freedom of movement on the playground and in gym (elementary school kids wear their regular clothes for phys ed, if they have it at all), and even in just sitting on the floor to hear a story. They force girls to worry about protecting their private parts from view, are cold in the winter and—like those Boys' and Girls' entrances of old—they emphasize gender difference to no good purpose. "Do we want to set it in stone that girls are always going to be teased about their underpants?" asks New York NOW's Galen Sherwin, who told me that feminist complaints about forced skirt-wearing got no response from the school board.

Uniforms are promoted as money-savers—an average ensemble costs between $100 and $200. But this is overstated, because kids still need the clothes they wear now, for after school, weekends, church. For school, they still need coats, jackets, boots, sneakers, hairpins, ribbons—so the class distinctions uniforms are supposed to erase can easily be transposed onto those items. Besides, if the Board of Ed can force parents to spend money in particular ways on their children, why not force them to do something that would help their children learn, like buying $100 to $200 worth of children's books? That the Board of Ed has promised to pay for uniforms for kids who can't afford them means that the school system will have even less money to pay for textbooks, library books, art supplies, musical instruments, athletic equipment, after-school programs.

But the parents want them, supporters argue. And many do—especially working-class, nonwhite and immigrant parents, many of whom grew up in uniformed school systems. Not all parents, though. There are big cultural, ethnic, racial and economic differences at issue here, and far from alleviating them, uniforms will exacerbate them. Already, three districts, disproportionately white, have vowed to challenge the uniform policy. Realistically, parents who are liberals, Jews, college professors, editors, artists, psychologists are not going to go along with uniforms any more than they would support school prayer or paddling, other nostrums favored by large numbers of parents.

Despite some claims—most prominently from Long Beach, California, which credits a move to school-color clothing in 1994 with reducing absences and disciplinary problems—there is no research, none, that shows uniforms improve academic performance. I'm suspicious of the Long Beach statistics too: There are years before the color code with attendance figures as good as the years after, and the change in the dress code was part of a whole package of improvements. The N.Y.C.L.U.'s Norman Siegel, NOW's Sherwin and City Council member Tom Duane put it the same, succinct way: Uniforms are a diversion.

They also represent something more, and worse: the regimentation of childhood as preparation for the regimentation of adult life. To the horror of child-development experts, many schools have abolished recess—playing, what a waste of time! An incredible two million children are on Ritalin. To win small grants for their underfunded schools, kids are forced to take part in promotions for Coke and other products, and to watch the execrable Channel One. Like most grown-ups, I'm not thrilled at every item I see on every child, including my own (platform shoes for a ten-year-old, what was I thinking?), but kids acting out through dress is an old tradition, and one that speaks much better for our country than the parts that come clad in uniforms—the military, McDonald's, sports teams, prisons, the police or for that matter the parochial schools and super-elite private schools that have long made their students dress alike.

A nation in which everyone who isn't a securities analyst is a security guard. Is that what we want?

April 27, 1998

VOUCHING TOWARD
BETHLEHEM

There are several intriguing aspects to the story of Jeanne Hearty, the devoted Catholic parochial schoolteacher in Cortlandt Manor, New York, who is being fired this June for marrying a divorced Episcopalian. There's the laity versus hierarchy theme, with parents and parishioners displaying a commonsense realism that, as so often, makes the clergy look demented. And there's the annulment theme, with the Catholic pastor advising Hearty to have her husband get his first marriage, the Protestant one, annulled. That struck me as bold: Should one religion intervene so forcefully into the sacraments of another? What if rabbis insisted that Christians who marry Jewish women must get circumcised? Ouch! By the time Ms. Hearty and her husband came to terms with the metaphysics of retroactively obliterating his first marriage, the monsignor said it was too late. Family values must be served, although it's a little hard to see how those values are fostered by declaring that a marriage never existed—no matter how sincerely it began, how long it lasted, how many children it produced. In her juicy autobiographical polemic, *Shattered Faith*, Sheila Rauch Kennedy, ex-wife (or perhaps not) of Representative Joseph Kennedy, argues against the hypocrisy of annulment as practiced in America, where 60,000—

three-quarters of the worldwide total—are granted each year. She makes a powerful case, if you can overlook the strangeness of a divorced woman talking about "saving the marriage" by preventing its annulment, and a Protestant calling on Rome to resist the lax ways of the American church.

The angle that interests me, though, is the labor angle. Title VII of the 1964 Civil Rights Act specifically exempts religious institutions from its strictures against religious discrimination. They are, for instance, permitted to hire only members of the sect (even for janitorial positions, as the Supreme Court determined in *Church of Jesus Christ of Latter-Day Saints v. Amos*), and to fire employees who violate religious laws in their private lives. Thus, every year Protestant and Catholic schools fire a few teachers for getting pregnant out of wedlock, for making the wrong kind of marriage, for converting to another religion or for voicing a nondoctrinal opinion. In some fundamentalist academies, women teachers are fired when they marry, period, because wives should be at home. The guiding principle is separation of church and state: a bargain by which religious organizations are permitted to follow principles that in the secular realm would be flatly illegal, and in return forgo government funding.

But then was then, and vouchers, which would rewrite this bargain, are now. Usually vouchers and other forms of government aid to religious schools are discussed through the lens of education and social policy. Will vouchers undermine the public schools or force them to improve? What happens to kids left behind? What about quality control—fly-by-night academies that take the money and run? And do private schools really do a better job of educating poor children? On the voucher issue, the Catholic Church has allied itself with some of the most reactionary forces in the land and, through a brilliant P.R. campaign, created the illusion that the main mission of parochial schools is to teach poor minority children who are often not even Catholics. (In fact, even in the New York archdiocese, which includes Manhattan and the Bronx with their large populations of African-Americans and non-Christian immigrants, only 20 percent of parochial school students are non-Catholic; nationally, it's 13.6 percent. Moreover, no more than 13 percent of Catholic schools are even located in the inner city.) The Christian academies of the South, whose main reason for existence is to perpetuate the all-white classrooms outlawed by *Brown v. Board of Education*, are not exactly panting to accept minority students.

Educationally and socially, vouchers are a bad investment. But there's more. Should public funds go to shore up, enhance and even create schools that not only evangelize their students in ways that would never pass muster in a public system—even in Alabama—but that also conduct their hirings and firings without due process, without legal recourse and along lines laid down in the seventeenth century? It's all very well for communitarian-oriented liberals to urge a benign view of religion and heap praise on "faith-based" institutions, to use the squishy religious-right propaganda term that is acquiring general currency. But cases like Jeanne Hearty's are what it all comes down to. Should government subsidize, with your tax dollars, employers who insist on the right to fire workers whose blameless private lives violate a religious teaching? What about expelling students (as in Ohio) who say they believe in legal abortion, or suspending ones (as in Florida) whose cars sport pro-choice stickers? Warm fuzzies obscure hard questions—questions that are on the table now.

The voucher bill for the District of Columbia, recently passed by both houses, answers such questions with a yes. By saying vouchers are not a form of federal aid, it exempts vouchered schools from Title VII's provisions against discrimination in employment and from Title IX, which requires equal treatment of students. If you consider how broadly "federal aid" has been interpreted—even student loans count—and how effective an anti-discrimination tool these Titles have been, you can gauge how much teachers and students stand to lose if the bill becomes law.

May 25, 1998

Race and Gender and Class, Oh My!

Are race and gender and sexual orientation distractions from basic issues of economic inequality and social class? In recent years a number of commentators—Todd Gitlin, Richard Rorty, Michael Tomasky, Michael Moore—have argued in *The Nation* and elsewhere that "the left" has gone up the garden path of "identity politics" when it should be focusing on unifying large majorities around the traditional Democratic Party agenda of strong unions, public spending and respect for patriotism, Christianity and the family. This has been the view of every writer in *The Nation*'s ongoing "First Principles" series except Barbara Ehrenreich, who is, perhaps not coincidentally, the only contributor to it who is not a white heterosexual man.

Unfortunately the debate over "identity politics" has become confused with debates over poststructuralism, cultural studies, postcolonial studies, the social critique of science and whether there are what Judith Butler likes to call "truths with a capital T"— the domain of the so-called academic pomo left. Thus, in his inaugural "ideas" column in *The Nation* two weeks ago, Eric Alterman asserted that there are two lefts: the good, if perhaps overly Whitman-loving "reformist left"—who used to be called liberals before that became a synonym for wuss—and the bad "Foucault-ian" [*sic*] left, whose chief exemplar is, of all people, Eleanor Roo-sevelt's biographer Blanche Wiesen Cook, whose previously unsuspected devotion to the divine Michel came as a big surprise to her fellow historians. The bookmark in my copy of *The History of Sexuality* is still where I left it (page ninety-five) in 1996, but I sup-pose on Alterman's chopping block I'd be sliced as a Foucauldian too, along with—let's see—Patricia Ireland, Barbara Ehrenreich, Adolph Reed, the Last Marxist and his fellow ultraleftists, Doug Henwood, Andrew Hacker, the Mexican American Legal Defense and Educational Fund and the long list of world leaders who have protested the impending execution of Mumia Abu-Jamal. (Like Michael Moore, Alterman identifies supporters of Mumia's cause with the far-out cultural left, as if saving black men from unfairly applied death sentences—remember the Scottsboro boys?—was not one of the oldest tropes of the American left!) On the other hand, I like Walt Whitman's poetry pretty well—too much to be happy to see it reduced to a patriotic anthem, even for Queer Na-tion, which, let's not forget, is where old Walt would probably be residing were he alive today.

Well, never mind poetry. Pragmatism is the byword on the left these days, so maybe a practical investigation of the race-class-gender question is in order. On my street, on the Upper West Side of Manhattan, the co-ops are owned by white people; the rental apartments taken by white, black and brown. Among the homeless, of which the neighborhood has quite a number, I'd estimate eight in ten are nonwhite. I dropped by a local food pantry a few weeks ago, and at least on that particular day the entire clientele consisted of black and Latin women with their children. Does economic class alone explain these facts? At McDonald's, Burger King, Hot and Crusty, Barzini's, Duane Reade, Rite Aid, Food Emporium, the cashiers, servers and cleaners are mostly black and Latin women; the supervisors and managers are men of many ethnicities. In the playground—recently refurbished with city and corporate dollars rounded up by extremely energetic wealthy moms—the baby-sitters are all black, barring the occasional European au pair; the babies are all white. When you do see a white parent, it's more likely to be a woman. In the Lifestyle sections, the Upper West Side may be at the cutting edge of the New Fatherhood; in real life the traditional domestic arrangements are alive and well.

What about schools? My district has two systems: elementary schools attended solely by children of color; and a few zoned schools and programs that, while racially integrated, cater to the white middle class. In this second system, parents raise hundreds of thousands of dollars to buy the "frills"—music, art and gym teachers, computers, counselors, books, science equipment—slashed by budget cuts. Even so, it's pretty spartan, and so we also have many private schools: cheap religious schools for blacks and Latinos, and fabulously expensive day schools and prep schools for whites. Is the racial division merely an accident of class?

I was chatting with a black mother at my daughter's school (public, magnet) the other day who was outraged at Mayor Giuliani's plan to replace school security with armed policemen. I asked her if she worried about cops going after her son. "Every day I worry. Of course! Every single day." How many white mothers of ten-year-old boys live with this fear? And let's not forget race, class and gender on "the left" itself. I work for a magazine that has hired exactly one black and one Asian-American editorial staffer, and one black columnist, in its 133-year history; except for Katrina vanden Heuvel, I am the only woman writer it has nurtured from a fledgling in the sixteen years I've been here, in which time maybe a dozen young white men, and only white men, have been given all sorts of tries at all sorts of topics and slots. The business side has a better record, but even there all the supervisors and department heads are white. How do you explain these interesting data without the concepts of race and gender?

All you have to do is look squarely at the world you live in and it is perfectly obvious that—as a host of scholars and activists, whom Alterman dismisses as "the racism/sexism/homophobia crowd," have documented—race and gender are crucial means through which class is structured. They are not side issues that can be resolved by raising the minimum wage, although that is important, or even by unionizing more workplaces, although that is important too. Inequality in America is too solidly based on racism and sexism for it to be altered without acknowledging race and sex and sexuality. Everybody sees this now—even John Sweeney talks about gay partnership benefits as a working-class issue—except for a handful of old New Leftists, journalists and mini-pundits, white men who practice the identity politics that dare not speak its name.

June 8, 1998

SCHOOL'S OUT

Another semester down the drain, which means the Last Marxist won't be moaning on the couch on Tuesday nights as he reads his students' papers. This term, in addition to his usual philosophy courses, he was handed a class in basic composition—punctuation, paragraphing, organizing ideas or, as he put it, "how to write more than one sentence at a time." His students came from Korea, China, Taiwan, Bulgaria, Nigeria and the Greek and Italian communities of Long Island, a place with its own distinctive folkways and vernacular. In expressivity, inventiveness and charm, the foreign-born students outshone the homegrown ones. Of course, their English was problematic, but they worked hard and it got better. In fact, everyone improved, even the Long Islanders. At semester's end, the L.M. handed out an assortment of grades, reminded everyone to observe the serial comma rule and sent his students off to seek their fortunes.

This was a course for credit, offered without controversy or apology at an expensive (if unprestigious) private university; it was roughly equivalent to what I remember of Mrs. Elliston's ninth-grade English class, and to courses, sometimes called remedial and sometimes called Freshman Composition or disguised as English 101, taught for credit at public and private colleges all over America. But not, beginning next year, at the ten four-year colleges in the

City University of New York system, whose board, acting at the behest of Mayor Giuliani and Governor Pataki, has just voted to ban them. Students accepted into CUNY will have to pass placement tests in reading, writing and math or be shunted off to remediate themselves at the system's community colleges, which are already overcrowded, or in no-credit summer crash courses, which will cost CUNY millions and do not yet exist. Nobody knows exactly how this will work, but overnight, CUNY, with its huge population of mostly working-class, immigrant and minority students, almost all of whom are working and many of whom are women with children, is supposed to become one of the most rigorous and inflexible undergraduate programs in the country. If you are ten years out of high school and have forgotten your algebra or, like many recently arrived Asian immigrants, are struggling with English but doing fine in the universal language of mathematics, you will be turned away.

Behind the CUNY reforms is a stereotype of its students as lazy underachievers fluent in Spanglish, Ebonics and welfare fraud, and of CUNY as a no-standards free-for-all, with students taking half their lives to graduate. Never mind that "open admissions" hasn't existed since 1976; that even in its heyday students who had less than an 80 average were steered into the community colleges; that the time-to-graduate rate (six years) is well within the national norm; that CUNY students pay in tuition and fees ($3,200 a year) a higher proportion of the actual costs of their education than students at most other public universities. Never mind, either, that CUNY students don't prep at Exeter.

Is it unfortunate that students have to learn basic math and English skills in college? Of course. Ask any professor, though, and you'll find that poor preparation is hardly limited to CUNY freshmen. For a lot of reasons, ranging from too much TV to teachers' overreliance on multiple-choice tests, too many kids—and that includes well-off suburban kids—enter college without knowing how to write a paper, how to think about a poem or story, how to spell—much less use the serial comma. "Think of freshman year as a kind of extra year of high school," a colleague of mine advised me when I was teaching freshman composition at an elite college a few years ago, "because that's what it really is now."

Mayor Giuliani argues that high school is the place to acquire the necessary skills for college. In the abstract, sure. But this is the same man who has slashed the public school budget, who supported Governor Pataki's veto of state funds for building new city schools, who tried to use public funds to send low-achieving students to private and parochial schools, and who, when informed that the Constitution disallowed that plan, helped raise the money privately. This is also the mayor who wants to cut $15 million from the public library budget—while giving $65 million in city funds to the Museum of Modern Art, a private institution already swimming in money. For the city's poorest and newest students, the bar is being raised, while simultaneously the rug is pulled out from underneath.

Told about a Vietnamese immigrant student who might never have succeeded at CUNY under the new rules, Herman Badillo, the once-"progressive" city pol who has spearheaded the campaign for the new rules, brushed aside concern. The young man had "drive," he told *The New York Times,* and people like that always rise to the challenge. Maybe so. But should you have to have the makings of an Olympic athlete or a Nobel Prize–winner to go to college? Maybe there are some people whom nothing can deter from their goals. Maybe Herman Badillo is one of those people. But why should a society make education a test of iron determination, like climbing K2? What about all the people who are less like Herman Badillo and more like my grandmother, who dropped out of night school in 1921, bewildered by math class and ashamed of her imperfect English, and for the rest of her life felt unable to claim for herself the education she revered in others?

My grandmother knew Yiddish, Polish, Russian, German, Hebrew and English. She was the only girl in her shtetl to go to high school, and brought all her siblings safely through World War I after her mother died. If a woman like this could be made to feel unworthy of a seat in the classroom, maybe it's easier than Badillo thinks to discourage people who haven't been raised to see college as their birthright.

June 29, 1998

FAR FROM CHILE?

Although women around the globe are slowly gaining access to legal abortion, there remain five countries, all Catholic, that forbid abortion even to save a woman's life—El Salvador, Malta, Andorra, Vatican City and Chile. Absolute prohibition is, of course, the official position of the Catholic Church, much to the embarrassment of the vast majority of the laity here, who do not accept church teachings on sexual matters and, indeed, have abortions at slightly higher rates than Jews and Protestants. What does it mean for abortion to be criminalized, and to such an extreme degree? In answer to that question with respect to Chile, the Center for Reproductive Law and Policy (CRLP) and the Open Forum on Reproductive Health and Rights, a Chilean group, have just co-published a booklet, *Women Behind Bars*. Every soi-disant pro-lifer, especially the ones who claim to be feminists, and every "progressive" who thinks abortion is a marginal matter of "identity politics," should read it.

Does criminalization stop abortion? Chile has 150,000 illegal abortions a year. That's one in three pregnancies, the highest rate in Latin America and slightly higher than the rate in this country. Criminalization means abortion is unsafe. One in five Chilean women who have abortions ends up in the hospital, and illegal abortion is the single biggest cause of maternal mortality—one-third of all pregnancy-related deaths.

Criminalization also means that women go to jail, along with abortion providers and, in theory, anyone who facilitates the abortion. Not all women, of course. Of the 157 whose cases were tracked by the researchers, all were poor—housewives, domestic servants, students, laborers. These are the women who self-abort or go to back alleys, usually to women as poor as themselves, and end up in public hospitals, where doctors and midwives report their injuries to the police, sometimes even withholding treatment until the woman "confesses." Middle-class and wealthy women go to private hospitals and personal physicians, who rightly keep their confidentiality. Eleven percent of the arrested women were turned in by relatives and boyfriends pursuing vendettas. Sixty percent had no legal counsel; in more than half the cases, judges refused bail, so even those eventually acquitted typically spent time in jail; and, since under Chilean law the absence of evidence does not necessarily result in acquittal, 70 percent were left under the legal cloud of "suspension" of their case. Abortion providers were dealt with even more severely, sentenced to up to 541 days in prison.

Fortunately, the United States is not Chile. Even the Christian fundamentalists recognize that the Human Life Amendment, which would criminalize all abortion except to save the life of the mother, is a nonstarter, despite its presence in the Republican platform. "The current right-wing strategy is to erode choice by choosing issues where they can create ambivalence," the CRLP's Janet Benshoof told me—so-called partial-birth abortion, for example, which strikes many as repellent, and which this spring became the subject of a ban in Wisconsin so sweeping and vaguely worded that it briefly caused all the abortion clinics in the state to close their doors. Abortions after twenty weeks constitute only 1 percent of all abortions, and they often involve the most desperate abortion seekers—girls and women whose situation has suddenly and disastrously changed, or who are too poor, too frightened, too socially isolated to deal with their pregnancy sooner. If late abortion is, in effect, criminalized, will these women find themselves in the back alley or jailed for trying to abort themselves, like the women of Chile? Will we see nurses informing on doctors they suspect of bending the rules?

Teenage girls are another target. Currently winding its way toward passage and the President's desk is the deceptively titled Child Custody Protection Act, which would make it a crime for anyone but a parent to take a minor across state lines to get an abortion unless she had first met the requirements of her home state's parental notification and consent laws. Proposals to exempt close relatives—grandmothers, aunts, stepparents—were voted down. Thus, a law supposedly intended to foster family communication will encourage, as in Chile, family disruptions of the most horrendous sort. And, also as in Chile, the fanatical determination to make abortion difficult leads to flagrant violations of constitutional law: Since when is one still subject to one's home state's laws in another state? It's as if Brooklynites couldn't gamble in Atlantic City because casinos are illegal in New York.

The ambivalence-exploitation strategy fits neatly with the right's aggressive moves to restrict women's reproductive options. Only 19 percent of federal employees are covered for all forms of contraception in their health plan, and a battle is shaping up for later this summer over minors' access to birth control under Title X. In June the House voted to bar the FDA from approving RU-486. And there's the continuing scandal of millions of state and federal dollars handed out for religion-drenched abstinence-only sex education, with even usually progressive organizations like the YWCA taking the bait. All of which will ensure that the harder it becomes to get an abortion, the more girls and women will need them. Far from Chile? Yes, for now.

July 27/August 3, 1998

MASTERPIECE THEATER

Angle of Repose, by Wallace Stegner, is a better book than *The Golden Notebook*, by Doris Lessing. *Deliverance*, by James Dickey, is a more significant, richer, deeper and more formally satisfying novel than *Things Fall Apart* by Chinua Achebe. *The Heart of the Matter*, by Graham Greene, is superior to *The Comedians, The Power and the Glory* and *The Quiet American*, also by Greene. Compare, contrast, discuss, dismiss.

Proof that there is indeed progress in human thought is the irritation that has greeted the Modern Library's list of 100 novels, supposedly the best of the century written in English. Eyebrows were raised by the makeup of the selection committee: nine white men (and what men! Daniel Boorstin, Christopher Cerf, Shelby Foote, Vartan Gregorian, Edmund Morris, John Richardson, Arthur Schlesinger Jr., William Styron, Gore Vidal) and one white woman (A. S. Byatt), average age 68.7. Anatomy may not be destiny, but it's no surprise that these particular people produced a list with only nine books by women, three by blacks and four published since 1975.

But that's the trouble with concepts like greatness, excellence and quality. They sound terrific in the abstract; who, after all, champions mediocrity? Once you get down to cases, though, they prove so flexible—What stories matter most and to whom? What is universal, what particular? What makes a prose style pleasurable? How important is pleasure, anyway?—that they leave you in much the same straits as if you didn't have those concepts. Thus, reviewer Richard Bernstein, a big defender of quality and excellence, announces in *The New York Times* that he finds *To the Lighthouse* (No. 15 on the list) "somewhat precious and dull" and prefers *Lord Jim* (85). Harold Bloom, who thunders like a critical Zeus, sets out to make a modern canon and finds that, by an amazing coincidence, much of it has been produced by his colleagues at Yale.

Still, it is hard to imagine the aesthetic criteria by which *Ulysses* is No. 1 and *I, Claudius* is No. 14. What we have here is an arbitrary selection of classics from the earlier part of the century (Joseph Conrad has four spots, Gertrude Stein none); middlebrow novels that seemed profound in high school, like *Brave New World* (5), *The Bridge of San Luis Rey* (37) and *Lord of the Flies* (41); dusty blockbusters like *Studs Lonigan* (29) and *Tobacco Road* (91). Add a few oddities (*Zuleika Dobson*, 59) just to see if anyone's still paying attention, and don't forget lots of books about men: at war (*Catch-22, The Naked and the Dead, From Here to Eternity*), at stud (*The Ginger Man*), on the road (*On the Road*). These are the books you'd find in a bed-and-breakfast run by a retired books editor of *Smithsonian* or *Time*.

Modern Library claims its list is heavily weighted toward the first part of the century because more recent books have yet to stand the test of time. So why call it the century's best books? On the other hand, if the novels had to stand the test of time, what about the listed books that have already flunked, like *Appointment in Samarra* (22)? But what's particularly galling about the list is that the only claim advanced on its behalf is the supposed cultural weight of the panel. If Arthur Schlesinger likes it, it must be good.

Francine Prose argued last month in *Harper's* that fiction by women is slighted in reviews and prizes, which are mostly controlled by men. Women who write about women's lives and "women's subjects" are marginalized, while women who write wild and woolly, formally ambitious, "difficult" books don't tend to get the sympathetic hearing accorded a David Foster Wallace or Don DeLillo. I think she's right, and the Modern Library panel proves it. Imagine a committee consisting of Susan Sontag, Mary Gordon, Margaret Drabble, Elizabeth Hardwick, Pauline Maier, Toni Morrison, Nadine Gordimer, Nell Irvin Painter and Joyce Carol Oates with Richard Howard in the A. S. Byatt role. Don't you think these distinguished writers and scholars would choose a different set of books? Might they not find *The Man Who Loved Children*, *The Making of Americans* and *Song of Solomon* at least as important as *The Maltese Falcon*? Would they have lavished two slots (!) on Aldous Huxley? Might they not have wondered if behind the exclusion of short stories—Flannery O'Connor, Katherine Mansfield, Alice Munro, Mavis Gallant and Hemingway's best writing—lay an idea of the novel as the big burly proving ground of genius, the boxing ring where Tolstoy is world heavyweight champ? Indeed, the mixed group of students in the Radcliffe Publishing Course produced their own Top 100, with one-third women and many writers of color, its own fair share of silly books (*Gone With the Wind*, *Hitchhiker's Guide to the Galaxy*) and, instead of three hard-boiled noirs, three children's classics. It wasn't a good list—doesn't anyone read hard books after they graduate from college?—but it was no less defensible than Modern Library's.

The point of the list? To sell books, of course. Modern Library, its parent, Random House, or others in the Bertelsmann group publish fifty-nine of the hundred. But surely the reason someone would serve as a selector, besides vanity, is the hope of shaping the process of cultural transmission: *Henderson the Rain King* (21), not *The Assistant* or *Pictures from an Institution* or *Their Eyes Were Watching God*. It is pleasant to dismiss canon-making as futile, like King Canute trying to stay the tides of literary history; unfortunately, as Gary Taylor brilliantly demonstrates in *Cultural Selection*, neither genius nor popularity suffices for a book to enter history. It has to fit a cultural narrative. Lists matter. Critics count.

It took me several days to track down a copy of *The Magnificent Ambersons* (100), which a friend found in the Yale Library, from which it has been checked out seven times in thirty years. I'm on the third chapter now, and to my ear its jocular, self-satisfied prose sounds like an endless after-dinner toast. I try to imagine the sensibility that thrills more to the work of Booth Tarkington than to *Mrs. Dalloway* or *Beloved* or *Tono-Bungay* or *Cry, the Beloved Country* or *Malone Dies* or *Memento Mori* or *The Waterfall* or *The Towers of Trebizond* or even the once-celebrated, now totally forgotten novels of May Sinclair, which I love. But I can't imagine it. I give up.

August 24/31, 1998

SEPTEMBER THONG

Like someone caught in one of those recurring dreams of having to retake a long-ago flunked math exam or catch a train naked without a ticket, President Clinton keeps apologizing but can't seem to get it right. But then, it's hard to sound sorry when you're really only sorry about getting caught, and when you know that in the real world, the off-camera, off-the-record world, the things you are said to have done, and have done, are not so unusual. The worst of Zippergate for Clinton, one former Democratic Party activist told me, has to be listening to all those male politicians thunder away while knowing that lots of them are up to monkey business too, and having to ask forgiveness of all those male ministers, priests and rabbis, who probably are no better than they should be either. And then there's the added torture of having to listen while former high-level staffers publicly profess themselves shocked-shocked-shocked. "What you read about the President makes it impossible to respect him," George Stephanopoulos told the *New York Post*. But Clinton's "character flaws" were already on full display in 1992, and so was "the cover-up": In the candid documentary *The War Room*, Stephanopoulos himself is shown cautioning a caller who claims to have compromising information about his man.

I go to maybe four parties a year, but I've heard tons of sexual gossip about President Clinton from people who knew him at Oxford and in law school, from other reporters, from neighborhood politicos. If I am five degrees of separation from someone Monica Lewinsky used to regale with her phone messages back when the President's men were calling her a stalker and a fantasizer, how could people who actually knew him, who moved in his world and worked for him twenty-four hours a day, not know that the President was an energetic philanderer?

Now, thanks to the magic of the Internet, we have a new political term of art: the yuck factor. Kenneth Starr must be betting that "the American people," up until now surprisingly resolute defenders of the public-pubic division of presidential morality, will be grossed out by the particulars of the President's affair with Monica Lewinsky when they see them written down in gynecological black and white. Certainly, commentators have been quick to mock and deride, to profess themselves elaborately puzzled and disgusted by what Jack Newfield of the *New York Post* calls "kinky sex." Adolescent, sure, but kinky? Come on. Aren't journalists supposed to be men and women of the world? The sex acts—or, as the President would have it, nonsex acts—that are supposedly so outré are pretty tame. Not to get too clinical here, a cigar may be an unusual erotic object, but lots of people use toys, purchased or improvised, in their sex play. There's a reason you can buy a vibrator in almost every drugstore in America. Lots of people taste each other's fluids, have sex in the office while others are nearby or while talking on the phone. One friend of mine says his friend Kathy claims men in politics are especially fond of receiving oral favors during phone calls. How does Kathy know? I asked. She used to be "sort of a hooker." It's a big world.

Like the vast majority of "the American people," I'm outraged that the Starr report has publicized the intimate details of the President and Monica Lewinsky's love life. (Of course, I'm fascinated too: You'd have to go to the novels of Philip Roth to find a narrative that more skillfully reveals character through sex.) I don't want to know such things about them because I don't want people to know such things about me. It's that simple. As for sexual harassment, you'll notice nobody's talking about that anymore. The supposed rationale of this whole investigation—if Monica, then Paula—gone in the flash of a thong.

Since this knowledge has been forced upon us, though, the least we can do is resist the heaving tide of sanctimonious flotsam that is sweeping over us. In *Newsweek,* the ever-clueless Dan Quayle compares the President's affair to a high school principal sleeping with a student—never mind that the President is not a principal, the White House is not a high school and Monica Lewinsky is not a student. In the *Daily News,* Letty Cottin Pogrebin calls on Hillary Clinton to "show us how a woman of dignity responds to personal humiliation"—not by getting a divorce, a decision the entire nation could understand and many women would cheer, but by lecturing her husband publicly on fidelity and citing her commitment to her marriage as proof of her superior family values! This is feminism? And what about the ubiquitous handwringing about the President as a poor "role model" and fussing over how to keep the kids away from the evening news? As if ordinary people model themselves on a President. And as if the real stuff of children's nightmares, the luridly made-up face of the murdered JonBenet Ramsey, were not on display at every checkout counter.

Of course, you could say that what goes around comes around. Clinton signed the Personal Responsibility Act, which forces poor women to name the fathers of their children as a condition of receiving welfare. Where was his concern for sexual privacy then? The same bill offered states $50 million annually for classes in abstinence—not birth control, not sex ed—for poor women. Clinton signed the Defense of Marriage Act, and has presided over the ousting of record numbers of lesbians and gays from the military. He fired Joycelyn Elders for talking about masturbation. He's in a poor position to rally the forces of sexual tolerance.

Can anything good come of Sexgate? Less respect for the presidency would be nice, and never has the case for abolishing the ridiculous "job" of being First Lady looked so persuasive. Short of that, we can look forward to a grand public airing of dirty laundry that will leave family values bigots of both parties looking pretty foolish. Dan Burton, scourge of Clinton, adulterous father of an out-of-wedlock child? Helen Chenoweth, militia pinup and sex-smearer of political opponents, a fornicating would-be home-wrecker? When Bill Kristol tells CNN that Republicans are more moral than Democrats because they commit adultery with women closer to their own age, you know that the self-appointed guardians of the nation's hearths are quaking in their boots about the revelations still to come. Well, they asked for it.

October 5, 1998

GREAT BIG BASKETS OF

DIRTY LINEN

After I read *Salon*'s report of Senator Henry Hyde's five-year affair with a married mother of three in the sixties—he was a married father of four at the time—I went to bed thoroughly depressed. Why hadn't Norman Sommer, the story's source, come to *The Nation* while making his dejected and rejected rounds of some fifty news organizations? What are we, I muttered, *Arizona Highways?*

You can imagine how I felt when I learned, the next morning, that *The Nation* had been offered the story in July—and turned it down. In the *New York Press,* our Washington editor, David Corn, explained that he could not establish that Hyde was a flaming family-values bigot while actually conducting the affair, so maybe he wasn't a hypocrite but underwent a postadultery conversion. Our own editorial pages have invoked the specter of "sexual Mc-Carthyism"; indeed, a few issues back a rather prissy item bemoaned the outing of fulminating congressman Dan Burton as the adulterous father of an out-of-wedlock child. Surely, the item tsk-tsked, Burton's deplorable record as chairman of the Government Reform and Oversight Committee should be enough for voters to send him packing. Right. The rest of the media may be Tripping all over themselves in pursuit of scandal—about as hard to find as lumps of coal in a mine, apparently—but not *The Nation*. No shiny black alluring lumps of coal for us. Over here, it's All High-Mindedness, All the Time.

I'm all for high-mindedness; that's why I work here. But in this case, I think *Salon* made the better call. As its editors wrote, "Ugly times call for ugly tactics"—this is partisan hardball now, and if Republicans are going to make a constitutional issue out of President Clinton's extramarital shenanigans, they have to expect the turnabout that is fair play. Apparently, we all need to know that Clinton doesn't believe having oral sex counts as a sexual relationship (a view held not only by Newt Gingrich when he was having a non-marital dalliance but by around 13 percent of all Americans and, at least according to one 1991 Kinsey Institute poll, 60 percent of undergraduates, suggesting that the President may indeed be a man ahead of his time). So why shouldn't we also know that Henry Hyde considers his affair with Cherie Snodgrass a mere "youthful indiscretion," since he was only a stripling of forty-one when it began? "Indiscretion," one might add, seems a rather Clintonian way of characterizing an affair that lasted longer than college, helped destroy the Snodgrass marriage and about which all five family members, some thirty years later, still seem bitter.

But beyond party politics, if family values are going to be used as a legislative and policy weapon by the opponents of sexual liberalism—Democratic, Republican, communitarian, whatever—then why should the hypocrites among them be protected by gentlemen's agreements like the one that both parties recently made denying funds to candidates who attack the "personal, private life" of an opponent? For me, the logic of exposure is the same as it was with the declosing of homosexual politicians, government officials and others who used their positions to support an antigay agenda. Nasty? Maybe, but a more effective reminder of what's at issue here than the high-minded option of praying for your enemies as they burn you at the stake.

I've written several times in this space that public figures should have their privacy as long as they allow the rest of us to have ours. But what if—like Henry Hyde, Dan Burton, Helen ("I've asked for

God's forgiveness and I've received it") Chenoweth and many more on both sides of the aisle—they don't? Year after year, bipartisan swarms of politicians and preachers parade their wives, dogs and children as proof of their sexual rectitude and use this image to lend gravitas to their attacks on the intimate behavior of ordinary citizens: teenagers who are sexually active, divorced people, homosexuals, single mothers, women on welfare, women who have abortions—the majority of Americans, actually. The media fall right into line. Not only post-*Salon* but also after stories by David Moberg in *In These Times*, the *Chicago Reader* and *The New Republic* detailing Hyde's involvement in a $67 million savings and loan fiddle more disastrous than the worst alleged of the Clintons' financial dealings, the press continues to treat Hyde as a figure of high moral probity.

I used to be for privacy, but now I think, Oh what the heck, let it all come out—as, given cable TV, shock radio and the Internet, it will anyway. Maybe that's the only way to get the virtuecrats, the homophobes and censors and woman-blamers and Church Ladies of both sexes to leave us alone. One pundit moaned that the Starr investigation has made it impossible for the President to lecture welfare mothers about their lack of sexual responsibility—that's the best thing to emerge from this whole sorry business. Maybe *Salon* has made it a little harder for Henry Hyde to call teenagers' confidential access to birth control "an egregious violation of family values" and "little less than legitimizing promiscuity." If a teenager, or a married mother of ten, should have to "pay for her mistakes" with childbirth and whatever further disasters that may entail, why shouldn't Hyde—whose eponymous amendment forbids the federal government to pay for abortions for poor women—pay for his "indiscretions" with a bit of public laughter?

And what of the press, which has turned Sexgate into a riot of sanctimonious smut? No shortage of hypocrisy there—editors who rave on about the evils of sex in the workplace but are famous for coming on to each new batch of interns, columnists who call abortion murder but avail themselves of its legality, editorial-office lovers who lambaste the ones in the Oval Office, and lofty commentators who exempt themselves from the strictures they apply to others. Maybe it's best if it all comes out about them too. Maybe if enough dirty linen gets dragged out of enough cupboards and closets, and we can all take a good long look at the great sweat-stained heaps of it lying there gray and steaming in the sun, we'll quietly decide to put it away and allow one another the freedom and privacy we would like to have for ourselves.

October 19, 1998

POVERTY:

FUDGING THE NUMBERS

Are poor people in America poor? According to "The Myth of Widespread American Poverty," a recent "backgrounder" by Heritage Foundation senior policy analyst Robert Rector, the Census Bureau is promulgating a false picture when it classifies some 13 percent of Americans—about 35.6 million people—as poor. "Pockets" of poverty aside, Rector argues, basically the poor are just like you and me. They have less money—at least some of them do—but not so as you'd notice.

"For most Americans," he writes, the word "poverty" means destitution, an "inability to provide a family with nutritious food, adequate clothing, and reasonable shelter." Actually, most Americans do not define poverty in this rock-bottom way. In a 1989 Gallup poll commissioned by the Center on Budget and Policy Priorities and the Population Reference Bureau, Americans placed the poverty line 24 percent higher than the Census Bureau (in 1997 the poverty line for a family of four was $16,400). Still, by making homeless vagrants and coatless children the standard of measurement, Rector is able to suggest that the large majority of poor Americans are in pretty good shape: 41 percent own their homes; 70 percent own a car; far from being undernourished, poor people are likely to be obese. Rector is particularly exercised by the diffusion of home technology. He finds it of note that 97 percent of the poor own a color TV and nearly half have two or more; nearly three-quarters have a VCR; 64 percent own microwave ovens, half have stereos and more than a quarter have dishwashers.

You don't need to be an economist to see what's wrong with those factoids. The home-ownership figure, for instance, reflects the fact that lots of old people surviving on small fixed incomes live in houses paid off in younger days. It may be that 750,000 officially poor people own houses worth $150,000 (not so luxurious given today's real estate market) and that nearly 200,000 lucky poor persons own houses worth $300,000 or more. In a total poor population of 35.6 million this represents a mere 2.7 percent. And who are these people? Working-class strugglers whose gritty urban neighborhood—or lovely rural county—has been discovered by yuppies? Recently divorced suburban stay-at-home mothers who will keep up the mortgage payments for a few years before defaulting?

Emphasizing that the census measures income, not wealth, Rector cites as statistically poor a businessman who earns nothing for the year but has a million dollars in the bank—you know, one of those banks that pay no interest. No one disputes that some people are only temporarily poor. But it's far more likely that the census understates rather than exaggerates the seriousness of poverty—think of the four million people it misses, many of whom are doubled up and illegally housed.

Rector's report brims with misleading references to other countries and other eras. Two-thirds of the poor have air-conditioning, he tells us, whereas thirty years ago only a third of Americans had it. Leaving aside that many high-rises, including some truly dismal public housing, have air-conditioning as their ventilation system, and that in many poor houses what we're talking about is one wheezing single-room air-conditioner, how excited are we supposed to be over this little bit of comfort? Shouldn't the standard of living be higher now than it was thirty years ago? Indoor plumbing used to be a luxury too. Are the poor no longer poor because they have toilets and bathtubs? Similarly, Rector favorably compares the average living space of the poor (440 square feet per person) to the quarters available to the average denizen of Paris (349), Athens (264), Tokyo (170) and Russia (about 100). But these places are famous for their tiny apartments. (And imagine making Russia a standard of comparison! Was the cold war fought for nothing?) Anyway, which would you rather have—three bedrooms in Buffalo or two in Montparnasse?

As for nutrition, Rector conflates figures on different populations to find the poor "super-nourished"—big, tall, fat—mentioning only in passing that 16 percent say they "sometimes" or "often" do not get enough to eat. In other words, more than five million people admit to going hungry well into our history's longest "boom." Home entertainment? America's poor may be able to watch a movie in their living room, but how many can afford to take the family to a movie theater? About crumbling schools, substandard medical care, the prevalence of guns and drugs, the decline of public transport, the fees now charged for many once-free public amenities and the many other ways life—air-conditioning and all—has become harder for the poor than a generation ago, and much more difficult in America than in the rest of the industrialized West, he has nothing to say.

What is poverty? Adam Smith, no bleeding heart, defined it as the lack of what "the custom of the country renders it indecent for creditable people, even of the lowest order, to be without." In my daughter's public school class last year one child would have missed the sixth-grade trip to Washington if the P.T.A. hadn't offered the family a subsidy, since they didn't have the $215 to keep their child from being left out of the most important school event of the year. It's not starving-in-Ethiopia poor or huddling-around-a-bonfire-on-the-Bowery poor. But in the richest city in the richest country in the world, it's poor enough.

Heritage Foundation "research" is so nakedly tendentious it's amazing anyone takes it seriously. Rector's "findings" about air-conditioners and VCRs and overeating have been repeated verbatim in several newspapers, and his Op-Ed summary version in *The Wall Street Journal* ("America Has the World's Richest Poor People") was touted in a *New York Observer* editorial as evidence that capitalism has won the war on poverty. Next stop: talk radio, resentment heaven, where the wealthy poor dining on steak in their electronic-device-laden $300,000 houses will join in angry-white-male folklore the welfare clients who get $36,000 in annual government benefits, the girls who have abortions to look slim in their prom dresses and the gays and lesbians who want "special rights" to molest your kids.

November 2, 1998

Murder, Inc.

On October 23, Dr. Barnett Slepian, who performed abortions, was shot and killed by a sniper while standing with his wife and son in his kitchen in the Buffalo suburb of Amherst, New York. They had just returned from synagogue. Dr. Slepian, father of four, beloved gynecologist and obstetrician, is now a statistic in the annals of anti-abortion violence: the seventh medical practitioner to be killed since 1992 in a wave of violence that last year touched one in four abortion clinics—arson, acid attacks, stalkings, assaults, death threats. His death leaves Buffalo, a city of 330,000, with only three doctors who perform abortions. As I write, two of them are "in seclusion."

Dr. Slepian's death is being treated in the media as an occasion for revelations about the violent wing of the anti-choice movement. It's great copy—in the past two days every reporter in America has probably visited the "Nuremberg Files" Web site, where, on pages decorated with pictures of supposedly aborted fetuses and lines of dripping blood, Neal Horsley of Carrollton, Georgia, maintains detailed personal descriptions, including photos, addresses and phone numbers, of abortion providers, as well as the names and ages of their spouses and children. On his list the names of the wounded are in gray; those of the dead are struck through with a line. Horsley, who calls himself a "journalist," denies that he advocates violence or is in touch with those who commit it, although Dr. Slepian's name was crossed out within hours of his murder. The press has also made much of the fact that Dr. Slepian was the fifth abortion provider (one other in Western New York and three in Canada) in the past four years to be shot in his home by a sniper around this time of year, apparently in honor of Veterans' Day—for Canadians, Remembrance Day—on which the anti-choicers mourn the "unborn."

Did you know about that? I didn't. Did you know that when New York's attorney general, Dennis Vacco, was the U.S. Attorney in Buffalo in 1992 and the city was targeted by Operation Rescue's "Spring for Life," he refused to prosecute Operation Rescue for continuing to block the entrance of Dr. Slepian's clinic despite a federal court order? Did you know that one of his first acts as attorney general was to abolish the Office of Reproductive Rights? Did you know that Senator Al D'Amato, recent recipient of endorsements from the Human Rights Campaign and from the influential black clergyman Floyd Flake, voted against the Freedom of Access to Clinic Entrances Act, or that his last narrow reelection came from votes on the Right to Life Party line?

A *New York Times* poll shows 69 percent of New Yorkers don't even know D'Amato is anti-choice. As *New York Observer* columnist Richard Brookhiser put it, the state's pro-choice majority forces the senator to keep quiet about "the good he does" and his "love of the unborn." But what kind of pro-choice majority needs eighteen years to figure out where its senator stands?

If zealots like the ones who burn down abortion clinics and kill doctors and stalk their children were committing the same crimes against, say, dermatology clinics or convents or the marines, you'd probably know all these things and more. You'd know about the annual White Rose Dinner in Washington at which the anti-choice advocates of murder celebrate their heroes. You'd know that four out of five of the doctors shot around Remembrance Day were Jewish. But then, if anti-abortion violence was treated like the terrorism it is, the perpetrators might have been caught by now. It was the National Abortion Federation, not the police, who warned area doctors of the Remembrance Day pattern.

We are always told that violent anti-choicers are a mere fringe. Obviously, few anti-choicers commit murder or arson. But, as the Matthew Shepard case reminds us, extreme vocabulary creates a climate of moral permission for extreme acts. This is a movement whose main spokespeople, many of them mantled in clerical or political authority, regularly use words like "baby killers," "murder," "holocaust" and "Nazis," thus legitimizing just about anything. After all, the conspirators who tried to assassinate Hitler are heroes. If anti-choicers are so opposed to violence, how come Eric Robert Rudolph, the suspect in the bombing of a Birmingham, Alabama, clinic, which killed a security guard and seriously injured a nurse, has had no trouble swimming like a fish in the sea of the people of North Carolina—even now that he's been charged with the Atlanta Summer Olympics bombing?

At the practical level, anti-abortion violence makes it harder to choose abortion, to find it, to afford it. Like all terrorism, it aims to terrify, in this case not just the amazingly brave doctors who perform abortions now but the doctors of tomorrow who simply choose another specialty, as well as support staff and, of course, women. (One woman whose abortion was delayed when John Salvi made his fatal assault on a Massachusetts clinic was so scared she never went back, had the baby—and is now suing the *clinic* for wrongful birth.)

More subtly, the violence makes "mainstream" anti-choicers look reasonable by moving the margin of debate ever further onto anti-choice turf. In Michigan this summer a prosecutor made a twelve-year-old who'd been raped by her brother a ward of the state to prevent her parents from taking her out of state for a late abortion. In Louisiana, a woman awaiting a heart transplant was denied an abortion by the hospital that had been treating her because the chances of her dying in childbirth weren't over 50 percent. Also in Louisiana, a mentally disabled seventeen-year-old was barred from having an abortion because her father, who had raped her, refused to consent to it. (Both eventually had abortions in Texas, thanks to the National Abortion Federation, which arranged and paid for them.) And these are the "hard cases"—involving rape, incest, risk to life—that the media assure us will always be protected!

The middle ground keeps moving right. And it will do so as long as pro-choicers leave activism to the other side. What can you do? Donate your time. Volunteer for clinic defense—a genuine grassroots political act. Donate your voice. Speak out—everywhere.

November 16, 1998

PRECIOUS BODILY FLUIDS

You religiously employ, with never a slip, some combination of pills, injections, implants, foams, gels and devices for, oh, twenty or thirty years with whatever side effects, inconvenience or expense each of these entails. *Or* you experience morning sickness, weight gain, varicose veins, stretch marks, childbirth and all that follows. *Or* you make your way through a swarm of screaming fanatics to a clinic for an abortion you may feel uneasy about. The ability to select, without legal coercion, from this menu of problematic and expensive alternatives is called having all the power in human reproduction.

That, at any rate, is what men's rights groups are calling it in the wake of the season's weirdest lawsuit, in which an Albuquerque man is suing his ex-girlfriend for breach of contract, fraud and conversion of property—his sperm—because, he says, she got pregnant against his will.

Peter Wallis, thirty-six, says he agreed to have sex with Kellie Smith, thirty-seven, only if she took the pill, and now charges her with "intentionally acquiring and misusing his semen" by secretly discontinuing her medication. Ms. Smith says taking the pill was *her* idea and that the pregnancy was an accident, but in any case, her lawyers argue, Wallis "surrendered any right of possession to his semen when he transferred it . . . during voluntary sexual intercourse." Maybe Ms. Smith should have gotten a receipt.

The theft-of-precious-bodily-fluids charge is too bizarre even for Wallis's defenders—shouldn't he be summoning a demonologist instead of a judge?—but on the central feature of his case, the refusal to have paternity or child support thrust upon him, Wallis has much support. In *Slate*, Scott Shuger opined, "A woman's promise to take charge of birth control and then not doing so remains the only form of monetary fraud . . . that is not only not punished, but is in fact regularly rewarded." If this is fraud, then should we call a man's insincere promise to "put it in for just a minute" assault? In *Newsday*, Sheryl McCarthy said that if Wallis is telling the truth, he should get a child-support reduction: "A deal . . . is a deal," according to the paper's headline writer. So little Taylor Smith should be punished with poverty because of her mother's deception?

Besides the he said/she said nature of the evidence, there's Wallis's mercurial behavior: He urged Smith to abort after learning of the pregnancy, then offered to marry her (she said no because she felt he didn't love her), then threw her out. Now, despite having filed a lawsuit against being named the father, he wants visitation, which is fine with Smith, who, by the way, is not asking for child support but only wants a formal declaration of paternity.

The state, however, may insist on child support in the future. One hopes that the point will not be lost on the judge that a victory for Wallis could mean the end of paternal support for out-of-wedlock children—every man could claim his girlfriend tricked him—and that, therefore, to treat one person's interpretation of a private conversation as an enforceable *contract* would be against the public interest. What's more, contracts must involve mutual obligations and sexual performance cannot legally figure in them, so how is Wallis's princely offer to have sex with Smith if she assumed all the risk of birth control—he does nothing, she does everything—a contract?

If Wallis wins, we will be on our way to redefining paternity as a relationship whose privileges and obligations can be claimed or refused by men as they see fit. Judges have already ruled that a male friend who donated his sperm to a lesbian couple and promised not to claim parental rights could change his mind and insist on visitation against the women's wishes. According to the courts, the importance of fathers to children outweighs the preconception agreement: A deal is not a deal. But what if the mother had fallen on hard times and sued the sperm donor for child support? Every pundit in the country would have written a column about women wanting rights without responsibilities.

Wallis says he insisted on the pill because it was the only method he considered infallible. But according to the Alan Guttmacher Institute, pills have an average real-life failure rate of 6 percent. You'd think that a man determined to control his fertility would know these things and do his bit to lower the risk. It's hard to feel too sorry for a man who couldn't be bothered to wear a condom.

What if Wallis is right, though, and Smith did deceive him? Well, just as pregnancy is a risk of sex, people behaving badly is a risk of love. All the more reason for men to protect themselves. How many women, after all, carry unplanned pregnancies to term because their boyfriends deceptively promise to marry them or otherwise support the child? It's the oldest story in the world! Most of those unwed mothers get no child support, and not much sympathy either. How far would a woman get in court if she charged theft of womb and demanded financial compensation?

In the quest to control their fertility, women have demonstrated in the millions, gone to jail, jammed the voting booth, put up with the side effects and health damage, and even died. They pay hundreds of dollars out of pocket every year for contraception and abortion, and donate millions of dollars and volunteer hours to Planned Parenthood, NARAL and other groups. How many of the men complaining that women have all the reproductive options have written a letter, given a dollar, joined a group, marched or demonstrated to get some for themselves? Every disease and condition in the country has its advocacy organization; where is the big fertile-male campaign to forward the development of a male pill or a reversible vasectomy? Is male-controlled contraception at the top of the list of demands of any men's rights group?

Women assume all the responsibility for birth control, and all the risks of its failure. This isn't women "having all the power." It's men having their cake and eating it too.

December 28, 1998

MAKE LOVE, NOT WAR

Last week will surely go down in history as one of the great ironic moments of our time. In the teeth of overwhelming opposition from every sector of the population except self-described conservative Republicans—the people who like to talk about themselves as "the real America" and everyone else as "the elite"—the House voted to impeach President Clinton for lying about having voluntary, non-coercive, non-sexual-harassment oral nonsex sex. Meanwhile, vowing not to leave office a nanosecond early, the President donned his war bonnet and carpet-bombed Iraq without so much as a phone call to Congress, much less the U.N. Security Council. So much for the contrast leftists, liberals and progressives of all stripes, including me, have been drawing lo these many months between Clinton's grade B failings and the serious breaches of the Constitution committed with impunity by undeclared warriors Johnson, Bush and Reagan. As usual, warmongering is proving to be pure political Viagra. Clinton's ratings, already stratospheric, now rival Christ's and Santa's.

The old-fashioned peace-justice/anti-imperialism activists, whom progressives-lite find so embarrassing, took to the streets in goodly numbers over the weekend and, to their great credit, some unions canceled buses scheduled to carry protesters to an anti-impeachment rally in Washington. But the main objectors displayed by the media were cynical right-wingers who feared being balked of their prey, like newly outed white supremacist Trent Lott—who was slammed for coming "close to the offense of treason" in a *Daily News* editorial because he wondered out loud about the convenient timing of the raids, as if *Wag the Dog* wasn't the joke at every office Christmas party.

From the liberal side of the aisle came the summons to rally round the flag. Richard Gephardt urged postponing the discussion until the bombs were all dropped, because it sent "the wrong message to Saddam Hussein." John Conyers said he was "personally outraged that we would decapitate the Commander in Chief at a time when we are at war abroad . . . to smear [him] when brave men and women are risking their lives for their country shocks the conscience." At war? Did I miss something? Sheila Jackson Lee offered thanks to "our American troops who are now fighting for our liberty." Saddam Hussein threatens our liberty? Is it too much to ask that a member of the House recognize that a President who bombs foreign countries without consulting Congress is the threat to liberty she ought to be worrying about? This is the sort of paranoid jingoism progressives can usually be counted on to mock. Not this time: Jesse Jackson, rallying the anti-impeachment crowd in Washington, passed over the airstrikes entirely in favor of weepy revivalism. Paul Wellstone told dismayed peace activists who staged a sit-in at his St. Paul office that he fully supported the bombing and did not feel called upon to represent Minnesota progressives, reducing to tears people who had worked with and for him for years. Betty Friedan and other feminists who convened in Washington to lobby ex-Speaker-elect Robert Livingston against impeachment registered no antiwar protest. Not a peep from the four hundred historians who signed Sean Wilentz and Arthur Schlesinger's anti-impeachment petition, with its reverential defense of the institution of the presidency, presumably even as embodied in some $500 million worth of airstrikes. Silence also from Toni Morrison, Elie Wiesel, Barbra Streisand and the other intellectuals and show folk who rallied against impeachment the previous week.

So here it is: A nation on the brink of tearing itself to pieces over adultery and miniperjury can unite around bombing "Saddam"—that is, the miserable Iraqi civilian population. People who have argued for months that our national oral-sex fixation has made us look ridiculous abroad don't mind a bit if the rest of the world stands appalled as, once again, a U.S. President ignores international consensus—and law—and plays the bully. If the United States can bomb Iraq because Saddam Hussein fails to comply with weapons inspections, can China bomb Israel, maker of secret nuclear weapons and imprisoner of Mordechai Vanunu, whose only crime was to tell the world about them? Can Russia decide to take on Pakistan, or France attack India? Why is it only the United States that gets to do whatever it wants with *its* weapons of mass destruction?

I've opposed this whole impeachment business for one reason: I don't want the Christian crazies, anti-choicers, gun lovers and racists—let alone Sam and Cokie—to have the satisfaction. I'd rather see them endlessly hoist with their own hypocritical petard by Larry Flynt, hero of the hour, whose million-dollar reward for Republican sexual scandal has already rid the stage of the maritally challenged Livingston. (By the way, his replacement, the ex–wrestling coach J. Dennis Hastert, hailed by the media as a paragon of geniality, honesty and fairness, has a voting score of 8.3 percent from the N.A.A.C.P.—even worse than Livingston's 16.7 percent.) But surely it is possible to protest trumped-up impeachment charges intended to forward some mad crusade against the twentieth century and *also* raise one's voice against the Iraq bombing? Why are "progressives" always the ones who rally around the President without getting—or even asking for—anything in return?

January 11/18, 1998

THE PEOPLE VS. LARRY FLYNT?

I didn't realize how much I was counting on Larry Flynt until I noticed I had spent Monday evening trying to find on the Web or TV a report of the much-anticipated news conference in which he had promised to offer up the names of several prominent right-wingers whose sex lives were at odds with their speeches. Trent Lott with the congressional page in the conservatory? Elizabeth Dole with the Viagra in the bathrooms of the Red Cross? (Don't laugh; one story did quote Flynt as saying not all the miscreants were men.) Arlen Specter with himself in a dress? A friend in the know had told me to expect something big. Coming on the heels of DNA tests that scotched last week's big poli-sex story—Bill Clinton's supposed thirteen-year-old love child—Flynt's promise to send more Republicans off to the Home for Retired Hypocrites was an exciting prospect.

Imagine my disappointment when I woke up the next morning and found out his press conference had fizzled: Bob Barr refusing to answer questions in divorce proceedings about his soon-to-be third wife is not exactly the stuff that screaming tabloid headlines are made of. Flynt's other charge, that Barr, an anti-choicer, went along with his second wife's abortion in 1983, hasn't clicked with the media either. Barr does seem to lead a charmed life, defended against those appalled by his speechmaking before the racist, eugenicist Council of Conservative Citizens by no less a liberal stalwart than Nat Hentoff. Hentoff wrote a column in *The Washington Post* portraying Barr, whose A.C.L.U. rating is 7 percent, as a civil liberties hero because he's against roving wiretaps and the proposed universal medical-data card.

No matter how loftily the anti-Clintonites resist the charge, the impeachment does keep coming back to sex. Maybe it shouldn't; maybe it should be about campaign finance abuses, or about bombing Iraq, as some leftists, including me, have said. (Historian Jesse Lemisch, who wrote a piece in the *Chronicle of Higher Education* attacking the Schlesinger-Wilentz petition, circulated his own petition to that effect at the recent convention of the American Historical Association.) Maybe it should even be about perjury and witness-pressuring, as conservatives keep insisting it is. But it isn't, and more than a year of haranguing and scolding by an army of preachers and politicos and pundits hasn't been able to change that. It's about sex, and everyone knows it. Why else, after all, does Representative Lindsey Graham intone that if senators only knew what was contained in documents that have not been admitted into evidence—documents that, we are given to understand, pertain to other, possibly violent sexual episodes in the President's past—they would vote to convict him in a heartbeat?

That this is all about sex is the only way to understand why the President and the First Lady are the most admired man and woman in the country, with Monica Lewinsky not far behind. The economy doesn't explain it, although Republicans now cling to the idea that Americans are too stupefied by prosperity to rise to the necessary heights of rock-ribbed sternness in service of moral principle. Besides, the people most opposed to impeachment are the people at the bottom, who've benefited the least from the boom and who have suffered the most from Clinton's co-opting of Republican issues.

The Republicans wanted a showdown on "morality" and they got one. In *The New York Times* William Safire devoted an entire column to marveling at the loyalty Bill Clinton inspires from people who ought by rights to be furious with him—his wife, Susan McDougal, Web Hubbell, Harold Ickes and the two out of three Americans who tell polls they plan to stick by the President even if the charges turn out to be true. Safire couldn't come to terms with the obvious answer: People cling to Clinton because they don't believe he's done anything so terrible, given that he is, after all, a politician; and they hate and fear Clinton's enemies, whom they see, correctly, as narrow-minded reactionaries with a dangerous agenda. It's not just that most people have skeletons in their own sexual closets, and if they don't their best friend does. It's that they don't have the strict, old-fashioned beliefs about sexual morality of the anti-Clintonites, and they know, moreover, that many of the anti-Clintonites don't have them either.

Everyone from Maureen Dowd on down has enjoyed attacking feminists for coming to the defense of the President. But on this issue, NOW and Feminist Majority are squarely in tune with American women, and the Independent Women's Forum and the Concerned Women of America—not to mention Linda Tripp and Lucianne Goldberg—are not. Maybe the truth is, women understand that powerful men are mostly creeps, and mostly get away with it. As *The Washington Post* reported in an insufficiently noted front-page story awhile back, the oft-repeated assertion that Clinton would have been quickly fired had he been a corporate CEO is just not true. So if one set of creeps attacks the head creep from the other side, something besides women's workplace equality is probably at issue. The President may not be God's gift to feminism, but as defenders of women, his attackers have no credibility at all.

I'm not going to worry that Larry Flynt has jumped into the ring, distracting "the American people" from listening to their betters—whether it's George Will fretting about the loss of "masculine" virtues like stoicism and hard work (who cleans his house, I wonder?) or the 160 religious academics, most notably Jean Bethke Elshtain, who signed a hand-wringing statement bemoaning the President's convenient deployment of the concept of Christian forgiveness. Of all the weird little corners to focus on! If "politics and morality are inseparable," as they declare, how come we didn't hear from these people when the President was gutting welfare? Or when Reagan was secretly funding the *contras* and illegally mining the harbor of Corinto? If the impeachment proceedings are really not about the Constitution or the presidency or the ability to keep a straight face in public life, much less History and American Destiny; if they're really a referendum on sexual liberalism, modern gender roles and "the sixties," Larry Flynt and the people are on the same side.

February 1, 1999

LET THEM SELL LEMONADE

Let's conduct an experiment but not keep records of the outcome.
That's the Giuliani administration's approach to the vast adventure
in social engineering that is welfare reform in New York City.
Mayor Giuliani has said that he wants his biggest accomplishment
in office to be the abolition of welfare in New York by the year
2000. In 1997 he hired Jason Turner, who helped carry out Wisconsin's draconian welfare reform program, as human resources commissioner to make his dream come true.

The Wisconsin plan, one of the strictest in the nation, requires
women to work at any job they can find beginning six to twelve
weeks after childbirth. Its much-publicized "individualized service"
exists mostly on paper. New York City's plan is similar: People are
expected to fend for themselves—to take any job (or any workfare
assignment), any makeshift child care. (Currently, 39,598 children
are on waiting lists for day care.) But unlike Wisconsin, which has a
small caseload and only 3.2 percent unemployment, New York City
has 745,800 people on welfare and 7.6 percent unemployment overall—10.8 percent among blacks and 12.5 percent among Latinos.
Asked how people could support themselves without welfare if
there were no jobs for them, Mayor Giuliani suggested they become
entrepreneurs: For example, they could "start a lemonade stand."
(Forget for the moment that in his determination to rid the city of

all that is raffish and down-market, the mayor has declared open war on our local microenterprises: sidewalk vendors and artists, hot-dog sellers, squeegee men.) And there's always returning soda bottles.

The city's new "job centers," staffed by "financial planners" (formerly known as caseworkers), have specialized in lowering the rolls by any means possible—and preventing new people from signing on. On January 25 a federal judge ruled in favor of a suit brought by the Legal Aid Society and the Welfare Law Center charging that these centers were depriving applicants of prompt access to food stamps and Medicaid (for which they are eligible under federal law), inventing arbitrary rules barring immigrants or teens or women unaccompanied by their husbands, rejecting anyone who arrived after 11 A.M. and so on. The judge's order, which temporarily stops the conversion of more welfare offices into "job centers," has put a crimp in the administration's plans. But there seems to be no doubt that the mayor will steam ahead with his millennial goal. The city caseload is already down by 36 percent. (Nationally, the numbers are down 44 percent on average, as President Clinton cheerfully announced on January 25.)

What happens to people who leave the welfare rolls? Reporting on a Wisconsin survey recently, Jason DeParle of The New York Times declared the question a draw between "dueling opinions." The good news: 62 percent of former recipients were working when surveyed, and 83 percent had worked "sometime in recent months." But is that news so good? The way I read the numbers, of those who'd been recently employed, 21 percent were unemployed on survey day. So how many of those counted as working are themselves likely to be unemployed before too long? Meanwhile, 47 percent of former recipients had trouble paying their utilities bills, 37 percent their housing costs, 32 percent their grocery bills. Most shocking, 5 percent of former recipients said they had been forced to "abandon their children."

We'll never know how many ex–welfare mothers have to give up their kids in New York, because the Giuliani administration collects virtually no data on what becomes of those who leave the rolls. One state survey showed dismal results: Only 29 percent of those dropped between July 1996 and March 1997 found employment in subsequent months—and employment was defined as earning $100 over three months! In a speech before the right-wing Manhattan Institute in December, Turner published as glad tidings the results of a survey conducted by his office's quality assurance unit. According to the report, co-written by noted antiwelfare political scientist Lawrence Mead of New York University, 39 percent of those sampled found full-time work, 15 percent were part-timers and the median wage was $7.50. That still leaves 46 percent without work, but even that gloomy statistic is understated. Out of an original random sample of 569 individuals, pollsters attempted to contact only those with current phone numbers; of that pool of 211, they located only 126—and it stands to reason that households with paid-up phones and stable addresses would be the ones most likely to be coping. Considering that 400,000 New Yorkers have left the rolls since 1995, it's hard not to see this survey as a social-science confidence trick.

So what *is* happening to ex-welfarites in New York? "Ten to 15 percent—max—are finding their way into paid employment," said Peter Laarman, the pastor of Judson Memorial Church and a leading figure in the fight against workfare. "A fair number have left the city. People are doubling up with friends or relatives, living off someone else's paycheck, returning to abusive partners. By deciding not to monitor, the Giuliani administration has given itself permission to lie. If there were lots of people going into well-paying jobs, the reformers would be pushing those people in front of the cameras. So where are they?"

Supporters of reform claim opponents' warnings of increased misery haven't materialized. Mickey Kaus even suggested in *Slate* that maybe ex–welfare mothers without jobs weren't working because they had married. It's true, you don't see children starving in the streets. But in January 1998, city food pantries turned away 59,000 people. Nationally, hunger is up, homelessness is up, child abuse is way up. And are Wisconsin mothers the only ones who can't afford to keep their kids under the new dispensation?

In New York, such questions are of no official interest. Apparently Giuliani figures that what we don't know can't hurt him.

February 15, 1999

WOMEN'S RIGHTS:
AS THE WORLD TURNS

Does it seem to you that feminism this past year was just one long gargle over the meaning of Monica? That the biggest women's issue was whether oral sex is sex? That too much time, energy and money were given over to P.R. stunts like the White House Project, which invited people to envision a passel of female worthies—including the antifeminist, anti-choice, fundamentalist-friendly Elizabeth Dole—as potential presidential candidates? (By too much time, energy and money, I mean a second, an erg and a penny.)

There have been times this past year when it felt to me as if everything were going backward: From now on, life would consist of an endless right-wing TV talk show, in which professional virgin Wendy Shalit and early-marriage enthusiast Danielle Crittenden would give dating tips to restlessly single Laura Ingraham ("Leopard-print miniskirts? Scary! No wonder guys don't call back"). How different the fight for women's equality seems when you consider the rest of the world, as I just did in honor of International Women's Day, March 8.

The struggle in the United States may seem stymied—as if the big shakeup of the seventies were settling into a new, improved, but still sexist, status quo—but abroad all sorts of things are happening, awful and hopeful. We tend to hear more about the former: You probably know about the Italian judge who ruled that women wearing blue jeans can't be raped because it takes cooperation to pull them off—sparking a protest by jeans-wearing female MPs. But did you know that in India the Supreme Court ruled for the first time that mothers, not just fathers, are the legal guardians of their children? Besides rectifying a major insult to women, this ruling has important implications for divorcing women seeking custody and child support. The same court ruled in January that sexual harassment violates women's rights and need not involve actual touching—a particularly interesting verdict, given that sexual harassment, along with legal abortion, is often seen as the obsession of a handful of U.S. feminists.

And speaking of abortion, recently two countries, Poland and El Salvador, made abortion harder to get. El Salvador, indeed, is now one of the only countries to enact in law the official position of the Catholic Church and the platform of the U.S. Republican Party, both of which reject abortion even to save the mother's life. But eight countries—Albania, South Africa, Seychelles, Guyana, Germany, Portugal, Cambodia and Burkina Faso—liberalized their abortion laws. And before you write those letters pointing out that Cambodian and Salvadoran women have bigger problems than abortion, consider that in Nepal, a desperately poor country where abortion is illegal, there are women, including rape victims, serving twenty years in prison for having abortions. Poor women have always needed liberal abortion laws the most, because they are the ones who seek the back alleys or who self-abort, and they are also the ones targeted by the police.

These positive changes—Senegal, Togo and three other African countries have banned clitoridectomy; Spain's Basque region pays battered women a "salary" to encourage them to leave their abusers—flicker like candles in a darkening room. Islamic fanaticism is sending women back to the Middle Ages. In the Taliban's Afghanistan, women are banned from schooling, jobs, health care and public life, and are subject to beatings and stonings. The new world disorder of the global economy has thrown millions of women and girls into prostitution, sex slavery and, well, slavery as housebound servants in foreign lands. The Asian economic collapse has caused millions of families to stop their daughters' schooling. War, refugee camps, AIDS, poverty, illiteracy, maternal mortality (one in thirty-eight women in Pakistan) are everyday realities for vast numbers of women. Culturally sanctioned coercion and violence persist—"honor killings," genital mutilation, forced marriage, wife murder (half the murders of women in India)—sometimes with a weird postmodern twist. In famine-stricken North Korea, women are being sold across the border to Chinese farmers unable to find wives because sex-selective abortion, female infanticide and neglect have skewed the national sex ratio. And the problem is worsening: A Chinese sampling in 1995 showed that there were about 116 boys four years old and under for every 100 girls that age.

Against these terrible tides, set the movement for women's human rights. Only a decade ago the idea that women's rights are human rights was dismissed as sentimental Western cant: Human rights pertained to state action, not to family, marriage or community norms, however cruel and oppressive. Today, academics—and they usually are academics—who compare clitoridectomy to male circumcision or footbinding to high heels are the ones who seem indifferent to reality. And slowly, as the result of immense effort on the part of millions of women and men, a new set of social and moral paradigms is being articulated.

On International Women's Day, the United Nations opened its first-ever session on violence against women with a teleconference broadcast around the world. "It was something to see," said a friend who attended, "all those heads of state having to listen to women tell them about the harm their laws had done to them."

I don't want to make too much of what is at least in part political theater. Behind all the talk about "empowering women" how much really changes? The Cairo conference in 1994 was supposed to overturn the population-control approach to family planning in favor of one that placed women's "empowerment" at the center, but how many clinics in Asia (or the United States) have shifted course? It will take a decade, Barbara Becker of the Center for Reproductive Law and Policy told me, or maybe even two, for practices to change. But little by little a language is developing that did not exist before, one in which new hopes can be voiced and new demands made. It's a language we could learn to speak in the United States as well.

March 29, 1999

A BRONX TALE

You're nineteen, single, on welfare. You breast-feed your baby because you know breast is best. When the baby fails to gain weight, your mother says not to worry, you were even smaller at that age. Twice you take the baby to your Medicaid HMO for checkups, but you're turned away: The baby's Medicaid card hasn't arrived in the mail yet. Finally, after two months, you rush the baby to the hospital, but it's too late; the baby, now weighing barely five pounds, dies in the taxi. A tragedy, surely, but manslaughter?

A lot of people had a hand in the death of little Tyler Walrond of the Bronx, but only one was put on trial: his mother, Tabitha Walrond. This is family-values America, where mothers and only mothers are held responsible for their children's well-being, even as fathers decamp and communities and social services fall apart. Walrond, prosecutor Robert Holdman argued in what must be one of the most misogynous accusations on legal record, was a woman scorned who starved her baby to get back at his father, Keenan Purrell, who abandoned her in mid-pregnancy.

The evidence of Walrond's malevolence toward the baby? Well, on first being dumped she considered having an abortion—as if a just-rejected pregnant teenager's momentary thought counted for more than the fact that she not only didn't have an abortion but was an exemplary prenatal patient—went to all her doctor's appointments, attended Lamaze class faithfully, decided to breast-feed, an unusual choice among poor urban women and, after this trial, likely to become even more so. Holdman brought out Purrell and his mother, who made allegations that were shown in court to be untrue: that Walrond had tried to prevent Purrell from seeing his son, that she ignored the baby, that they had given Walrond money. The prosecutor didn't explain why the father, or his mother, weren't also to blame for Tyler's death. They could have whisked him off to an emergency room themselves if they were as worried as they later claimed to have been.

And then there were the doctors. Walrond's lawyer, Susan Tipograph, showed that Walrond's numerous doctors failed to give her appropriate information, even though the breast-reduction surgery she had undergone at fifteen was a major risk factor for breast-feeding failure. Most culpable of all, though, were the Medicaid managed-care system and its clinics. By law, babies whose mothers are enrolled in Medicaid are supposed to be automatically enrolled as well. But no prosecutor full of baby-protection zeal thought to bring charges against HIP, Walrond's plan, though its contract with the city stipulates that it will see babies within two weeks of birth, card or no card. "There's no reason for that baby to have died," Elisabeth Benjamin of the Task Force on Medicaid Managed Care told me. "This is a tragedy of privatized health care. The name of the game is to deny care."

The jury rejected the murder-by-breast scenario but convicted Walrond of criminally negligent homicide after a mere two and a half hours' deliberation. "No matter what, she was the mother," one juror told *The New York Times*. "She was failed, but she should have been strong enough to do more." That's the pure spirit of the Personal Responsibility Act talking, but it rings a bell, I'm sure, with a lot of well-meaning liberal middle-class people who, like the jury, were horrified by photographs of Tyler's wizened day-old corpse (Tipograph was unable to enter into evidence photos of the baby taken shortly after death, in which he looked less ghastly). How could Walrond not have seen that her son was starving when she saw him every day? How could she not have found some way to get to a doctor?

It all seems so unlikely from the perspective of people who know how to demand what they need—who know what phone calls to make and to whom to complain. But is it so unlikely? If you live with someone every day, you can miss or explain away even quite alarming gradual changes—denial is a powerful force. And, according to Dr. Marianne Neifert, a lactation expert, starving babies can look more or less OK for quite a while, and then crash suddenly. After all, whatever happened with Tyler, Walrond's mother, who also saw him every day, missed it too.

Once the scorned woman hypothesis is off the table, there's no reason to see Tyler's death as anything but what it was—a tragedy set in motion by ignorance, poverty, social isolation and a deliberate policy of depriving the city's needy of social services. It should never have been prosecuted. Last spring in Brooklyn, the district attorney wisely decided against going forward with the very similar case of Tatiana Cheeks, another poor young black woman whose breast-fed baby died.

"People think of breast-feeding as an intuitive, natural thing," Galen Sherwin, head of NYC-NOW, told me. "But we're not cats." Advocates of breast-feeding have done a good job of making women feel guilty if they don't opt for it, but there's a reason that it's mostly prosperous women who choose it and stick with it. (See Linda Blum's *At the Breast: Ideologies of Breast-feeding and Motherhood in the Contemporary United States,* just out from Beacon, for an enlightening discussion of the cultural and social contexts of breast-versus bottle-feeding.) You need a lot of information and a lot of support, and we're not living in villages where these things are part of the social fabric, where breast-feeding is a part of life and every woman is able to instruct new mothers. Even well-off, well-educated women can run into trouble without realizing it. Tipograph told me she received many letters from such women with stories much like Walrond's. The difference is that those women had private pediatricians, and their babies' problems were caught in time—although sometimes only just.

The women's movement is always being accused of not caring about poor women of color, but virtually the only advocates for Walrond have been feminists: NYC-NOW, which staged demonstrations at the courthouse, the N.Y.C.L.U. Reproductive Rights Project, City Council member Ronnie Eldridge.

June 14, 1999

WAR AND MEMORY

Regret to Inform, Barbara Sonneborn's documentary about American and Vietnamese widows of the Vietnam War, was a standout at the Human Rights Watch Film Festival in New York. In candid and complex interviews, the Americans are soft and a bit clueless, cherishing memories of early love and not eager for answers to the questions about what their men had done; the Vietnamese, tougher, deeper, more politically astute. Sonneborn intercuts their words with film of her rail journey through the hallucinogenically beautiful Vietnamese countryside to Khe Sanh, where her own husband met his death, and with documentary footage of the atrocities perpetrated by the U.S. and South Vietnamese armed forces—torched villages, maimed and murdered women and children, beaten prisoners, Agent Orange. One old Vietnamese woman describes losing nine members of her family, including her husband and children, to the war. Others describe being tortured, watching friends die in agony, losing their husbands to prisons from which they never returned; they tell stories of children forced to witness their parents' brutalization, of turning to prostitution to survive, of a five-year-old boy shot when thirst drove him from a bomb shelter where he was with his teenage cousin—who, now middle-aged and in California, still blames herself for letting him go.

Those atrocities defined the war for millions in the sixties and seventies, but who talks about them now when the "lessons" of Vietnam are chalked on the policy blackboard? Vietnam is a "mistake," a "tragedy," a "failure." Aging boomers call for restoring the draft; the twenty-four-karat-gold plating of Henry Kissinger's reputation gets more lustrous with each volume of his self-serving oeuvre, with the doctor regarding himself vindicated by William Shawcross, who in 1994 wrote that he feels his important antiwar reporting was soft on communism. Nobody talks about strategic hamlets, or napalm, or throwing prisoners of war out of helicopters, or the Phoenix assassination program, or anti-Viet racism, or the deaths at U.S./ARVN hands of at least three million "gooks," two-thirds of them ordinary people in a nation of thirty-eight million. At journey's end, Sonneborn finds that her husband died in a freefire zone, where soldiers were told to shoot anything that moved. Of the area's 167 villages, all but 30-odd were totally destroyed.

For a decade, millions of Americans believed that going thousands of miles away to a country most could not have located on a map the week before was an act of self-defense. They did not distinguish between their country and its government, as Americans routinely expect citizens of other nations to do. U.S. soldiers, by and large, did not revolt, throw down their guns, refuse orders that violated the Geneva conventions, nor do we honor today the ones who did, who fragged their officers or deserted.

I think Barbara Sonneborn meant to tell a moving story about the losses women endure in war, about their strength of character and hopes for peace. What the movie said to me was more specific: that not so long ago, Americans did the same things for which we now place the Serbs in Kosovo beyond the pale of humanity. Like the Serbs with their "war psychosis," their "victimization mentality," millions of Americans believed we were endangered by people who posed no threat at all. Like the Belgraders quoted in news reports, lots of Americans denied the massacres or justified them by appealing to the confusion of war, the stress of combat or the lone crazed soldier. Except for the case of Lt. William Calley, who served only four years under house arrest for My Lai—there were no war-crimes trials of U.S. soldiers, much less of the men who set the policies and gave the orders. "We weren't the murderers," said one Viet vet after the film. "The people at the top were the murderers. We were just their tools." O.K., but would you accept that from a Yugoslav draftee?

We never made good on our moral debt to Vietnam. Kissinger promised financial aid; it never materialized. The army never accepted its responsibility to the thousands of Amerasian children fathered and abandoned by U.S. servicemen, or to their mothers. Land mines and leftover bombs still kill or maim about a thousand people every year. The U.S. government, which could easily spend some of its vast stores of humanitarian energy dismantling them, won't even sign the anti-land-mine convention. You would think our history in Vietnam would give us special insight into Serbia—another country whose young men do terrible things that don't register strongly enough back home; where many people have trouble withholding loyalty from their government; where people think more about what's done to them, in fantasy or reality, than about what's being done in their name; where resisting war makes you an outcast, not a hero.

July 12, 1999

NATURAL BORN KILLERS

It didn't take long for the press to connect twenty-one-year-old white-supremacist multikiller Benjamin Smith with the all-purpose explanation du jour: violent entertainment, in this case the computer game Dungeons & Dragons. This replaces the explanation, given by his mentor, Matt Hale, leader of the World Church of the Creator, that Smith was driven to shoot minorities in the Midwest over the July 4 weekend—six Orthodox Jews, at least three blacks, two Asians—because political correctness prevented him from expressing his racial theories verbally. It turns out Smith expressed himself verbally quite a bit: His views were widely known to his fellow students at Indiana University. He expressed himself physically too: He had been forced to withdraw from the University of Illinois after beating up a girlfriend in the dorm. As with the Columbine killers, there were plenty of warning signs. One neighbor from Wilmette, Illinois, where the Smith family lived during Benjamin's teen years, said she was afraid of him and was relieved when he moved away.

Of course, even if Dungeons & Dragons had totally warped Smith's mind, which I doubt, you can't kill many people driving around with a virtual sword. For that you need guns. In the wake of

Columbine, it looked for a moment as if Congress would be shamed into at least token gun-control legislation, but in the end John Dingell—a Democrat, for those of you who still like to blame the Republicans for all our woes—saved the nation from the dreadful prospect of having to wait for a background check before buying a personal arsenal from an unlicensed dealer at a gun show. The kind of serious, comprehensive legislation it would take to make a significant dent in the easy availability of firearms—a feature unique to the United States among Western industrialized nations—is decades, maybe lifetimes away.

So forget gun control. Media violence is the trendy cause now. In *The Washington Post*, Michael Massing declares it's beyond question that the media are connected to real-world violence, although I find it hard to believe that the movies he singles out—*L.A. Confidential* and *Pulp Fiction*—had anything to do with the inner-city violence that he says shaped his views: crackheads throwing children off rooftops, teens killed in penny-ante drug deals (besides, isn't rap music the usual suspect here?). Still, you won't find me defending art films loaded with stylized killing, hyperviolent action films, super-gory horror flicks, misogynous heavy metal and rap, violent computer games, slap-happy cartoons, sadomasochistic fashion spreads or sexist music videos. Whether or not you can connect this cultural effluvia to specific acts of violence in a one-to-one causal way, thousands of hours of it can't be good for the soul.

But realistically, what does one do with that insight beyond curling up with a good book? The government is not about to censor pop culture, a huge commercial enterprise, any more than it's about to enact real checks on guns, another huge commercial enterprise. And there's another problem with fighting media violence. You wouldn't know this from the way the issue is presented by proponents of media uplift, but most Americans don't disapprove of the current media fare—they love it! The anti-slash-and-sleaze constituency is small and getting smaller. According to a recent Associated Press poll taken during the post-Columbine debate over media violence, only one-third of Americans said violence is the biggest problem with current movies. (The same number cited ticket prices.) And the 40 percent who said violence would make them less likely to see a film is down from the 60 percent who gave that answer a decade ago. Moreover, most of those in that 40 percent are women, old people and people who hardly ever go to the movies.

It skews the issue to present the problem as one of "youth culture"—worried, disapproving parents falling asleep over Preston Sturges reruns while their crazy kids watch *Natural Born Killers* with one eye and update their racist Web site with the other. Much of America is deeply fascinated by violent entertainment. The whole family watches *COPS* and *NYPD Blue* and *Homicide*, and idolizes athletes, musicians and actors with records of brutality against women. Massing mentions *Home Alone*, which struck me too as containing rather a lot of supposedly humorous physical cruelty for a movie aimed at small children. But so what? *Home Alone* was the eleventh biggest-grossing movie ever.

Or take wrestling. It's violent, racist, sexist and witless—Americans can't get enough of it, and now their kids can't either. Recently, a seven-year-old in Dallas killed his three-year-old brother when he tried a wrestling move he'd seen on TV—a pretty clear demonstration of a connection between media violence and the real thing—but how far do you think a campaign to confine televised wrestling to the postbedtime hours would get? The idea that Americans have been imposed upon by entertainment moguls who have seized control of culture is much too simple. That's why Massing's proposal that "we" shame Hollywood into cleaning up its act won't work. First, Americans would have to stop watching. Look at the Southern Baptists. This rich, politically powerful organization of millions hasn't been able to bring off its boycott of Disney. The urge to ride Space Mountain is even more powerful than homophobia.

Violent and stupid entertainment is popular because it corresponds to reality, which is often violent and stupid. Take a society in which half the population is armed; with astronomical rates of rape, domestic violence, child abuse and murder; which fights one war after another and glories in it, has a bad case of jock worship and Lord knows how many white people marinating in racial resentment like Benjamin Smith; in which the vast majority of parents hit their kids and think that's fine. Take a society in which people are told they should be able to have whatever they want, but only if they can pay for it and if they can't they're losers. Why wouldn't the inhabitants of such a society thrill to watch their psychosocial dramas enacted on screen?

It's always the same story: We meet the enemy and he is us.

July 26/August 2, 1999

No Males Need Apply?

Does feminist theologian Mary Daly have the right to exclude men from her "Introduction to Feminist Ethics" course at Boston College? Gloria Steinem, Ellie Smeal and other well-known feminists say yes, she does, and so—to my complete astonishment—does *The Nation,* which ran Laura Flanders's "Feminist De-tenured" as a signed editorial. Title IX, which guarantees equal access to education for both men and women in schools that receive federal funds, has probably opened more doors for girls and women than any other statute on the books. Now it's being tossed aside in a casuistical orgy of special pleading that confirms every media stereotype of feminists as separatists, victimologizers and hypocrites.

A bit of background. This past spring seventy-year-old Mary Daly was summarily de-tenured by Boston College when she refused, as had been her practice for a quarter-century, to admit a male student into her feminist ethics course. In previous years Daly had accommodated the occasional male by giving him a private tutorial. But twenty-two-year-old Duane Naquin—perhaps because he was a Young Republican backed by the right-wing Center for Individual Rights (C.I.R.)—insisted on being a full member of the class and threatened to sue. When Daly would not admit him,

Boston College struck her courses from its course guide and insisted—falsely, Daly says—that she had resigned.

Daly's lawyer, Gretchen Van Ness, argues persuasively that Daly has been denied due process by the college (at least I found her arguments persuasive; Middlesex Superior Court judge Martha Sosman was unimpressed and ruled against Daly in May). But procedural violations are not why Daly's case is a cause célèbre. If administrators fired or pushed into retirement a male professor who barred women from his class on male small-group psychology, or nonwhites from his whiteness studies seminar, I doubt anyone but his lawyer and the American Association of University Professors (which has sided with Daly) would be interested in the niceties of his case.

Daly's supporters portray her as a radical feminist star forced to struggle alone against the patriarchal Jesuits of Boston College. (For the record, BC has a majority female student body at undergraduate and graduate levels; its tenured arts and sciences faculty is 26 percent female.) Star or no—Daly's books after *Beyond God the Father* strike me as self-indulgent gibberish, and her essentialist views of gender are far removed from contemporary scholarship—she's certainly had star treatment: no tedious committees, fourteen leaves of absence in thirty-three years of teaching and tacit permission to violate Title IX. ("A nerdy turdy legalism," Daly called Title IX—this from a woman who wants the world to care about the fine points of tenure law!) Then she was caught, however, and the administration had to back away or risk being sued itself. This, I submit, was the moment for Daly to gracefully accept that pesky male instead of falling on the rusty sword of seventies-style separatism and embarrassing the whole feminist movement.

But that would violate Daly's belief that a coed classroom is not a "safe space" for women. "Even if there were only one or two men with twenty women, the young women would be constantly on an overt or a subliminal level giving their attention to the men, because they've been socialized to nurse men," Daly told reporters. Amazingly, this insulting generalization has become "the" feminist position—never mind that there are thousands of feminist professors, and, as far as I know, Daly is the only one who bans male students. Surely a professor of Daly's stature and experience should be able to handle the psychodynamics of having—horrors!—one man in her seminar? How odd that this fire-breathing feminist assumes any man would inevitably dominate the classroom, that students and professor alike are helpless before the awesome power of testosterone to compel feminine deference. That really *is* "victim feminism." Whatever happened to feminism's insistence on rejecting gender stereotypes?

As for Naquin's being antagonistic and possibly even fomenting lawsuits—if Daly had accepted students regardless of gender, she would have been in a better position to exclude him as an individual; at worst, she would have had one student who was a pain in the neck. Big deal! Everyone who teaches, as I myself sometimes do, has the occasional hostile or arrogant kid in class. Why should Mary Daly get to teach only students who already like her?

I'm not arguing that single-sex discussions aren't sometimes useful—for both sexes. But an academic course is not group therapy; it's the place for vigorous discussion, where students should learn to deal in an adult way with a wide range of views, including ones that make them, to use their favorite word, "uncomfortable." It's also the place for which all students pay tuition. If Daly had wanted to provide students with an all-female "safe space" she could have hosted discussions in her living room.

Much has been made of C.I.R.'s involvement. It is indeed galling that these reactionaries should seize the moral high ground. C.I.R.'s role makes Daly's behavior even more irresponsible. In a world in which right-wingers are trolling for lawsuits, potential targets have to mind their *P*s and *Q*s. Daly had had previous run-ins with the administration over this very issue. How could she think she could violate established law forever? And contrary to what some of her supporters claim, it is established law. A professor unilaterally deciding to run a women-only class is not at all the kind of narrowly tailored compensatory goal Justice Ruth Bader Ginsburg mentioned as possibly justifiable in her majority opinion against Virginia Military Institute's males-only admissions policy.

How smart is it for feminists to rally around Daly? Title IX works in women's favor 99.9 percent of the time—it's fueling the explosion in women's college athletics even as I write—and that's why C.I.R. wants to get rid of it. By refusing to play fair when egalitarianism means giving something up—even something as eccentric as letting teachers ban men at will—feminists give credence to their already considerable public reputation as expert practitioners of the game of heads I win, tails you lose.

August 23/30, 1999

WEIRD SCIENCE

My first thought upon hearing that the Kansas state education board had removed evolution from its mandatory curriculum was: Go ahead! Be like that! Handicap your kids for life. Let the "secular humanists" have all the good colleges and get all the good jobs. I know this was an unworthy thought—Darwin's demotion was a political maneuver by Christian conservative politicians, not a grass-roots effort by Kansas parents, much less their unfortunate children—but there you are. As a rootless cosmopolitan, I get tired of being expected to pay homage to "the heartland" as the moral center of the universe.

And creationism, honestly! In 1999! All summer, serious newspapers have felt it necessary to publish casuistical Op-Eds by apologists for "creation science"—and the Old Testament is the only biology textbook you really need, these clever fellows always forget to add. What's going on? As Stephen Jay Gould pointed out in *Time*, in no other Western country is the teaching of evolution regarded as controversial. Throughout the world, one way or another, most Christian denominations have managed to reconcile belief in God with belief in the mechanisms of natural selection. A French or German or Scandinavian politician who called for students to entertain as a reasonable deduction from existing evidence the proposition that Earth is at most 10,000 years old would be bundled off to a mental hospital.

Creation science is religion, no matter what its apologists say; let's start from there. No one looking at the physical record would determine that dinosaurs and humans co-existed, that fossils represent the creatures drowned in Noah's flood and so on. The only way those notions would even occur to you is if you considered the Bible an unerring historical document—but why would you think that unless you accepted the Bible as divine revelation of factual truth? The *Topeka Capital-Journal* asserted that "creationism is as good a hypothesis as any." Because no human witnessed the beginning of life on Earth, one guess is as good as another. Of course, a great deal of science involves making inferences about phenomena no human has witnessed—the birth of stars, the interior of the sun, subatomic particles. And, as one wag asked in a letter to *The New York Times,* would creationists argue that the vast majority of crimes, which occur unwitnessed, should not be prosecuted?

As Theodore Schick Jr. and Lewis Vaughn explain in their wonderful book *How to Think About Weird Things,* the theory of evolution fulfills all the scientific criteria of adequacy: It is falsifiable, it predicts, it leads to further discoveries, it is conservative, and it fits what we already know. That isn't to say a better theory might not come along someday, but it won't be creationism, which fails all those tests in spades. To call creationism science (or to call evolution religion, as *National Review* seemed to be doing when it recently said Darwinism and creationism are equally "fundamentalist") is to destroy the whole concept of science. After all, if the creationists are right, not just biology must go but also geology, archaeology, astrophysics, physics; so must radiometric and carbon-14 dating. Indeed, creationists should be protesting every natural history museum in the country that uses public funds to promulgate the "secular humanist" doctrine of geological time.

In a better world, science teachers would teach creationism along with evolution as an exercise in critical thinking. But critical thinking is not what creationists are interested in. Nor, so far, are the usual people who love to weigh in on educational scandals. In fact, that's one of the most interesting aspects of the creationism flap. Al Gore, who bills himself as Mr. Science, finds himself unable to speak out on Kansas, saying that the decision to teach evolution should be left to local school boards (the same position taken by George W. Bush). And where are the doughty soldiers in the science and education wars who profess to uphold standards and truth against the irrationalist hordes? Where are the customary bemoaners of educational "fads" and politicized curriculums—Michael Kelly, William Buckley, Bill Bennett, Maureen Dowd? Sparring on ABC with a refreshingly rational George Will, William Kristol said teaching creationism was understandable enough.

If, as so many commentators maintain, it's good for black students to read *Huckleberry Finn* even if Huck's use of the n-word hurts their feelings (and I would say it *is* good), why isn't it good for the children of fundamentalists to study modern biology even if that unsettles their faith? If standard biology is adequate to show that breast implants don't cause autoimmune diseases, why is it useless to help us decide if eohippus is the ancestor of the modern horse? The ferocious defenders of the scientific method were quick to take to the word processor to congratulate Alan Sokal when he succeeded in publishing a parody of left-academic science critique as the real thing a few years ago. They don't seem to see that the mainstreaming of creationism presents some of the same issues as the "postmodernism" or "antifoundationalism" they despise: Both stances reject the idea of the "master narrative" of science based on reason, evidence and expertise in favor of cultural relativism; both accept the idea that "truth" is social and political and provisional, not "out there." For both, knowledge is a social construct. Creationism is just as political, and just as damaging to real education, as "Egyptian mathematics" and other self-esteemful tidbits tossed out by schools to placate powerless but angry constituencies or flatter liberal psyches. But it's infinitely more likely that incontrovertible evidence will someday show that the Egyptians really were black, that the Iroquois really did inspire the U.S. Constitution and that women ruled in the Old Stone Age than that creationism will ever meet the standards of verifiability by which the contents of our nation's textbooks are supposedly judged.

Maybe the science wars in academia focus on the "left" because they are partly a struggle over academic turf. In the universities, fundamentalists are irrelevant. In the real world, though, fundamentalists have lots of power and lots of votes, so no one wants to alienate them. Just ask Al Gore and George W.

September 20, 1999

POLYMARITALLY PERVERSE

I've always vowed I would never be one of those people—and you know who you are!—who cancel their A.C.L.U. membership in a fit of pique over a single issue. So I'll just say that I was surprised to learn recently that the organization has a policy opposing laws against polygamy: "The A.C.L.U. believes that criminal and civil laws prohibiting or penalizing the practice of plural marriage violate constitutional protections of freedom of expression and association, freedom of religion, and privacy for personal relationships among consenting adults." A footnote explains that "plural marriage" is a gender-neutral term.

Unfortunately, in the real world, it's not. The A.C.L.U. policy was framed in 1991 in response to a child-custody case in Utah, where at least 25,000 fundamentalist Mormons still follow the path of Brigham Young, husband of twenty-seven, and where "plural marriage" means only one thing—polygyny, or one man with multiple wives.

Depending on whom you talk to, polygyny is either openly tolerated in Utah—until this year no one had been arrested for it in half a century—or severely stigmatized. Polygyny became a hot topic there last year when a sixteen-year-old girl belonging to the secretive Kingston Order sought to leave her "marriage"—she was her uncle's fifteenth "wife"—and was beaten unconscious by her father. After a major brouhaha—Republican governor Mike Leavitt seemed surprised to learn that polygyny was illegal—the uncle was convicted of incest, and the father of child abuse. Polygyny itself was never at issue. The girl, who had been pulled out of school in the seventh grade, is now in protective custody, catching up on her education and being a teenager.

The girl's story is not uncommon, says Carmen Thompson, a former polygynous wife who directs Tapestry of Polygamy (www.polygamy.org), an eighteen-month-old volunteer organization that assists women in flight from polygynous marriages. Tapestry has aided some three hundred "refugees" just since the start of this year, and their stories are hair-raising: incest, abuse, children who have no birth certificates and are never sent to school, threats of "blood atonement" (death) made to fleeing wives. This reality recedes from view, though, when you put on libertarian glasses. Then the important testimony comes from Elizabeth Joseph, poster girl for "feminist polygamy." As she put it in a *New York Times* Op-Ed, you get to have your career, a co-wife watches your kids and the children have a strong paternal authority figure. A feminist touting the virtues of patriarchal dads makes me a bit suspicious, but in any case, Joseph, a lawyer and radio-station operator who isn't a Mormon and who entered her "marriage" with one man and seven other women as a mature adult, is hardly a typical polygynous wife.

What's wrong with legalizing polygyny? Consider the phrase "consenting adult." After much Sturm und Drang, Utah raised the age of consent last year from fourteen to sixteen—fifteen with the permission of a judge, who is barred by law from asking questions that might uncover coercion. Girls cannot refuse to be "home schooled," and school authorities don't insist that such schooling means math and history and English and science, with progress measured by tests. Instead, they look the other way when girls are pulled from school to work for free in clan businesses, as was the Kingston girl, while awaiting the summons to marry.

One Utah Civil Liberties Union board member said my arguments were "ethnocentric." Leaving aside the appropriateness of the term (last time I looked, living in Utah was not an "ethnicity"), nobody would argue that cultural diversity is an absolute value overriding every other consideration. No one I spoke with at the A.C.L.U. had a problem with rejecting religious or cultural defenses of child abuse, domestic violence or female genital mutilation. "Violence is different," A.C.L.U. director Ira Glasser told me. But if the A.C.L.U. is going to draw a line at all, why only there? Why not see polygyny as a human rights violation, a contract so radically inegalitarian—he has fifteen wives, each wife has one-fifteenth of a husband; she can have no more mates, he can have as many as he likes—that it ought to be illegal? That some women may find this arrangement acceptable doesn't mean the law should permit it, any more than the law should let people work for a dollar an hour, or sell their kidneys, or clean houses off the books and wind up with no Social Security.

So what is the A.C.L.U. doing? Outside Utah, plural marriage is not an issue. But gay marriage is. Every person I spoke with connected the two issues, on the grounds that if you accept restrictions on the legal definition of marriage in the one case, you have no standing to argue against such restrictions in the other. "So if polygyny is the price of gay marriage, you're willing to pay it?" I asked Glasser. Yes, he replied. But except for the fact that neither one is included in the legal definition of marriage, plural marriage and gay marriage have little in common. Two same-sexers are entering into the same contract as two heteros. That's why people who argue gay marriage will "threaten marriage" can never say exactly what the threat is. But plural marriage is fundamentally different. It would redefine all marriage contracts, because every marriage would be legally open to the addition of more partners.

Of course, as Glasser and others were quick to point out, monogamous marriage is also often exploitative and harmful to women, and fifteen-year-old girls can be pushed into monogamous marriage too. Right! But those facts suggest that there's something amiss with the whole strategy of trying to expand the marital population. Shouldn't the real libertarian position be that marriage itself has to go? There's something deeply contradictory about accepting the state's right to privilege married people while denying it the right to decide who those people will be and to define what marriage is.

In a world where the age of consent was, say, thirty, where teenage girls had real autonomy, where all women were well educated and able to support themselves and their children, and where people were less isolated and easily trapped, the libertarian position would make more sense. Polygyny, I suspect, would be a rarity—and maybe marriage too.

October 4, 1999

CATHOLIC BASHING?

My father disapproved of the "Sensation" show at the Brooklyn Museum of Art. He thought it was bad for the Jews. Who owned the art, including Chris Ofili's *Holy Virgin Mary*—the elephant dung–decorated representation of the Madonna surrounded with cutouts from porn magazines that thanks to Mayor Giuliani has become the most famous religious painting since *The Last Supper*? Charles Saatchi. And who is in charge of the Brooklyn Museum? Arnold Lehman. Two Jews. "Anti-Semitism's just gone underground," my father warned, "but it's still there, and this will bring it out." I felt as if I had wandered into a Philip Roth novel—and my dad's a Protestant!

A prescient one at that. "Why are a Jewish collector and a Jewish museum director promoting anti-Catholic art?" asked Camille Paglia in a subhead since deleted from her *Salon* column, adding a Nixonian touch to her usual insinuating boorishness. Um, I don't know, Camille. Because they killed Christ? Because they think they're so smart? Because they want to make a fast buck? Like most pundits who've inveighed against "Catholic-bashing" art in the show—Peggy Steinfels on *The New York Times* Op-Ed page, Terry Golway in the *New York Observer*, Cokie Roberts ("it's yucky"),

George Will, not to mention John Cardinal O'Connor, William Donohue of the Catholic League for Religious and Civil Rights and the mayor himself—Paglia hasn't bothered to make the trip to Brooklyn, but she knows "Catholic bashing" when she reads a one-sentence description of a painting in a newspaper. Besides, she saw Lehman on TV and found him to be a "whiny slug."

Well, I saw the "Sensation" show and guess what? It's pretty interesting. True, thanks to the mayor, my sensibilities were heightened by having to go through a metal detector, and the presence of a pair of chic Italian journalists interviewing each other in the museum's entranceway no doubt further piqued my sense of anticipation. Still, I've seen a fair amount of trendy contemporary art, and I was prepared to come away with gloomy thoughts about what Milan Kundera calls the Uglification of Everything. Hadn't a wonderful novelist friend said to me, just the other day, I'm tired of defending bad art? But, then, my friend hadn't seen the show either.

The Holy Virgin Mary is a funny, jazzy, rather sweet painting, in which the Virgin Mary is depicted as a broad-featured black woman in a blue dress shaped like a leaf. The porn cutouts—mostly too small to distinguish—swarm around her like flies or butterflies, and one of her breasts is represented by that celebrated lump of pachyderm poo, decorated, as is much of the painting's surface, with beads of paint for a Byzantine mosaic effect. It's absurd to call it anti-Catholic—Chris Ofili, an Englishman of Nigerian extraction, is himself a practicing Catholic, and the Virgin Mary was not a Catholic, and isn't even a uniquely Catholic symbol. To me, the painting suggests the cheerful mother goddess of an imaginary folk religion—an infinitely happier image of female strength and sexuality than the pallid plaster virgins and Raphael copies on display at Saint Mary of the Intact Hymen. As for the elephant droppings, there are four Ofili paintings in the show and every one employs it. *Affro-dizzia,* an *hommage* to black pop culture, features balls of dung emblazoned with the names of Miles Davis, James Brown and other figures, and no one has said Ofili meant to insult them. *Holy Virgin Mary* may not be a painting for the ages—elephant dung biodegrades pretty quickly—but it's fun to look at, even behind bulletproof glass.

Once again, the people of New York have proved their superiority to the pundits. While phony populist commentators label the show "elitist," people are flocking to see it. Teenagers, usually not to be caught dead in museums, are going. Black people—for whom an Africanized Madonna does not automatically signal blasphemy—are going. Steinfels warns that provocative art risks rousing anti–First Amendment beasts and may end in major cuts in arts budgets—a point made also by William Safire, who hadn't seen the show—but in fact, Giuliani's play for votes has backfired. A *Daily News* poll showed that only one in three New Yorkers supported him on this. There is no outraged vox populi in this story. There are only headline-seeking politicians and power brokers, and opinion mongers too lazy to get out of their chairs.

Is there awful, even repellent, art in the "Sensation" show? Yes, although there won't be much agreement about which works those are. I, for example, found Jake & Dinos Chapman's mutilated and deformed mannequins truly disturbing—but they haven't even been mentioned in news accounts. Too hard to reduce to a sound bite, perhaps. Damien Hirst's shark in formaldehyde makes a better target. It's the sort of conceptual art that unimaginative people think they could have thought up themselves, the way they think their four-year-old's finger paintings are as good as Jackson Pollock. If Hirst palls, one can always profess oneself grossed out by Marc Quinn's sculpture of his own head made from his own frozen blood. In fact, those works bear almost no relation to the mental picture conjured up by the sneers. The shark is eerily beautiful, lonely, fragile, strange; the sculpted head has the dignity of a Roman portrait bust or a death mask.

Aesthetic and political conservatives have been complaining about modern art ever since there was any. It's not uplifting or patriotic or healthy; it's the work of fakers, perverts and commies; it's promoted and paid for by elitists (i.e., people who actually know something about art) and, as Paglia points out, by Jews. The history of this critique should give us pause—it's certainly led more often to bonfires than to artworks of lasting interest—and it's irritating that it evokes so much automatic sympathy in the *bien-pensant* media. On the positive side, though, the strain of holding such patently ridiculous views seems to be driving Mayor Giuliani over the edge: In the October 13 *New York Times* he's quoted ranting against putting "human excrement" on walls because "civilization has been about trying to find the right place to put excrement." I guess the mayor still hasn't been to see the show.

November 1, 1999

HOME DISCOMFORTS

Isn't it curious how often the policy disaster that is posited as the thing that will never happen takes place within minutes? Thus, no sooner had New York mayor Giuliani insisted that welfare mothers in homeless shelters work or be evicted and lose their children to foster care than Jason Turner, who directs the city's welfare-to-work program, pooh-poohed its possibility. What mother (that is, what mother who deserved to keep her children) would refuse to work when faced with such a threat? Fortunately, the policy was enjoined by the courts before it could be implemented, leaving the mayor to console himself by having a buildingful of artists evicted just before Christmas.

But by that time, the thing that was never going to happen was already all over the news. In Suffolk County, Long Island, which had implemented the very rules blocked in New York City, young Eve Engesser had her two sons taken into foster care when she lost her shelter place because of a missed workfare appointment—her third minor run-in with the byzantine welfare regulations (one due to a sick child, the other a bureaucratic error). God himself could not have arranged a better poster child for the evils of the policy of requiring work for shelter: Ms. Engesser was white, sober, by all accounts a good and loving mother—not the unruly black addict whom welfare reformers obsess about; her parents were solid working-class people who, priced out of Long Island's tight housing market, also became homeless; her defender was a local Presbyterian minister. None of this prevented the county from removing her sons, whereupon they became understandably upset and withdrawn; the eight-year-old apparently was not sent to school. If it were not for the generosity of a nonprofit agency that came forward with housing and job offers, who knows what would have happened to those kids—not to mention their mother?

To all this John Tierney, the conservative "Big City" columnist for *The New York Times,* was cheerfully oblivious. Why on earth, he wondered, do people object to the work-for-shelter rule? After all, it's working so well to restore the self-respect of the ex-addicts and former convicts now sweeping city streets for the Doe Fund, a private charity that helps them back on their feet in return for low-wage work. "Why would anyone want to protect someone's right to lie around a shelter doing nothing?" as the head of the Doe Fund told Tierney. It's worth noting that Doe Funders volunteer for the program, but in any case, women with children are not like single men with no ties: They are *already* working, taking care of their kids and maybe other family members also. One can only equate homeless mothers with addicts and criminals if one has already decided that, for them, domestic labor is not real—their kids can go to foster care because they are not the sort of mother any child would really miss. At the bottom of the social scale family life is invisible; all that matters is paid work, never mind if slogging long hours for low pay means your kids suffer.

At the top, though, domesticity is making a big comeback, at least on paper. There's Martha Stewart, a cross between an arts-and-crafts counselor and Marie Antoinette in shepherdess mode (make envelopes out of birch bark! ice your child's birthday cake with molten gold!). And now there's Cheryl Mendelson, with her wildly successful 884-page guide to housework, *Home Comforts: The Art and Science of Keeping House.* Larded with tributes to housekeeping as the source of order, beauty, pleasure and happiness, Mendelson's book provides unbelievably detailed instructions on everything from how to dry a wineglass to how to hang wash on a line (yes, there is a right way and a wrong way). Beneath her portrayal of domesticity as a satisfying and enjoyable pastime is what one Amazon.com reader calls "a relentless paean to obsessive practices." Mendelson wants us to sanitize our sponges and disinfect our dish towels after every use, change the kitty litter every other day, put on fresh pillowcases twice a week, vacuum our mattress pads whenever we change the sheets and unplug and wash the refrigerator once a week!

Taken seriously, this is domesticity as paranoia—oh, no, a germ! Taken in small doses, it's housekeeping as a hobby for busy professionals, like gourmet cooking, or (more likely) a fantasy: one more self-improvement project that lasts a week and makes you feel guilty forever. Naturally, conservative commentators such as Danielle Crittenden have been chatting it up as proof that working women are wasting their lives. Vacuuming can be fun! Somehow I doubt that Crittenden, who has plenty of hired help and works like a stevedore producing antifeminist drivel, is spending much time sanitizing sponges. As for elegant Elizabeth Fox-Genovese, whose blurb for *Home Comforts* rhapsodizes that "she helps to restore dignity, value and craft to the work that creates and sustains the private space that nourishes our humanity," I can't imagine a woman less likely to wash the kitchen floor on hands and knees, as Mendelson recommends.

Put Eve Engesser's story together with Cheryl Mendelson, and what you have is domesticity and motherhood as class privileges. For poor women, take a "job" or lose your shelter and your kids. For the well-off, running the house becomes a holy task, than which nothing of which the human spirit is capable could possibly be more important.

January 24, 2000

THE DEATH PENALTY
IN THEORY AND PRACTICE

That the death penalty is applied unequally in this country is be-yond dispute—except, unfortunately, in the view of the legal sys-tem itself, which dismisses statistics showing that nonwhites convicted of killing whites are vastly overrepresented on death row, and sees nothing amiss with persons accused of capital crimes being represented by lawyers whose only qualification is that they are alive, if not always awake. Lots of people are charged with hor-rible crimes in the United States, and some of them are even guilty, but the ones who get the death penalty are mostly society's cast-aways—the ones who can't afford a Dream Team. Of the thirteen condemned men exonerated in Illinois, ten were poor blacks or Latinos.

This fundamental inequity doesn't matter to some death penalty fans—victims' families in search of the ever-elusive "closure"; the Last Marxist's students, who, under his shrewdly Socratic question-ing, decided that a ratio of one innocent person executed for every seven guilty ones was a fair price for the deterrent magic of lethal injections. In a *New York Times* Op-Ed, David Frum, the right-wing ideologue, heaped scorn on death penalty opponents for throwing sand in the machinery of death, thus thwarting the "popular will" and destroying faith in government, as if the sand—writs, appeals, protest campaigns—were not guaranteed us by the Constitution, and as if the Constitution were not also an expression of the will of the people and, at least marginally, a more considered expression of said will than polls, talk radio and drunken yahoos cavorting outside prisons on execution night.

A number of e-mails crossing my screen this past month brought home both the importance of fighting the death penalty on its unfairness case by case and the limits of that strategy. There was a bulletin urging letters to "compassionate conservative" George W. Bush on behalf of Betty Lou Beets, the sixty-two-year-old great-grandmother scheduled to die in Texas on February 24 for the murder of her fifth husband. Given the governor's enthusiasm for executions, it would be a miracle worthy of his favorite political philosopher if this campaign were to be successful, but it should be. Twice her death sentence was struck down, only to be reinstated.

Then there's Eugene Colvin-El, next in line on Maryland's death row, a black convicted burglar and heroin addict sentenced to die by an all-white jury for the 1980 murder of an eighty-year-old white woman in a burglary. Unless the Supreme Court overturns his sentence, which like Beets's has been set aside twice only to be reinstated, Colvin-El will be the first person in the state executed solely on the basis of circumstantial evidence: no witness, no confession, no evidence placing him at the murder scene. His fingerprint was found on broken panes of glass from a basement door, but the door was blocked and could not have been the point of entry; he was shown to have pawned two cheap watches, but he could have got those elsewhere. Colvin-El's lawyer, who had argued exactly one felony trial in his life, was so ineffective that Colvin-El petitioned the original trial judge, unsuccessfully, to have him taken off the case.

We're hearing a lot now about factual innocence, but death row is full of people like Betty Beets, who did not get a fair trial but who is almost certainly guilty of killing—in fact, two killings (when they found husband number five buried in the garden, they also found husband number four under the patio)—and who, like many on death row, grew up in poverty and violence and is a deeply dam-aged person (she tried to blame her children for the killings). As for Colvin-El, it's hard to know what his story was, but the truth is, it shouldn't matter. It's a scandal that a man may be executed on cir-cumstantial evidence after a three-day trial (Beets's was four), but even if he were found guilty beyond a shred of doubt after a vigor-ous defense by Clarence Darrow, his execution would still be wrong. And it would be wrong even if white burglars who kill eighty-year-old black women stood a statistically equal chance of drawing the death card, and if the only women executed really had killed their husbands for the death benefits Beets was wrongly sup-posed to be after.

Still, people trying to save particular inmates have no choice but to argue their particular cases. That's one reason I don't agree with Marc Cooper's attack (in *New York Press* and on the *Mother Jones* website) on the movement to save Mumia Abu-Jamal. Cooper ar-gues that the movement is hero-worshiping, sectarian and obsessed with the case of Mumia and his putative innocence (which Cooper thinks improbable) rather than with the larger issue of the death penalty.

It's true that for a long time the only people who cared about Mumia were Maoists and black nationalists—and good for them, I say—but little by little this supposedly quasi-loony cause has gath-ered a lot of mainstream support: Amnesty International, the pope, the International Longshore and Warehouse Union, the pacifist Anabaptists of the Bruderhof Communities, the conservative columnist John Leo (albeit limitedly), not to mention the thou-sands here and abroad (8,000 in Berlin just a few weeks ago) who regularly turn out for demonstrations. I'm not so sure, either, that it takes away strength from the anti–death penalty movement proper. More likely the reverse: It's introduced to death penalty protest countless young people who would certainly not show up for an A.C.L.U. teach-in. As for hard-core political Mumia supporters, why knock their preoccupation with Mumia, a former Black Pan-ther and one of their own, any more than one would knock advo-cates of battered women for involving themselves in Beets's case or

Native Americans for focusing on Leonard Peltier? Their insistence on his innocence may be misguided tactically—if he were guilty, would his trial be less of a travesty, the death sentence less heinous?—but the amazing thing is that the Mumia movement has outgrown its sectarian cradle. Surely that's cause for optimism, not a rebuke! As John Morris, Colvin-El's appeals lawyer, told me when I asked if he believed the Mumia movement drained resources from other cases, "This isn't a zero-sum game. All these cases stand on their own merits, and they all make the same argument: We shouldn't be doing this."

March 6, 2000

REGRETS ONLY

On March 12, the first Sunday in Lent, Pope John Paul II apologized to God for assorted bad things done in the name of the church over the past 2,000 years. Although he employed carefully vague language, he seemed to be saying that he was sorry about, *inter alia,* the Crusades, the Inquisition, forcible conversions in South America and Africa and the denial of equal rights to women, "who are all too often humiliated and marginalized." This marks something like the ninety-fifth time the pope has said he was sorry for acts performed in the name of Catholicism—he has apologized for the hard time Galileo got for saying the earth goes around the sun, and recently he regretted the burning at the stake in 1600 of Giordano Bruno, who, he nonetheless reminded the world, really was a heretic. For John Paul, being the pope means always having to say you're sorry.

And yet, as so often with apologies ("if anyone was offended, that was not my intention"), what is given with one hand is taken back with the other. For many, the big news was that once again the pope failed to acknowledge the silence of Pope Pius XII in the face of the Holocaust. "Until he comes to terms with that, everything is cosmetic," the novelist Mary Gordon told me. True, the pope was apologizing on behalf of "sons and daughters of the church," not the church as an institution. But who are these sons and daughters the pope has in mind if not the bishops, cardinals and popes who preceded him? Whether in the twelfth century or the twentieth, Sicilian marketwomen and Irish farmers and Bavarian housewives had little power to forward or retard the great evils to which the pope alluded. By blaming the people, as if the church were a town meeting in which everyone gets one vote, John Paul II has taken the hard-won democratic reforms achieved by Vatican II and used them to avoid institutional responsibility: When everyone's equally at fault, nobody really is.

Some have suggested his reticence was intended to preserve the distinction between the earthly church and the church as spiritual ideal, the Bride of Christ, without "blemishes and wrinkles," as St. Augustine rather dermatologically put it. But these entities are theologically and organizationally connected: That is how it is possible to even talk about a fallible human pope who can nonetheless make infallible statements on matters of doctrine *ex cathedra*, something no rabbi or Protestant minister would claim to be able to do. Yet the pope left undiscussed the involvement of assorted popes and/or saints in the activities he describes, raising the interesting question of where on the ontological scale these worthies belong: If they are guilty humans who act in history, why not mention them? If they are part of the church as perfect spiritual entity, how could they have promoted torture and enslavement? One wonders who indeed was minding the store.

Apologies about past misdoings are all the rage. The Southern Baptists apologized for slavery, and so has President Clinton, who also apologized for Monica Lewinsky, for the Tuskegee experiments and for permitting genocide in Rwanda. Australia has National Sorry Day, to send its regrets to the aborigines. But what does it mean to regret a hundred-year-old crime, or a five-hundred-year-old crime, or even the murder of millions after it is too late to help them? Apologies of this sort usually mean the person who makes them is trying to close the books, not open them. Thus, President Clinton could simultaneously regret inaction in Rwanda and stay aloof as Central Africa goes up in flames. The Southern Baptists can regret slavery, but take no stand on restitution—paying black Americans for their lost inheritance, the fruits of that 250 years of labor, education and normal citizenship stolen from their ancestors. And in the same way, the pope can regret the Catholic role in anti-Semitism and fascism while simultaneously moving to sanctify 10,000 pro-Franco Spanish priests, nuns and brothers and to canonize Pope Pius IX, who, among other misdeeds, forced the Italian Jews back into the ghetto and actually kidnapped and raised as his own son a Jewish child on the grounds that he had been surreptitiously baptized by a maid. (An attempt to canonize Pius in 1954 was derailed when evidence came to light that he had seriously mistreated the child.)

The case of women is even more egregious. It's all very well to apologize for the sins of the past—burning witches, opposing suffrage, telling battered wives they had no choice but to stay with their husbands and so on. But what about now? The church continues to oppose "artificial" birth control, even condoms in AIDS-plagued Africa; abortion, although women in some Catholic Latin-American countries have illegal abortions at higher rates than U.S. women have legal ones; divorce, no matter how abusive the marriage; opening the priesthood to women. In a church in which every position of theological power is held by a man, women are not equal, they are inferior. In *First Things* magazine, Mary Ann Glendon, a Harvard law professor who headed the Vatican's delegation to the U.N. Beijing Conference on Women, argues that feminist critics of the church forget the great advance for women early Christianity represented over paganism. Maybe so, but that was 2,000 years ago.

The most interesting question about the pope's apologies is why he felt the need to make them. No leader makes ninety-five-plus apologies unless he really has to—Stalin never said he was sorry for the Moscow show trials, Mao never apologized for the Cultural Revolution. That the pope decided to acknowledge the historical wrongs of the church shows how weak it has become. As reported in the ultraconservative *Latin Mass Quarterly,* which holds that the rot set in when Latin went out, since 1970 the church has lost ground throughout the West in virtually every area: numbers of priests, nuns, brothers, seminarians, schools, marriages and baptisms. In Latin America, Pentecostalism is making major inroads. The pope can rail against contemporary Catholics for secularism and religious indifference all he wants, and blame the people in the pews for the actions of the hierarchy, but modernity is stronger than he is: Look who's apologizing.

April 3, 2000

PROGRESSIVE PRESIDENTIAL POLITICS

(CONTINUED)

Remember Barry Commoner's presidential campaign in 1980 on the Citizens' Party ticket? I thought not. There's a long tradition of high-minded progressives making principled but hopeless runs for the White House. Sometimes they aim for the Democratic Party nomination (Jesse Jackson, Jerry Brown, the pseudoprogressive Bill Bradley); sometimes they go the third-party route (John Anderson, Dr. Spock, Commoner, Ralph Nader). Either way, progressives nationwide gallantly rally round; if they have doubts about the man or the program (remember Jackson and Hymietown? Brown and the flat tax? Bradley and the contras?), they suppress them, along with whatever intimations of futility they may feel about the whole project. For months, or even, in the case of Jackson, years, activists work their tails off. The primary or the election comes along, rank and filers troop to the polling booths and vote their conscience—and that's it for another four years.

Left-liberals may think they are building a movement by focusing on the highly visible presidential election. But are they? In the Democratic Party, the progressive who had the closest thing to a real organization and a popular constituency was Jesse Jackson. But where is the Rainbow Coalition now? As critics charged and supporters hotly denied, it turned out to be all about Jesse Jackson himself and faded away when his candidacy did; today Jackson is a devoted Clintonite whose main preoccupation is getting Wall Street firms to hire more black stockbrokers. And what about the third parties? The most successful third-party candidate in living memory, Ross Perot, is a conservative lunatic; he got twenty-eight times as many votes in 1992 as Ralph Nader got in 1996. Despite the generally right-wing orientation and white-suburbanite membership of Perot's Reform Party, many progressives saw great potential in it and in its one success, Minnesota governor Jesse Ventura. Today the Reform Party is a national joke, and Jesse Ventura, despite his macho swagger and gift for colorful sound bites, is becoming a mainstream politician faster than you can say bodyslam: As I write, he just came out in favor of permanent most-favored-nation status and WTO membership for China, which must sorely disappoint those who saw him as a standard-bearer for the "anticorporate populism" that is supposed to replace the supposedly outmoded left.

My skeptical comments about Ralph Nader evoked a mini-cascade of furious mail. But if something hasn't worked the last ten times you tried it—the last third-party presidential candidate from the left to get enough votes to actually make a dent in national politics was Bob La Follette in 1924, with 16 percent—doesn't it make sense to wonder whether going back to the drawing board with the same box of chalk is really such a good idea? Maybe there are reasons why challengers from the left—even a widely admired, universally recognized figure like Nader—don't get very far as presidential candidates and don't leave much behind, and it would be useful to think about them.

Personality is part of the story—of the candidates I've mentioned, only Jesse Jackson was a natural politician who enjoyed connecting with voters. If a run is purely symbolic, like Dr. Spock's, it may not matter that the candidate always looks like he wishes he were somewhere else. But to come from the outside and get anywhere in politics today, you have to be a vivid extrovert or, as the Last Marxist puts it, "a full-of-life psychopath"—someone like Bill

Clinton or Jesse Ventura or John McCain. The left doesn't produce many people like that, because that kind of person wants to be on the winning side, where the action and the money and the girls are.

More important than the candidate's personality, though, is the nature of electoral politics itself. Robert Kuttner recently quoted Tammany leader George Washington Plunkitt, who observed way back in 1905 that "politics is as much a regular business as the grocery or the dry-goods or the drug business." It's about arranging national affairs to suit the (sometimes) competing agendas of organized interests: corporations, banks, Wall Street, small business, unions, homeowners and so on, all the way down the list—way down—to the Christian Coalition, the National Organization for Women and the Audubon Society. At the local level, third parties can sometimes take on this job, usually by performing a complicated dance with one of the two major parties; that's what the Liberal, Conservative and Right to Life parties do in New York State, where fusion tickets are permitted, and what the Working Families Party hopes to do. But at the national level, third parties have no chips to get into the game: That's why the A.F.L.-C.I.O. is not keen on the Labor Party, and why Bernie Sanders, nominally a socialist, votes like a Clinton Democrat. And that's also why ordinary citizens do not flock to third-party standards, although they may throw caution to the winds and vote—once—for a man-of-the-minute like Perot.

Intuitively, people understand what electoral politics is really about, what it can and can't do, so when the two-party system offers them nothing, they just stop voting. The people who remain at the polls are the ones for whom the system works at least some of the time. It's all very well to say that the two parties are Tweedledum and Tweedledee: Both serve corporate interests, favor free trade and so on. But if you're a public school teacher, the anti–school voucher Democratic Party really will protect your job better than the Republican Party; if you're a white small-businessman, the tax-cutting anti–affirmative action Republicans really will do more for your bottom line than the Democrats. The differences between the parties may be small, but they're quite concrete. There are reasons why most black voters are Democrats.

To detach voters from the current setup would take a lot more than a candidate, however charismatic. It would take a huge political movement that could credibly promise voters that it would fulfill the needs currently supplied, however imperfectly, by the existing parties. Focusing on the White House has never created such a movement before. Has anything changed that would enable it to do so now?

April 17, 2000

ABORTION HISTORY 101

Thirty years ago in early April, three years before *Roe v. Wade*, male politicians—urged on by doctors, lawyers and lobbyists—struck down New York State's restrictive abortion law, under which nearly all abortions were illegal. The measure was supported by Republican governor Nelson Rockefeller, defended by a senator who had witnessed the death of a young girl from complications of an illegal abortion, and it passed because one assemblyman changed his vote—Democrat George Michaels, who trembled as he told his colleagues that he knew he was signing his political death warrant. Weren't those men brave and noble to take such risks for women?

Yes, they were—if only we had more like them today! But something is missing from what seems to be emerging as the official version of events. In a long front-page story ('70 ABORTION LAW: NEW YORK SAID YES, STUNNING THE NATION, April 9), *The New York Times* recalled New York State's historic moment through the voices of ten people: all but two of them men, all but two of them politicians. On National Public Radio and on the air in Albany, the focus was the same. You would never know that women played a role in their own liberation. Indeed, Barbara Shack, then an organizer with the New York Civil Liberties Union, now president of the board of NARAL, helpfully told the *Times* that "the campaign to change the law was largely run by men."

As a policy matter among politicians, lobbyists and doctors, that's true. But policy change doesn't happen in a vacuum—physicians, and politicians too, had watched women die from illegal abortions for decades without being willing to do anything about it. What's missing from these accounts of legalization is the feminist activism that made it happen. Beginning in 1969, radical feminists held speakouts on abortion, at which hundreds of women went public with their own experiences: "I spoke first," recalls historian Rosalyn Baxandall of the initial speakout in New York, held at Washington Square Methodist Church, "and was totally scared—I could lose my job or go to jail. Who knew?" While the legislature was stymied—minor reform bills had been proposed in 1967, '68 and '69 but had been defeated in the Assembly—women lawyers mounted a federal court challenge to the New York State law that had the 1970 legislature terrified of being left with no abortion law at all, recalls Emily Jane Goodman, now a judge. There were demonstrations, a feminist speakers' bureau, lobbying efforts in Albany and brilliant and tireless organizing by Lucinda Cisler, cofounder of New Yorkers for Abortion Law Repeal. There was a flourishing abortion underground—from Jane in Chicago to the Clergy Consultation Service at New York City's Judson Memorial Church—and around the country, people knew about it. In 1969, feminists invaded and disrupted the New York State legislature's "expert hearing" on abortion law reform (the experts being fourteen men and a nun) and insisted on a total repeal of the law, not the minor reforms then under consideration. This dramatic action was widely, if not always respectfully, reported—GALS SQUEAL FOR REPEAL, was one headline. "The very moderate reform law of 1969 failed to pass," notes Ellen Willis, who took part in that disruption, "yet just a year later the same legislature passed the most liberal law in the country. Guess all those guys just had a spontaneous change of heart."

Feminists have labored so hard to make women visible, it's galling to see them erased from the legalization narrative—while they are still alive, yet. These are the same women—New York Radical Women, Redstockings—who have gone down in history, inaccurately, as the notorious "bra burners" at the 1968 Miss America pageant in Atlantic City, and whose slogan "the personal is political" is now so widely ridiculed. If the memory of activism and struggle fades so quickly, it's little wonder that legal abortion feels to so many women like a gift from on high, another in the long list of things over which they have little control and which they are constantly being told in one way or another isn't all that important anyway. After all, the reason the University of Arizona hospital doesn't perform or teach abortion today is that in 1974 the university agreed to ban abortion from its premises in return for $5.5 million from the state legislature to build a football stadium—so women's health matters less than college sports, just the way contraception matters less than Viagra when insurance companies decide what to cover. Similarly, Arianna Huffington quotes Marc Cooper's quip that the two parties are so alike, they should change their names to "the Pro-Life Corporate Party and the Pro-Choice Corporate Party"—imagine casting a vote along such trivial lines! Actually, more accurate names would be the Pro-Confederate Flag Party and the Anti-Confederate Flag Party—but racism, even symbolic racism, isn't a laugh line. Women's lives are.

Why does it matter if the role of activism is dropped from the historical record? History denied repeats itself. Today, abortion rights and abortion access are under threat on a hundred fronts—legislative bans on "partial birth" abortions, Catholic-secular hospital mergers, denial of insurance coverage, not to mention arson and violence and a constant barrage of anti-choice propaganda. Young women need to know that abortion rights and abortion access are not presents bestowed or retracted by powerful men (or women)—Presidents, Supreme Court justices, legislators, lobbyists—but freedoms won, as freedom always is, by people struggling on their own behalf. "Don't tone it down, be moderate or ladylike, or accept the lesser evil," says Baxandall today. How will people get that message if the news media tell them that women's major contribution to legalizing abortion was to say thank you after it was over?

———

Around the country, abortion funds help poor women pay for abortions. You can help these always-strapped grassroots efforts by sending a contribution to the National Network of Abortion Funds c/o CLPP, Hampshire College, Amherst, MA 01002.

May 1, 2000

Underground Against
the Taliban

The atrocities of the Afghan Taliban toward women have been widely reported in the Western press: women banned from work; forbidden to leave their homes unless shrouded in the burkha, a voluminous top-to-toe covering with a mesh grid over the eyes, and accompanied by a male relative (this in a country filled with widows, 30,000 in Kabul alone, after twenty years of constant warfare); girls' schools shut down; medical care denied, even in life-threatening emergencies. Human rights organizations have made important gestures: In 1998 Physicians for Human Rights did a well-publicized study of Afghan women's health, showing grave depression and suicidal tendencies; Amnesty International has declared the entire female population of Afghanistan prisoners of conscience. But mostly we still construe Afghan women as victims, passive and silent under their burkhas. We don't hear much about them organizing politically and taking action on their own behalf.

That's why it is so refreshing and stirring to meet the two young Afghan women who call themselves Sajeda and Sehar, who are currently traveling around America representing the Revolutionary Association of the Women of Afghanistan. RAWA, which was founded as a women's rights group in 1977 and is now based in the refugee areas of northwest Pakistan, has had the audacity to oppose not just the Soviet occupiers and the Taliban but all the foreign-backed fundamentalist warlords who have made Afghan life a misery; it supports human rights for women—and for men, too—and dares to imagine (although the particulars get a little vague here) that Afghanistan might someday be a secular democracy. Meanwhile, RAWA runs secret schools for girls inside Afghanistan and open schools for both sexes in the refugee camps. It has also started mobile health-care teams and income-generating projects, such as carpet-weaving, that women can do while confined to their homes. In fact, Sehar and Sajeda arrived in the States lugging six darkly beautiful but rather cumbersome carpets to sell in order to raise funds, which gives you an idea of the modesty of RAWA's budget.

And then there is the video. Contrast the Orientalized image of the passive, mysterious Muslim woman enticingly hidden behind her veil with this reality: Last November, when the Taliban summoned the women of Kabul to witness that city's first public execution of a woman, a RAWA member brought a camcorder under her burkha—which would seem to have its uses—and taped the grisly proceedings. If she had been caught, she would have been severely beaten, perhaps even killed. Similar risks attend RAWA members who teach girls in secret classes, who provide medical care undercover in remote districts or who demonstrate against the Taliban in Pakistan, where their spirited rallies are regularly assaulted by Taliban and Pakistani police. What do you do when they come at you with sticks, I asked the slight and very serious Sehar, who seems about as aggressive as a fawn. "We hit them right back," she replied with a little smile. "We have sticks too."

Together with Feminist Majority Foundation and the National Committee of Women for a Democratic Iran, RAWA held a small but vigorous rally in Lafayette Park in front of the White House on April 28, anniversary of the triumph of the warlords in 1992. Under an overcast spring sky, two women in turquoise burkhas held a long banner adorned with gruesome photographs—women begging in a marketplace; a child with amputated legs tied off like balloons; a grinning boy with a string of severed hands slung over his shoulder.

Eleanor Smeal spoke eloquently, without notes; there were messages of support from Representative Carolyn Maloney and Senator Harry Reid; Sajeda, refusing the sunglasses that were supposed to protect her from being identified by the Taliban, called on the U.N. to enforce peace and democracy—a utopian demand if ever there was one. Troops of white, middle-American tourists—families, high school kids on their class trip—stared at the burkhas and the banner and the angry orating women for a moment and moved on.

Tacitus famously wrote that the Roman army made a wasteland and called it peace. America, it might be said, creates its wastelands by proxy. It romanticizes as noble freedom fighters thugs and fanatics who throw acid on unveiled women's faces and have no interest in anything but their own power, and then looks at the result with puzzlement, as if Afghanistan were as distant and strange as the surface of the moon. There are those who argue that the Taliban simply represent Afghan culture, which has always been deeply Muslim: The burkha is nothing new; only a small percentage of girls, mostly those in cities, ever went to school. True enough, but if the Taliban were in accord with the local views, why the Kalashnikovs? Why the beatings in the streets? Before the Taliban took power, women in Kabul were 40 percent of doctors, 70 percent of teachers and 50 percent of the civil service; there were many thousands of female university students. In fact, the Taliban represent a modern and extreme version of Islam that was historically unknown in Afghanistan. (Ahmed Rashid's *Taliban: Militant Islam, Oil and Fundamentalism in Central Asia*, just out from Yale University Press, gives an excellent political and historical account of the movement's rise to power.) And the Taliban, who are mostly Pashtun, impose Pashtun ways on other ethnicities in what was once a more mutually forbearing ethnic patchwork. Like the warlords, the Taliban are supported from abroad, until 1996 by the United States—yes, the same Clinton administration that now courts feminist votes made no protest when the Taliban threw thousands of girls out of school after taking control of the city of Herat in 1995; now they are financed by Pakistan, Saudi Arabia and the United Arab Emirates—American allies all.

You can find out more about RAWA at www.rawa.org. In devastated Afghanistan, small donations go a long way: For $25 a month you can subsidize a teacher in an underground school; for $30 a month you can support a woman in a yearlong underground literacy and health-education course. Send cash or check, payable to "Support Afghan Women," to Support Afghan Women, PMB 226, 915 W. Arrow Highway, San Dimas, CA 91773.

May 29, 2000

Moms to NRA:
Grow Up!

In the end, after months of waffling, I violated my principles and went to the Million Mom March for gun control—make that "commonsense gun control." I've never liked maternalist politics: It relies on an image of women as basically apolitical homebodies, roused from the stove only by a threat to the nest and the nestlings. Maternalism takes the ancient sexist categories that exclude women from the public realm and uses them to win women a hearing there—children, it is generally conceded, are the one subject about which women know a thing or two—but it leaves the categories untouched. Under the rubric of maternalism, women can fight for kids but not for themselves. Thus there was no mention at the march of the thousands of women killed and injured each year with guns, or the connections, noted by Susan Faludi in *Newsweek,* between far-right militias and anti-choice zealotry. Meanwhile, maternalism subtly shifts responsibility away from men, which in the case of guns seems particularly unwarranted: The gun culture is a highly masculine preserve, and so is most gun violence—drive-by shootings, mass murders by school kids, racist killing sprees, domestic murder-suicides. Who leaves those loaded guns around for kids to play with, anyway? Shouldn't it have been a Million Dad March?

The march has been portrayed as a soccer mom extravaganza, and certainly there were lots of nonpoor white women—although the ones I knew, not to mention myself, seem to have missed out on the McMansion and minivan that "white women" are so often gifted with in the media. The afternoon had a family-holiday feel, like a monster playground fair—there were lots of strollers and double strollers, and cheerful, slightly self-mocking evocations of middle-class maternity like the chant "Time Out Chair/for Wayne LaPierre" (executive vice president of the NRA). Best mass-produced sticker: "Actually, guns do kill people"; best handmade sign: "I'm here because my husband is an idiot." Raffi, the preschooler's answer to Pete Seeger, had everyone singing "This Little Light of Mine."

Not surprisingly, all this sweetness and light made Camille Paglia blow her last remaining gasket in *Salon:* "The average citizen doesn't want national policy determined by packs of weeping women led by a shrill dimwitted talk show host (Hillary sycophant Rosie O'Donnell)"—or, as she is known to the NRA, Tokyo Rosie. Actually, poll after poll shows the average citizen is wildly in favor of the modest measures supported by the moms—registering handguns and licensing owners, background checks at gun shows and so on.

Still, it was certainly true that the march doubled as a Democratic Party rally—just as my reluctant companion, the Last Marxist, had predicted long before it was widely publicized that founding march organizer Donna Dees-Thomases is the sister-in-law of Hillary Clinton's close friend Susan Thomases. Along with O'Donnell, Reese Witherspoon, Anna Quindlen, Sarah Brady and other luminaries, a bevy of Democratic politicians took the podium: Maryland's Lieutenant Governor Kathleen Kennedy Townsend; Representative Carolyn McCarthy, whose husband was killed and son grievously injured by a gunman on the Long Island Rail Road; Bobby Rush, the congressman and former Black Panther whose son was murdered last year in Chicago. The President appeared via video; Tipper and Hillary worked the crowds. You would never know that the Democratic Party purposely seeks out pro-gun candidates to run in conservative districts or that it was a powerful Democratic congressman, Michigan's John Dingell, who killed last year's bill calling for seventy-two-hour waiting periods on gun show purchases. With women supporting gun control by 75 percent to men's 50 percent, Al Gore certainly isn't going to remind them.

The only speaker I heard who related gun violence to poverty and racism was Susan Sarandon, but all you had to do was look around and the connection was obvious. Black and Hispanic parents of murdered kids were everywhere—alone, with family members, or representing inner-city support groups, which typically have dozens of members. Some displayed memorial quilts bearing the faces of their dead children; one mother had mounted her poem mourning her dead son on a pole. I had a taste of what a fundamentally creepy job reporting is as I asked parents for their stories—the son about to go to college who was killed with a Saturday Night Special because his friend went out with someone's former girlfriend; the son who left the house and was dead fifteen minutes later, reason unknown, killer never found. These are the kids the NRA discounts in racist fashion as not really children, not really innocent, drug users and gangbangers. In other words: Not only do guns not kill people, they don't kill *people*.

Listening to these tragic stories of waste and folly, I saw the other side of maternalist politics: its ability to cut through flimflam and get to the heart of an issue. After all, the decades of good-government lobbying for gun control have achieved very little: Of the dozens of bills introduced in Congress after Columbine last year, not one passed. Maybe the passion of wounded ordinary people is what's needed; maybe the image of the bereaved and angry mother is the only one weighty enough to counterbalance that of the male hunter and patriot deployed so successfully by the NRA.

The sad thing, though, is that the Million Mom March brought so many people together—three-quarters of a million on the Mall and thousands of others at local rallies around the country—and under the guise of empowering them, disempowered them. Write your representatives, urged speaker after speaker. Remember in

November. Vote. But beyond scribbling a postcard—pink-and-white ones were thoughtfully provided—and pulling a lever six months from now, no one suggested anything resembling activism: picketing gun stores and gun shows, organizing with other parents to chuck the NRA's Eddie Eagle "gun safety" programs out of your kid's school or joining with other students to force your college to divest from the gun industry. It will take more than once-a-year gestures, whether marching or voting, to turn mom power into people power.

June 20, 2000

THE POLITICS OF
PERSONAL RESPONSIBILITY

On August 22, 1996, just before the last Democratic convention, President Clinton signed the Personal Responsibility Act, the Republican-authored welfare reform bill, and, as he had long promised to do, ended "welfare as we know it," while racking up a few more unnecessary points over Dole, the hapless future Viagra pitchman. Four years later, as the Democrats come together to anoint Al Gore, one of the Administration's more aggressive advocates of the PRA, welfare reform is widely deemed a huge success. Welfare rolls are way down all over the country. Unemployment too. The media ceaselessly promote stories of single mothers pushed and pulled into employment by tough-loving jobs counselors, who find them baby-sitters, get them off drugs and raise their self-esteem.

But how accurate is this sunny picture? In December of last year, *The New York Times*'s Jason DeParle glowingly depicted as a secular saint a Milwaukee case manager employed by the Virginia-based Maximus Corporation, the nation's largest private welfare-to-work contractor. A few months later, the paper reported that Maximus was being investigated for corrupt bidding practices in New York, had botched its contracts in Connecticut and had a history of slashing benefits in a cruel and capricious fashion.

In another welfare-reform triumph story in early June, *Times* reporter Robert Pear kvelled over the Manpower Demonstration Research Corporation's evaluation of the Minnesota Family Investment Program. By urging recipients into work, even low-wage work, while letting them keep part of their grant, MFIP seemed to validate the underlying ideology of welfare reform: After three years, poverty was down, marriage rates were up, kids were doing better in school and domestic violence and child abuse had both decreased. Conservatives liked the program because it emphasized work and family values; liberals liked it because it provided more money for families. The *Times* was so wowed that it repeated the study's highlights in an editorial.

The only problem with this beautiful story is that the MFIP discussed in the Manpower study, a pilot project in seven counties, no longer exists; it was shut down in 1998. The state program that replaced it, also called MFIP, is cheaper and much harsher. Under the pilot program, there were no time limits, recipients could keep a chunk of their welfare grant until they reached 140 percent of the poverty level and all families received the maximum amount of food stamps—in cash. Sanctions for "noncompliance" with the rules were mild. By contrast, the actually existing MFIP imposes time limits and cuts off benefits at a much lower level of earnings—a parent with one child loses all benefits on a wage of $6.26 an hour. Even though federal law requires that food stamps be given according to need, MFIP now gives all recipients the average amount, so that more than half of families get less than before—as much as $80 a month less. MFIP places enormous power in the hands of individual counselors, who decide, for instance, whether a client can count education as work. Mostly the answer is no: At any given time, fewer than 6 percent of the MFIP caseload are allowed to get postsecondary education or training, and of the nearly half who lack a high school degree, only 4 percent are permitted to receive basic education—to get their GED, for instance. Sanctions for noncompliance are severe and meted out with staggering unfairness: St. Cloud Area Legal Services found that of seventy-eight recipients facing sanctions, only six met the criteria. Nonetheless, said Deb Konechne of the Minnesota Welfare Rights Coalition, a grassroots group of low-income people, "When the Manpower report came out, Jesse Ventura came to the press conference and state politicians tried to pass it off as a report card on the whole program. It was a highly orchestrated fraud." And the *Times* fell for it.

What else do we know about Minnesota since welfare reform was introduced? As is true all over the country, homelessness is up—Hennepin County, home of Minneapolis, has had to double its budget for homeless people. (Ominously, George W. Bush, in his address to the Republican convention, called homeless shelters the "next bold step of welfare reform.") According to the Minnesota Food Bank Network, hunger is up as well. Not all of this can necessarily be laid at the door of the PRA—both hunger and homelessness were on the rise well before the law took effect. Welfare reform is one part of a national picture in which those at the top are doing very well, while those at the bottom are still struggling in heavy water. As the tale of two MFIPs shows, the problem with welfare reform is its basic structure: It throws women off the rolls into jobs that are too ill paid and too unstable to support a family, while denying them the education and support they need to advance. It creates a permanent class of low-skilled, low-wage workers—a kind of reserve army of the semi-employed.

On July 1, 2002, Minnesota's five-year lifetime limit on welfare kicks in, and people who have used up their sixty months will begin to be dropped from the rolls. "I think we'll see a crisis in this state," said Konechne, "with lots and lots of children who are homeless, who are hungry, who are suffering in ways we haven't seen in my lifetime." Will this prove to be the legacy President Clinton has been so busily seeking? Something to think about while watching the spectacle in LA.

August 21/28, 2000

Freedom from Religion, *¡Sí!*

"The Constitution guarantees freedom of religion, not freedom from religion," Senator Joseph Lieberman told a rapturous audience at a black church a few Sundays ago, just after being chosen as Al Gore's running mate. Given that the whole purpose of Lieberman's nomination was to detach Gore from Clinton's scandals by public displays of family values and sanctimoniousness, you can't blame him for starting right in—and so far the gambit seems to be working (Monica who?). Still, you would think the first Jewish major-party VP candidate in U.S. history might hesitate to cast to the winds the traditional secularism of American Jews. And that's what the Anti-Defamation League thought too, rebuking Lieberman for excessive use of "expressions of faith." After all, right-wing Christians are the 800-pound gorilla of U.S. church-state relations today, and given their triumphalism—"every knee shall bow" and all that—does one really need to encourage them? When a Jew endorses, or seems to endorse, an intrusive public role for religion, the Christian right is inoculated from charges of bigotry. No wonder Lieberman has drawn praise from Jerry Falwell and Jewish-banker-conspiracy fan Pat Robertson—even though, of course, they know he's going to hell for refusing to accept Christ as his personal savior.

But that's the official American civic religion at the opening of the twenty-first century: What religion you have may be your own business—rather literally so, in the case of Scientology—but it's society's business that you have one. Modernity may have eroded some of the distinctions between previously antagonistic belief systems—Quick! Explain the difference between Presbyterianism and Methodism!—as is suggested by the increasing replacement of the word "religion," with its connotations of dogma and in-groupness, by the warm, fuzzy propaganda term "faith." Facing the common enemy, secularism, devout Christians and Jews dwell lovingly on their similarities as part of a "Judeo-Christian" ethos, when historically the ethos of each faith was precisely that it wasn't the other.

In fact, Lieberman is wrong about the Constitution—it does protect us from religion. In their useful book *The Godless Constitution,* Isaac Kramnick and R. Laurence Moore remind us that the Founding Fathers carefully considered and rejected the idea of inserting religious language into the Constitution: "The nation's founders, both in writing the Constitution and in defending it in the ratification debates, sought to separate the operations of government from any claim that human beings can know and follow divine direction in reaching policy decisions." The Constitution specifically prohibits religious tests for political office; evidently Washington, Madison and Jefferson did not think civic virtue required belief in God. Still less did they sympathize with Bible-based politics. Looking for political guidance in the Bible is like looking for it in the entrails of birds—you can always find what you want if you squint hard enough. Think of abortion, about which neither testament has a single word to say, yet both anti-choicers and pro-choicers claim religious justification for their positions. Lieberman thinks Gore's prescription drug proposal for seniors fulfills the commandment to honor thy father and mother; someone else might argue that God wants you to honor them by buying their medications yourself, or by putting them out on an ice floe to re-enter the cycle of nature. Since every position can find a godly rationale, bringing religion into the public sphere in practice simply means that the biggest and best organized religion gets to use the public realm—public facilities, public money—to advance its own sectarian agenda.

Consider some of the recent entanglements of church and state. Last June the House passed and sent on to the Senate the Noncommercial Broadcasting Freedom of Expression Act, which would permit religious organizations to purchase noncommercial radio stations and substitute religious for educational programming. "Charitable choice" legislation, supported by both Bush and Gore, not to mention a muddled opinion piece in *The Nation*, would permit religious organizations to bid for federal contracts to deliver a wide range of social services—antidrug programs, literacy programs, marriage preservation, housing—while permitting them to hire, fire and dispense services according to their religious dictates. Already permitted in welfare-to-work programs, charitable choice is under legal assault in Texas, where Jews and civil rights advocates have charged one church-based program with giving Bible classes, urging clients to build a personal relationship with Jesus and offering a course titled, "Who's the Boss? All Authority Comes from God."

Because the most energetic religions tend to be the ones most invested in keeping women subordinate, women in particular have nothing to gain from the burgeoning involvement of religion in the public sphere. The wave of mergers between Catholic and secular hospitals is already depriving women of crucial reproductive services, from contraception and abortion to in vitro fertilization and the morning-after pill, even for rape victims. Indeed, wherever you look, religion is the main obstacle to providing women with modern reproductive healthcare: The fig leaf of "conscience" becomes a justification for denying others basic human services. Thus the Catholic Church throws its weight against making health insurers cover contraception (Viagra's fine, though) and anti-choice pharmacists claim the right to refuse to dispense birth control, emergency contraception or, should it be approved by the FDA, RU-486. What about the idea that if my "conscience" doesn't permit me to do my job, maybe I'm in the wrong line of work? Would an orthodox Jew take a job at Virgil's Barbecue and then refuse to serve the pork ribs? Maybe Lieberman will give us his views on the matter. But I hope he doesn't.

SOCIAL PSEUDOSCIENCE

Every five years the psychologist Judith Wallerstein updates her ongoing study of 131 children whose parents were going through divorce in Marin County, California, in 1971, and every five years her warnings about the dire effects of divorce on children make the headlines, the covers and the talk shows. Her new book, *The Unexpected Legacy of Divorce,* ups the ante: She now believes that parents should grit their teeth and stay together, so traumatized were her interviewees even into their twenties, contending with drugs and drink, bad boyfriends, unsatisfactory jobs, low self-esteem and lack of trust in relationships. Before you young cynics out there say welcome to the club, remember: This is not a moralistic sermon dreamed up by Dr. Laura, the Pope, your relatives or even Judith Wallerstein. This is science.

But what if it isn't? Scholars have long been critical of Wallerstein's methods: She had no control group—kids just like the ones in her study but whose unhappily married parents stayed together. (In her new book she has attempted to get around this flaw by interviewing a "comparison sample" of people from intact families who went to high school with her subjects, but the two groups are not carefully matched.) She generalizes too quickly: Can sixty

Marin County families really stand in for all America? Are the seventies us? Doesn't it make a difference that fathers today are more involved with their kids both before and after divorce, that mothers are better educated and better able to support themselves, that divorce is no longer a badge of immorality and failure? It never occurs to Wallerstein, either, that the very process of being interviewed and reinterviewed about the effects of parental divorce for a quarter-century by a warm, empathetic and kindly professional would encourage her subjects to see their lives through that lens. "Karen" may really believe divorce explains why she spent her early twenties living with a layabout—blaming your parents is never a hard sell in America—but that doesn't mean it's true.

The media tend to treat such objections rather lightly. Wallerstein's critics "don't want to hear the bad news," wrote Walter Kim in *Time*'s recent cover story. The real bad news, though, is the way Wallerstein has come to omit from her writings crucial information she herself presented in her first book about her research, *Surviving the Breakup*, published in 1980.

How did Wallerstein find her divorcing couples, and what sort of people were they? In her new book, she writes that they were referred by their lawyers "on the basis of their willingness to participate." *Surviving the Breakup* gives quite a different picture: "The sixty families who participated in this study came initially for a six-week divorce counseling service. The service was conceptualized and advertised as a preventive program and was offered free of charge to all families in the midst of divorce. Parents learned of the service through attorneys, school teachers, counselors, social agencies, ministers, friends, and newspaper articles." In other words, Wallerstein was not just offering people a chance to advance the cause of knowledge, she was offering free therapy—something she today vehemently denies ("Naturally I wanted to be sure that any problem we saw did not predate the divorce. Neither they [the kids] nor their parents were ever my patients"). Obviously, people who sign up for therapy, not to mention volunteering their kids for continuing contact, have problems; by choosing only therapy-seekers, Wallerstein essentially excluded divorcing couples who were coping well.

Today, Wallerstein provides no information about the psychological well-being of the parents before divorce, but in her 1980 book, she is very clear about how troubled they were. Only one-third displayed "generally adequate psychological functioning." Fifty percent of the men and almost as many women were "moderately troubled"—"chronically depressed, sometimes suicidal individuals . . . with severe neurotic difficulties or with handicaps in relating to another person, or those with longstanding problems in controlling their rage or sexual impulses." Fifteen percent of the men and 20 percent of the women "had histories of mental illness, including paranoid thinking, bizarre behavior, manic-depressive illnesses, and generally fragile or unsuccessful attempts to cope with the demands of life, marriage, and family." Some underwent "hospitalization for severe mental illness, suicide attempts, severe psychosomatic illnesses, work histories ridden with unsatisfactory performance, or arrests for assault." It's not for me to say whether a sample in which two-thirds of the participants range from chronically depressed to outright insane represents the general public—but attributing all their children's struggles to divorce is patently absurd.

The way Wallerstein describes her sample has changed also. In a table in her 1980 book, she places 28 percent of the families in the two lowest of five social-class rankings, as defined by the Hollingshead index, and 23 percent in the highest. In the new book, these figures are mentioned in passing, but at the same time she calls all the families "middle class"—including a famous wife-beating TV executive and his former spouse, a wealthy travel agent who spent her life globe-trotting. All are now "educated," as well, including the substantial percentage of parents (24 percent of the mothers and 18 percent of the fathers at initial contact in 1971) who hadn't been to college. Gone too are such relevant facts from the earlier book as that one-third of the couples had "rushed into a precipitous marriage because of an unplanned pregnancy" and that half the wives, "because of their age and lack of job experience, were viewed realistically as unemployable."

In short, what we have here are not generic white suburbanites who threw away workable marriages in order to actualize their human potential in a Marin County hot tub. We have sixty disastrous families, featuring crazy parents, economic insecurity, trapped wives and, as Wallerstein does discuss, lots of violence (one-quarter of the fathers beat their wives; out of the 131 children, 32 had witnessed such attacks). How on earth can she claim that divorce is what made her young people's lives difficult? The wonder is that they are doing as well as they are.

October 23, 2000

NOTES

CLARA ZETKIN AVENUE

3 Some lefty prankster: I discovered later that the signs were put up by Gabriela, a Filipina feminist organization.

4 in Pakistan: "Unveiled," by Melissa Robinson, *The New Republic,* March 9, 1992, pp. 11–12.

NATIONAL TULIP CONVERSATION

10 62 percent: D. Boyer and D. Fine, "Sexual Abuse as a Factor in Adolescent Pregnancy and Child Maltreatment," *Family Planning Perspectives* 24 (1992): 4–11.

OPINIONATED WOMEN

23 Barbara Ehrenreich: Barbara Ehrenreich, *Fear of Falling: The Inner Life of the Middle Class* (New York: Pantheon, 1989).

DEADBEAT DADS: A MODEST PROPOSAL

36 men over the age of twenty: M. Males and K.S.Y. Chew, "Adult Fathers in School-Age Childbearing," paper presented at the annual meeting of the Population Association of America, San Francisco, April 8, 1995.

WHERE ARE THE WOMEN WE VOTED FOR?

78 two major studies: One was from the Department of Health and Human Services, the other from the Office of Management and Budget. Both predicted that welfare reform would push at least 1.2 million more children into poverty—not overnight, but as recipients reached the proposed five-year lifetime limit on welfare.

POMOLOTOV COCKTAIL

114 Ross's well-known claim: See, for example, "Science Backlash on Technoskeptics," *The Nation*, October 2, 1995.

UTOPIA, LIMITED

122 many studies: In 1997, the Luxembourg Income Study gave the United States first place in percentage of children in poverty (24.9) in a list of fourteen industrialized western European countries plus Canada (15.3) and Australia (15.4). In France, the child poverty rate was 7.4; in Germany 8.6; in the Scandinavian countries 5 percent or less. The Luxembourg study also measures the degree to which social welfare and income transfer programs reduce poverty. Only Italy did less to keep children from being poor than did the United States, where government programs reduced child poverty by a mere 13.2 percent. In France, by contrast, the reduction was 73 percent. In 1999, *Child Poverty Across Industrialized Nations*, by Bruce Bradbury and Markus Jantti (Unicef International Child Development Centre, Florence), using different measurements, placed the United States (26.3) second after Russia (26.6) in a list of twenty-five industrialized nations.

THE STRANGE DEATH OF LIBERAL AMERICA

125 only about 6.7 percent: Rebecca Blank, *It Takes a Nation: A New Agenda for Fighting Poverty* (Princeton, N.J.: Princeton University Press, 1997), p. 153.

125 only 9 percent: *Welfare Myths: Fact or Fiction?* (Welfare Law Center, 1996).

GO FIGURE

170 If men's annual earnings: Lawrence Mishel, Jared Bernstein, and John Schmitt, *The State of Working America: 1996–1997* (Economic Pol-

icy Institute, M. E. Sharpe, 1997), p. 148. Four years later, in 1999, women earned 69 percent of men's 1979 annual earnings: conversation with John Schmitt, July 2000.

WHEN I'M SIXTY-FOUR

177 prenatal care: "Early Prenatal Care and Low Birthweight, 1997" (table B8) in *The State of America's Children Yearbook* (Washington, D.C.: Children's Defense Fund, 2000).

HONK IF YOU LIKE ART

190 Last year Americans: *The Arts in the GDP,* National Endowment for the Arts publication, February 1997.

192 thirty-eight cents: "Costs of Culture," by Kenneth Baker, *San Francisco Chronicle,* December 9, 1997.

192 what kind of rocks: Actually, it turned out I knew lots of people who had a passionate interest in space exploration, and who took great exception to this assertion.

MÄDCHEN IN UNIFORM

211 Long Beach, California: According to *The New York Times* ("Taking a New Look at Uniforms and Their Impact on Schools," by James Sterngold, June 28, 2000), Long Beach school officals have backed away from their more extravagant claims for uniforms, and have also broadened the range of acceptable "school-color" dress.

FAR FROM CHILE?

223 five countries: "A Global Divide on Abortion Splits Poor from Rich," by Barbara Crossette, *The New York Times,* June 7, 1998. Actually, a total of forty-three countries, mostly in Latin America and Africa, ban abortion with no explicit exception to save a woman's life, although in most of them the laws are arguably open to a broader interpretation: conversation with Laura Katzive, Center for Reproductive Law and Policy, July 2000.

GREAT BIG BASKETS OF DIRTY LINEN

235 13 percent: *Newsweek* poll, January 29–30, 1998.

WOMEN'S RIGHTS: AS THE WORLD TURNS

261 the platform of the U.S. Republican Party: "The unborn child has a fundamental individual right to life that cannot be infringed. We

support a human life amendment and we endorse legislation to make it clear that the Fourteenth Amendment's protections apply to unborn children." If the "unborn child" has a "fundamental individual right to life that cannot be infringed," abortion would have to be illegal under all circumstances, including to save the woman's life.

262 women in Pakistan: "Raising a Healthier Population in Pakistan," World Bank Group Essay, June 1998.

262 murders of women in India: L. Hiese, *Violence Against Women* (World Bank Population Health and Nutrition Division, 1997).

262 a Chinese sampling: "In America: China's Missing Girls," by Bob Herbert, *The New York Times,* October 30, 1997.

A BRONX TALE

267 On September 8, 1999, Judge Robert H. Straus rejected the prosecutor's request for a six-month jail term and sentenced Walrond to five years' probation, with mandatory psychological counseling. Although he said he had received nine hundred letters from around the world, all supporting Walrond, including ones from lactation experts and women who had experienced similar traumas, he said they had not influenced him: "The mother is the bottom line. The buck stops here."

NATURAL BORN KILLERS

273 *COPS* and *NYPD Blue:* An astute *Nation* reader made a convincing case that these shows were not gratuitously violent, and that it was only my lack of television savvy that had made me single them out. The reader is invited to substitute in his or her own mind whatever programs in the current lineup seem the most thuggish and dumb.

ABOUT THE AUTHOR

KATHA POLLITT is a poet, essayist, and columnist for *The Nation.* She lives in New York City with her daughter, Sophie, and the writer Paul Mattick.

A NOTE ON THE TYPE

The principal text of this Modern Library edition
was set in a digitized version of Janson,
a typeface that dates from about 1690 and was cut by Nicholas Kis,
a Hungarian working in Amsterdam. The original matrices have
survived and are held by the Stempel foundry in Germany.
Hermann Zapf redesigned some of the weights and sizes for Stempel,
basing his revisions on the original design.